THE
ARCHAEOLOGY
OF CORNWALL

THE
ARCHAEOLOGY
OF CORNWALL

The Foundations of Our Society

CARADOC PETERS

CORNWALL EDITIONS
FOWEY

To Nata and Dewy

CORNWALL EDITIONS LIMITED
8 Langurtho Road
Fowey Cornwall
PL23 1EQ UK

01726 832483
www.cornwalleditions.co.uk
Publisher: Ian Grant

This edition was first published in the United Kingdom in 2005
by Cornwall Editions and is limited to 1100 copies, of which 1000 are for sale

Number...**421**.................

ISBN 1-904880-13-4

FRONTISPIECE The castle at Tintagel
ENDPAPERS Photograph by Simon Cook

Typeset in New Caledonia 11/18pt

Art Director: Roger Bristow
Editorial Director: Yvonne McFarlane
Consultant Editor: Maurice Smelt
Managing Editor: Judy Spours
Production: Madeleine Day

Designed by Roger Daniels and Roger Hammond
Illustrations by David Ashby and Eric Thomas
Cartography by ARKA Cartographics
Index by Sue Lightfoot

Pre-press by Butler and Tanner, UK
Printed and bound by Butler and Tanner, UK

CONTENTS

FOREWORD

Caradoc Peters has set himself the formidable task of examining the archaeology of Cornwall from the Palaeolithic some 400,000 years ago to the present day. The text is scholarly yet approachable and is up to date – qualities rare enough in an academic book to be of particular note.

Cornwall is fortunate that its archaeology has been the object of great antiquarian interest over the last three centuries and that this interest and activity have continued and quickened, especially since the 1960s. Many counties, like Cornwall, have active archaeological societies and have annual journals and field and lecture programmes. There are few areas, however, that feel quite so different and quite so identifiable – and quite so special.

It is therefore unsurprising that there have been no less than six books on the archaeology of Cornwall and Scilly since 1932, but with the exception of Philip Payton's historical review of 1996, these previous studies finished somewhere between the end of the Roman occupation and the Norman conquest. Two significant issues set Caradoc Peters' book apart.

The first is probably the most straightforward and at the same time very time-consuming – the availability of new material. There has been an extraordinary amount of archaeological exploration and research since the last detailed review of archaeological work undertaken for the 1985 Silver Jubilee Volume of *Cornish Archaeology*. The Cornwall Archaeological Unit (now Historic Environment Service, Cornwall County Council) has carried out over 1200 projects since 1975 and recently we have seen the publication of great excavations from the past, such as Mawgan Porth, Davidstow Airfield, Trethurgy and Halangy. Over the next few years we can expect the publication of substantial reports on the excavations at Trevelgue Cliff Castle, Gwithian and Launceston Castle. Caradoc Peters has had available to him an unprecedented amount of new material through which to sift. Somehow he has managed to create from these sources a new and engaging story that binds together long-held and durable narratives with new and challenging interpretations. Hard facts are interwoven with new ideas. Readers are invited, for instance, to consider the increasing evidence from the Neolithic and Bronze ages that natural features in the landscape were of special significance, and that aspects of life deliberately mimicked nature. We are also led through the complex worlds of ritual and religion and the everyday world of domestic life.

The second issue is equally challenging and has to do with Cornwall's place in the world. Is it a uniquely distinctive place; can its inhabitants be regarded as an ethnic group; is it an ancient or modern Celtic country or both; has Cornwall ever been a separate state, and if so when; and who on earth was King Arthur? These are all contentious issues that cannot be solved by DNA studies alone. No one else has attempted to match together the known archaeological facts with the received myths and associated stories in dealing with two thousand years of history. The author threads his way carefully through this tangled world of prejudice, myth and known facts to provide us with a story that is a best fit with the available evidence and yet does not do irreparable damage to the belief that there is something very special about this peninsula. We are essentially British folk who adopted a Celtic culture and language in the centuries before the Roman occupation and whose tribal kin stretched far beyond the Tamar. The story of Cornwall as a distinctive place is effectively based on the relatively light touch of the Roman empire on these folk and the late and reluctant absorption of the area we now know as Cornwall into the growing English state. The stories of both Arthur and the Cornish in Brittany are explored, as is the emergence of modern celticism, perhaps as evidence of, or as the result of, industrial confidence in the nineteenth century.

The up-to-date archaeology is all here, and is used to create a distinctive narrative history. This is both a reference book and a good read. What makes it attractive and takes it beyond the normal archaeological world is that its subject is culture but culture with a very Cornish twist.

NICHOLAS JOHNSON, *County Archaeologist*

INTRODUCTION

OPPOSITE
St Michael's Mount, a tidal island in Mount's Bay, is deceptive. It looks like a Victorian stately home but in fact the island contains remains from at least the Neolithic period onwards, including a medieval Benedictine monastery.

THIS BOOK IS A JOURNEY THROUGH the whole of Cornwall's human past. It looks at Cornwall as a series of unfamiliar and exotic cultures separated by time. From the land of hunter-gatherers of its distant prehistoric past through to the touristy surfer paradise of the present, Cornwall has frequently changed its personality.

This study is also the archaeology of an ethnic group, the Cornish, as they emerged during the historic periods. Their relationship with the notion of 'Celtic' and with their neighbours in the British Isles and on the Continent is at the root of modern Cornish identity. The book investigates where this sense of identity has come from and where it is leading. The material past is particularly fascinating as it brings people in touch with past cultures in a direct way. A careful inspection of Cornwall's past structures and artefacts reveals its colourful ancient societies and brings life to its ancient cultural landscapes

The archaeology and origins of Cornwall

This is the first book ever to cover the whole of the Cornish past in archaeological terms. Archaeology is multi-disciplinary, using ideas from botany (for instance, pollen analysis), geology, chemistry, anthropology, ethnography, history, historical linguistics, psychology, philosophy, art, architecture and nuclear physics (such as radio-carbon dating). Archaeology is also essentially the study of the human past with emphasis on its material remains. So the buildings, artefacts, traces of past environments and landscapes, and the physical remains of people will form the backbone of this work. Yet the aim of the book is not to be an inventory of things, but a chronicle of people. It sets out to show how the people of Cornwall in past ages led their lives socially, economically, philosophically and religiously. It looks at the natural and

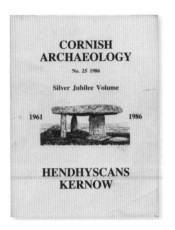

The Silver Jubilee Volume of
the journal Cornish
Archaeology *was published in
1986. New archaeological
information and ideas are
regularly placed in the
journal itself, but the lack of
subsequent overviews
necessitates this book.*

political world they inhabited. In later chapters, it also makes occasional forays overseas to see what happened to emigrants from Cornwall, and what their going meant to those they left behind.

What has happened *before* is not the only explanation of what happens *after*, for the present is shaped by its own times as much as by times past. There is no familiar, nostalgic place or state of being to which the present might one day return. *The Past is a Foreign Country* – the title of a book by the archaeologist David Lowenthal[1] (itself relating to the opening lines of L.P Hartley's novel *The Go-Between*) – spells it out: no one now lives in the past, no one has yet returned to it. Memory works only in the short run, not over the tracts of time explored in this book, and *continuity* means only a process of forever reinterpreting the remains of the past including, in later periods, documents. But though each age is uniquely itself and distinct from its imaginings of its past, no age is static: each has its own struggles, conflicting trends, ideas, desires and hopes. Nothing is inevitable; the idea that what happens first can only lead to what happens next is good hindsight but dubious logic. The book moves chronologically from the time of the earliest hominids to the present day, and includes interpretations that are very recent.

Current ideas in archaeology

Since *Cornish Archaeology*[2] published its Silver Jubilee volume in 1986, ideas in archaeology have undergone great changes. They stem partly from redefinition of what constitutes archaeology, partly from new methods and new approaches. Today Cornish archaeology does not stop anywhere, but ranges from the most remote human past to the present day. Its scope is also wider, taking in maritime archaeology and integrating it into the same framework as land archaeology. Moreover, continuing a trend since the Second World War, it has become ever more eclectic. Material evidence is still at its heart, but it will happily look for other sorts of evidence (and insights) from history, geology, anthropology, physics, chemistry, linguistics and botany. Finally, there has been change, which still continues, in its underlying philosophy.

That change has to do with the rise of a new movement, tongue-twistingly called Post Processualism.[3] Its predecessor (Processualism) saw archaeology as a *process* of historical development, every period producing the conditions from which they evolved. Its proponents studied such factors as social and economic change, political events and environmental developments to explain each evolution. Post-Processualists, however, challenge the idea that history is so important. They argue that different people often have different views of the same past, and that the past is what people think happened, not necessarily what did happen. They contend that the past (or rather the perceived past) is only one of many factors to be weighed, and that

Monuments are traditionally seen as dating from one period only. The folly of this view is demonstrated by Chun Quoit, a Neolithic dolmen subsequently modified in the Early Bronze Age by a low cairn heaped up around its base.

people are much more concerned with their daily lives. To ancient people, what mattered were the immediate influence of neighbouring groups and the immediate social, economic and natural environment.

My own standpoint challenges the idea of history being so important, but with reservations. I am concerned, for example, that Post-Processualism can overuse the word *memory* and treat ancient people as if they had modern mindsets. *Memory* has become a synonym for *history*, but many societies do not – as we do – regard the past as gone beyond retrieval. They think that the dead have gone to another dimension. Polynesian societies, for example, believed that dimension to be the ancient homeland of their ancestors, who could at any time return to the living in the form of dreams,[4] and were thus very much part of the here and now. Australian Aborigines do the reverse:[5] they can return to the Dreamtime when their world was created, a time beyond tenses – both past and present – and in effect another dimension. All this implies that some societies can re-invent monuments and artefacts so that they become part and parcel of their own lives and times. So, if an Early Bronze Age monument still stands today, it has been a monument in every period between; its survival must be explained, and its present form need not necessarily be the same as it was when originally constructed.

Finally, Post-Processualists see chronology as suspect, so a book like this – chronological as it must be and yet on the whole Post-Processualist – seems like a contradiction in terms. But the movement's strictest adherents must use chronology because dating demands it and thus – like it or not – they reinforce the very labels they repudiate. My own chapters adopt the Processualist model (Late Neolithic, Early Bronze Age) rather than the 19th-century period system (Bronze Age, Iron Age). Although archaeologists need chronologies to order their evidence from the past, the idea that they were living their short and changing lives in this or that period never struck anyone at the time. No one living on the cusp of what later generations have defined as two periods can have had the least awareness of moving from one to the next.

Timescales

I have divided the prehistoric periods into broad categories: Palaeolithic (Old Stone Age), Mesolithic (Middle Stone Age), Neolithic (New Stone Age), Bronze Age and Iron Age. These subdivide into, usually, three smaller units: EBA (Early Bronze Age), MBA (Middle Bronze Age), LBA (Late Bronze Age). The meanings of these prehistoric periods are explained as they arise in the text. As for the historic periods, these are Early Medieval, Late Medieval, post-Medieval, Industrial Period and Consumer Age. 'The Dark Ages' confusingly cover a range of different periods in different countries, and the term does not appear here. Instead I use the older and simpler 'Early Medieval' for the period AD 400–AD 1000, in line with current archaeological practice. 'Late Medieval' covers AD 1000–AD 1500.

Geology and landscape

Cornwall is a long tapering peninsula ending in two major headlands, the Lizard and Land's End in West Penwith.[6] Together with part of western Devon, it largely consists of slates and shales in low-lying areas surrounding large hilly areas of granite. The slates and shales began as sea sediments on a continental shelf that were transformed when magma pushed up into them from under the earth's crust. Later, seas eroded the upper levels of the slates and shales, exposing the granitic massifs as hills, and leaving a lower plateau of slates and shales. The granitic massifs became areas of poor upland soils, whilst the slate and shale plateau supported richer vegetation. Two areas are quite different – the Lizard, and the Culm Measures. The Lizard is a complex collection of rocks formed from deep sediments including gabbro, from which comes a type of clay used by prehistoric societies. Erosion by the sea when it was at higher levels has left it as a raised plateau. The Culm Measures are in the far north of Cornwall; they are folded and raised shales that drain poorly. (They possibly get their name from 'col', an old English dialect word for coal, because there is some sooty anthracite in them; or alternatively culm may be related to a Welsh word *kwlm*, meaning knot, in reference to the contortions and folds in the rock.[7]) Both the Culm Measures and the Lizard complex form areas of rough ground, like the granite moors but flatter.

Later erosion and weathering have produced river valleys running off the central spine that stretches the length of the peninsula to West Penwith. The northern coast is all shallow sandy bays and estuaries – the sand deposited by offshore glaciers in the Ice Ages. Deep arms of the sea cut inland into the south coast, creating the creeks of the Fal and Helford rivers. The granite hills have weathered to expose the living rock as tors on the summits or as boulders and loose clitter on the slopes. West of the mainland, the Isles of Scilly are the westernmost of the granite hills, surrounded by sandbanks, but have continuously eroded and broken up since the end of the last Ice Age. The incoming sea has drowned ancient landscapes of fields and settlements. Between these islands and the mainland are many lower rocks, just above or just below the surface, and further to the north-west are the Haig Frais seamounts[8] – important because around their base are the deposits which are source of much of the flint washed up on Cornish shores and fashioned by prehistoric cultures into tools. Cornwall's landscape is varied, and before modern transport lent it unity it was highly regional in its topography and natural resources. It is no surprise that people's view of it should be equally varied.

Definitions of the Cornish and Cornwall

At some stage – and this will be discussed in the book – an ethnic group emerged who called themselves the Cornish. They did not always stay in Cornwall (and their migrations are also here), but even in exile they have seen Cornwall as home. As an ethnic group they certainly feel ties of kinship and ancestry, and they acknowledge a common culture.

The idea that the Cornish can therefore claim nationhood is more contentious – not because they have no right to do so, but because the nation (a recent concept) is not necessarily equated to ethnicity anyway. The essence of nationhood is sovereign power in a state, which by no means always contains only a single ethnic group, even if it usually has a dominant one. Equally there are plenty of ethnic groups that have never wanted to become nations. So if the Cornish have had this idea of themselves as a nation for the last 350 years,[9] it is worth asking why. It could be from a sense of uneven-handed treatment first by England, then by the United Kingdom. It could be resentment at the pretence by governments since the late 17th century that the Cornish did not even exist as an ethnic group. One cannot interpret everything in the Cornish past as relating to a struggle for nationhood, nor can one interpret it as if it were simply English.

Cornwall can be a confusing term because it is sometimes used as a geographical expression, sometimes as a political entity and sometimes as shorthand for the Cornish. I shall not use it in this last sense. Politically it can either mean the Earldom/Duchy or the County.[10] The Earldom, later the Duchy, is a royal fief held these days by the heir to the throne. It by no means includes the whole County, but it has property in Cornwall (and elsewhere), as well as investments in other assets than land. The local government area – the Cornwall of signposts and maps – is the

The Revd William Borlase (1695–1722) was a discerning antiquarian, but his views on a supposed Cornish trade with the Phoenicians have since been displaced by clear evidence to the contrary.

*Changing sea levels have
produced rugged, wild cliffs
by eroding the plateau of
slates and shales that
surround the granite
moorland hills inland. During
the ice ages, these cliffs would
have been inland themselves.
Through the millennia, they
have inspired defence,
religious awe and leisure, and
been a good source of stone.*

15

County. County boundaries have changed and are in any case recent in archaeological terms; go back far enough and there was certainly no such thing as a county, probably no word or concept to stand for Cornwall. The Tamar was a river, not a frontier. A broad and flexible, yet critical, approach is needed when considering the cultural landscape, and generalisations must be tempered by an awareness of natural variations in resources and topography.

Cornwall is and has been a dynamic and changing place. We can look at the diversity of its landscape from the high cliffs and steep valleys of North Cornwall to the flat plateau of the Lizard. We can note its changing image through time from the flint scatters of distant prehistory to the 'space age' domes of the Eden Project. Rather than creating a false sense of timelessness, we are better off appreciating the creativity and dynamism that makes humanity so interesting.

Cornish archaeology – facts and fables

I attempt to present the ways in which people in each period viewed themselves and their past. We in our age have our own mythologies of the past. Three of these mythologies illustrate how attractive stories can entice people into co-opting the physical remains of the past as illustrations of their fantasies. The first is that of the supposed trade between the Phoenicians and Cornwall, which will not feature at all. The second is the legend of King Arthur, which I will treat not as 6th-century 'fact'

Sometimes the most obvious monumental constructions are ignored in the face of powerful popular legends. There are clear ruins of a significant Late Medieval castle at Tintagel, north Cornwall, yet even archaeological attention has focused on less obvious earlier remains that may or may not involve King Arthur.

but as a significant Late Medieval legend. The third and final theme is that of the Celtic origins of Cornwall, which I will discuss – but in a more disciplined and better defined way than comes to us in popular culture and in older archaeological literature. The last two themes are so interwoven in people's minds that one is unimaginable without the other. Yet they spring from different historic mind-sets, and it is more useful to consider them separately.

The supposed trade between the Phoenicians and Cornwall

Europeans in the Renaissance were curious about their origins and, with no archaeology to supply the answers, looked for them in the Classics and the Bible: as an ancient people about whom little had been written, the Phoenicians were likely candidates.[11] The idea of British trade with the Phoenicians goes back to the 15th and 16th centuries, and in England the humanist John Twyne thought the Phoenicians had settled Britain. But it was Aylett Sammes in his *Britannia Antiqua Resaurata* who first suggested a connection with south-western Britain, and another famous antiquarian, Camden,[12] in his work *Britannia*, who developed the long-standing but erroneous theory of the Phoenician trade with Cornwall. In Cornwall, the Revd William Borlase,[13] applying Enlightenment principles of reason to test his hypotheses, accepted Phoenician trade with Cornwall on the grounds that the *menhirs*, or standing stones, found in profusion in Cornwall were copies of Phoenician stelae. Unfortunately they are not.

The 19th-century British[14] made a connection between the great Phoenician trading empire and their own. Paintings of ancient Phoenician traders in Cornwall were hung in the Palace of Westminster (1840) and the Royal Exchange (1894–95), and a supposed Phoenician link to the Great Zimbabwe helped to justify British claims to that part of Africa. But by the end of the 19th century scholars agreed that the racial heritage of the Anglo-Saxons was Germanic.[15] Lacking Germanic heritage and any clear understanding of its past, Cornwall could now lay claim to its very own Phoenician connection. After all, the Phoenicians introduced clotted cream and saffron cake – except that they are post-medieval products; and a tin ingot found at St Mawes was surely part of the Phoenician tin trade – but again the date is wrong.[16]

When Hugh O'Neill Hencken, the author of the first archaeology of Cornwall,[17] brought archaeological rigour to the question in 1932, he could find no evidence of the Phoenicians in Cornwall. Items like the St Mawes ingot were found to be either of the wrong date or explainable in terms of already known and substantiated cultures. He went to Spain and learnt from Phoenician specialists there that the Phoenicians were only found in the south and on the Mediterranean coasts of the Iberian peninsula. As for the ingot, Neil Beagrie has more recently confirmed its date as Late Medieval.[18]

The Phoenician civilisation consisted of Phoenicia proper and its colony, Carthage. When the Assyrians conquered the Phoenician homelands in the Levant in the 7th century BC, Carthage became the centre of this trading empire.[19] A basic reading of Phoenician and Carthaginian archaeology reveals that any Phoenician presence would be archaeologically conspicuous. Phoenician sites include monumental architecture such as temples, stelae and statues, painted tombs, stone-built houses, pavements, cisterns, drains and harbours. Also, the finds of the sites include such artefacts as pottery vessels that are as varied as Roman or Greek ones; coins, lamps and amphorae; jewels of cornelian, obsidian, coloured glass and coral; metal vessels and tools. The story of Hanno, the Carthaginian king who sailed beyond the 'Pillars of Hercules', is sometimes used to suggest a connection with Cornwall. It is much more likely to refer to the Phoenician settlements along the 700-kilometre (435-mile) stretch of the Atlantic coast of Morocco as far as the Phoenician colony of Mogador.[20]

The legend of King Arthur

The Late Medieval literature that includes the legend of King Arthur was the earliest to notice the Cornish past and made no attempt to look at it critically – unlike modern history or archaeology. Myth and legend, whether written or passed down by word of mouth, were believed to the same extent as any legal document or administrative record. The past was as much for moral instruction and entertainment as for information, if not more so.

Geoffrey of Monmouth's *History of the Kings of Britain*[21] and the various tales of King Arthur and his Round Table supplied the framework for Cornwall's past. Geoffrey sought Cornwall's and Britain's origins in ancient Rome and ultimately Troy. The Arthurian legends contained references to Cornwall, and one Anglo-Norman author, known simply as Beroul, set the Tristram and Iseult legend entirely within Cornwall.[22] Geoffrey of Monmouth mentioned Tintagel as Arthur's birthplace, thus giving Tintagel and Cornwall a clear and special place in a folklore that had the widest currency. Arthurian legends, alongside the Bible, were the manuals of etiquette and courtly morals. Versions of them were written in Welsh, French, German and Italian and were well known all over Europe.

Medieval myth and legend began to be questioned in the Renaissance. All that had ever been written could now be printed, published across Europe and its colonies in the New World – and exposed to criticism. In the light of new ideas and new data, people could reappraise all the old unquestioned legends and, by the time

King Arthur and his knights have long been depicted in shining armour, which had not even been invented in the Early Medieval period when Arthur was supposed to have been alive.

of Borlase, other writers were already seeing Arthur as more imaginary than real. Borlase himself refers to Arthur as having been King of Britain only in a footnote[23] – yet that idea is still popular belief.

Some 20th-century historians have tried to fix dates for the Arthurian period from short references to Arthur in the *Welsh Annals*.[24] But these are notoriously hard to date accurately, and include entries inserted hundreds of years later by well-meaning but not very helpful monks. Even then the authors have not used, and never intended to use, the Arthurian legends as the basis of reliable narrative.

The Celtic origins of Cornwall

The concept of the 'Celtic' emerged in the early 17th century. Abbé Pezron first used it in the modern sense to compare the Breton and Gaulish languages. There was then a growing interest in comparative linguistics in Europe,[25] and an antiquarian called Edward Lhuyd took up the term in trying to trace connections between the people of the northern and western British Isles.[26] In Cornwall it was Borlase who connected the Cornish with the family of Celtic peoples and, as the idea of nation-states became ever more potent,[27] it was no accident that pan-Celtic nationalist movements, political and cultural, had emerged by the end of the 19th century, and included Cornwall. Archaeologists of the time linked the mention of Celts in Classical sources with finds from excavations, and the consensus was that the late prehistoric cultures of La Tène and possibly Hallstatt material were the physical remains of ancient Celtic people.

John Collis[28] and Simon James,[29] two present-day archaeologists, however, have argued that the Classics give no warrant for the use of 'Celtic' as a label for a whole range of people in a range of periods from the Iron Age to the present day. Classical authors used the word not to draw any serious ethnographic or linguistic lines, but in the same casual way that Europeans in the days of empire spoke of 'Indian' – Red Indian, West Indian, East Indian and so on. When Caesar and Tacitus wrote about Gauls and Britons specifically, that is what they called them – not Celts. In literature from the Early Medieval until 1700, neither Celts themselves nor outsiders referred to Celtic people as 'Celtic'.

All this is part of a wider debate about whether modern ethnic groups or nations have deep roots in the past or whether they invent ancestries to justify the politics of the present.[30] J.V.S. and M.R. Megaw,[31] Australian archaeologists, have criticised Collis and James as being English chauvinists who are hostile to Europe and who want to strip their less powerful neighbours of their identity by denying that there were Celts in the Iron Age on the European continent. Heinrich Härke,[32] a German archaeologist, has also suggested that English archaeologists want to distance themselves from Germany and its recent past, and that is at least partly why they have been trying to establish indigenous origins for themselves. Even so, there is no doubt that Collis, James and others[33] have brought much greater clarity to our understanding of the past.

The term 'Celtic' usefully conveys the linguistic connections between various groups in the British Isles and ancient Gaul. It also serves to name people who choose to describe themselves as Celtic. But as Collis and others have shown, its indiscriminate use has clouded our appreciation of the complexity of European pre-history. For example, a famous cauldron found in a Danish peat bog, the Gundestrup Cauldron, often appears in textbooks as Celtic, yet recent analysis shows it came from Romania (not associated with Celts). Iron Age Europe was involved in wide-spread traffic of goods and ideas, and to give them all just one label is simplistic.

More than simplistic, it is misleading if it smuggles in the idea that the Celts were some sort of racial group. In any work on Cornish prehistory the reader finds almost obligatory references to Ireland, Wales, Scotland and above all Brittany (well before the migrations from Cornwall to Brittany in the Early Medieval period) and the hyperbole goes far beyond what they had in common. For Cornishness and Celtic-ness are only linguistic and ethnic concepts, and ethnicity is only a shared sense of common ancestry or kinship. It does not imply genetic purity. Members of an ethnic group commonly marry outsiders, and outsiders can become insiders by marriage or adoption. A study by Harvey and others[34] showed that the Cornish had great biolog-ical affinity not only with people in other Celtic-speaking areas but also with their neighbours in south-west England. Curiously, the closest match to Cornwall turned out to be South Wales. Despite the title of their article – 'How Celtic are the Cor-nish?' – the authors did not claim that there could be any racial category of Celts.

Shorn of a few fallacies, 'Celts' can become a useful term because its tenable uses are precise. First, the last three centuries of the Cornish past can unquestionably be called Celtic. It is the word people have used for themselves, and connections with other Celtic people have been very real. Second, the Celtic-speaking peoples of the British Isles in the Early Medieval period retained or revived elements of the Iron Age La Tène style in their artwork,[35] and maintained trading networks among them-selves and with the Mediterranean, to the exclusion of the incoming Anglo-Saxons.[36] They also maintained religious differences with most of the Anglo-Saxons (except in Northumbria). However, while the Cornish may well have been able to communi-cate effectively with the Welsh and Bretons, they would have struggled with the Irish, Manx and Scottish Gaelic languages. Indeed the language of the so-called Celtic Church (not a contemporary term) was an old-fashioned version of church Latin,[37] and therefore the main literary language. The bonds between these areas may have been due to linguistic and cultural affinities, but they may also have reflected a common identification with the Mediterranean after centuries of a Roman presence. Another example of continuity is the link between Cornwall and

Brittany throughout the Medieval period into the post-Medieval – and to some extent later, especially today. As for prehistory, with no written record of its language or even whether Cornwall was called Cornwall, little can be meaningfully said.

In the chapters that follow, therefore, Celtic will be used in discussion of the last three centuries of Cornish archaeology, and avoided completely for prehistory; Celtic-speaking will be used of the periods from the end of the Roman period to the present. The terms will not be used to imply that they denote a race, but only as descriptors of ethnicity or language.

For many, this view of a prehistoric stone circle in Cornwall will conjure up powerful images of a mystic and mysterious Celtic culture. Unfortunately, the term as currently used to mean those cultures speaking Celtic languages is only 300 years old.

CHAPTER ONE

NATURAL AND HUMAN WORLDS ON THE EDGE OF THE ATLANTIC

Palaeolithic (400,000 YEARS AGO–10,000 BC)
& Mesolithic (10,000–3500 BC)

THIS CHAPTER COVERS A PERIOD OF HISTORY over seventy times longer than any discussed in other chapters. It is long enough to make even geology look dynamic! At the beginning of this period, the present-day area of the county was just a hilly promontory overlooking an extensive tundra plain in a continental zone of permafrost. At the end it was a mild, temperate peninsula deeply dissected by creeks, overlooking an ocean stretching to the horizon. At no point in this period would anybody have seen much difference between one day and the next, but over its whole span people's experience of this landscape changed enormously. One fact unifies the period: its people were hunter-gatherers. This term and its use in archaeology have recently been the subject of intense debate.

Hunter-gatherer societies of early prehistory

At a simple level, people at the end of the Palaeolithic followed herds of horses and deer on their annual migrations. During the Mesolithic they gathered wild plants in season, and hunted animals where fodder and water were plentiful.[1] They undertook fishing inshore, and they gathered other seafood in the form of seaweed, shellfish and sea urchins. However, these days hunter-gatherer societies are seen as varied and more complex, as ethnography and new archaeological evidence have revolutionised our views. As one archaeologist put it, Mesolithic people should be seen as more sophisticated than simply having meaningful relationships with hazelnuts.[2]

Instead of patiently waiting for nature to provide, the hunter-gatherers of Cornwall are likely to have given nature a helping hand.[3] They could transplant what they gathered to new, more convenient places. They could burn, or more probably clear, woodlands to make room for useful plants – and those would certainly include the kind of plants that attract grazing animals. They could create mussel and limpet beds

for easy harvesting. Far from being passive occupants of some ecological niche, hunter-gatherers respond to change and promote it, to turn haphazard sufficiency into reliable abundance.

From the Late Mesolithic we find larger and more lasting base camps where people presumably gathered for seasonal ceremonies – perhaps like the gatherings of the so-called 'harvester people',[4] who lived on plentiful and reliable supplies of wild rice in the swamp lands to the west of the Great Lakes in North America. Similarly, at the end of the Ice Age a pre-agricultural people in the Levant called the Natufian could settle because they were surrounded by a profusion of wild cereals.[5] It could be that regular return to the same places at the same important seasons became possible in Cornwall as fishing and the shoreline yielded more food, and as people taught nature to be more productive.

Hunter-gatherers have used a range of technologies, some of which applied in Cornwall. The Natufian culture discovered how to grind stones into shape – a practice which in Europe is usually associated with the first farming communities. The Late Mesolithic people in Cornwall knew nothing of agriculture but they too made some tools by grinding stone: these certainly included pebble hammers (or 'mace heads'). There was probably no strict division of labour between the sexes or age groups in the periods covered here. Firmly established social and economic roles only come about when people can build up surpluses of food and other resources; and adequate surpluses only come about when people stop living literally from hand to mouth. Ethnographers watching present-day hunter-gatherers like the !Kung in southern Africa have seen how flexibly they behave.[6] If women and children out gathering fruit and roots come across prey they can kill, they kill it; if men out hunting find an edible plant, they gather it. That said, there may have been minor variations from the Early and the Late Mesolithic in Cornwall; when there were surpluses of food and resources there would be at least a tendency for people to specialise.

Finally, there was religion. Hunter-gatherer groups do not necessarily share the same beliefs as one another, and groups living at different times in the same area can also have different beliefs. I shall argue that that was the case in Cornwall, and that there was a major shift in religious belief from the Early to Late Mesolithic. A recent idea that hunter-gatherer cultures could generally – or often – be described as shamanistic has met resistance because it uses the word too loosely for the wider archaeological community to take up. Among the few to aim at a sharper definition are Neil Price and his fellow authors of *The Archaeology of Shamanism*, published in 2001. Shamanists think that priests or 'shamans' can leave their bodies and commune directly with fellow shamans, nature spirits, animal spirits and ancestors; and that others can commune with these spirits in less direct ways. It cannot be ruled out that some of the finds from Late Mesolithic sites in Cornwall may be shamanistic.

Until recently, archaeologists discussing the Mesolithic of north-western Europe have either said nothing about its religion, on the grounds that it was unknowable, or settle for bland statements about nature worship. What follows is my attempt to offer a view of the Palaeolithic and Mesolithic in Cornwall in the round, covering the full range of its different ecologies, its economic activity, the technologies it used, its social behaviour – and religious beliefs.

Traces of the Palaeolithic (400,000 YEARS AGO–10,000 BC)

The Palaeolithic in Cornwall is represented by loose surface finds, and occasionally by stone tools. Unfortunately, these are not from actual sites, except the Upper Palaeolithic site at Booby's Bay, just south of Trevose Head and north of the village of Constantine.[7] This uncertainty means that our picture of the Palaeolithic in Cornwall has to rest more heavily on other knowledge – about the impact of environmental change and human behaviour patterns over south-west Britain as a whole.

The last interglacial – the period between the last Ice Age and the one before that – saw higher sea levels than those of today. Around the coast of Cornwall, a raised, wave-cut platform marks the line of this earlier sea level, and the temperature was higher. The bones of warm-climate animals like hippopotamus are found in Britain.[8]

During both the last two ice ages, however, the coast lay much further out – at its furthest, in the last Ice Age, about 150 kilometres (93 miles) beyond its present line.[9] Lying between areas of higher ground, what are now the Celtic Sea and the English Channel were plains dissected by rivers, with floodplains and a few gorges. The Rhine followed its present course, then bent south and ran parallel with what are now the coastlines of Dorset and Devon, then still further south and away from Cornwall.[10] As rivers made a benign environment, that deviation may help to explain why Palaeolithic remains are scarcer in Cornwall than in Devon and Dorset. Glaciers in the last Ice Age reached only as far as south-west Wales, leaving the Severn to flow down through the Bristol Channel and Celtic Sea to the north of Cornwall. So Cornwall was the end of a hilly promontory in the middle of a tundra plain, between the two major river systems of the Rhine and Severn.

Elsewhere in the south-west, seasonal campsites have been found in caves and on river terraces. Cave sites include Kent's Cavern, Kitley and Tornewton in the Torbay area, and Gough's Cave, Cheddar and Wookey Hole in North Somerset.[11] These are sheltered locations, especially those around Torbay, with the Dartmoor massif between them and the polar winds. Kent's cavern, in a sheltered valley in Torquay, is probably the best show-cave for visitors interested in archaeology. A line of river-terrace sites, exposed by 19th-century gravel digging, lies in the Axe valley on the Devon/Dorset border and is part of a recent study by Southampton University.[12] The site at Broom gives an idea of what open-air sites in Cornwall might have been like.

The Palaeolithic period is generally represented in Cornwall by chance finds of flint lying on the ground surface. The handaxe, a large triangular-shaped tool with two long sharp sides, was a multi-purpose tool carried by people who were travelling light as they followed herds of game animals.

These sites are typical of the Palaeolithic in Europe, and would have been on the route of animals such as horses and reindeer, migrating to summer pastures in the uplands – the herds being not only prey in themselves but guides to other sources of plant and animal food. No doubt Cornwall has more riverside sites than have been found, probably hidden under the extra layers of silt washed down as waste. The Fal valley, incidentally, had a deep gorge on its northern (St Mawes) side.[13] Most of the finds cluster on the south coast facing the Rhine.

Ecology has been the big question (perhaps because it offers clear cut answers), but there are plenty of others. What were the various people of the Palaeolithic like physically? What did they do; indeed, what could they do? *Homo erectus* and then Neanderthals were the people of the earlier Palaeolithic and the first hominids to live outside Africa.[14] Their human qualities are much debated. *Homo erectus* could produce fire and make spears, but probably not speak as modern humans do – their mouths and throats look wrong for the purpose. Elsewhere Neanderthals[15] have left visible signs of ritual burial, and the apparently ritual arrangement of bear skulls. The Torbay caves show no sign of burials, but that anyone chose to make stone tools in caves may point to a ritual purpose.[16] Only now are archaeologists beginning to grapple with social and ritual life in these periods.

Kent's Cavern in Torbay has produced evidence that handaxes were made there.[17] Handaxes account for much of what the Lower and Middle Palaeolithic have left behind, and the main find comes from Cornwall. In spite of their name these were

This map shows all the known find spots of Palaeolithic tools in Cornwall. There are only 15 recorded find spots and one site, Booby's Bay, from a period lasting about 400,000 years. The overall picture is limited by the nature and quantity of the evidence.

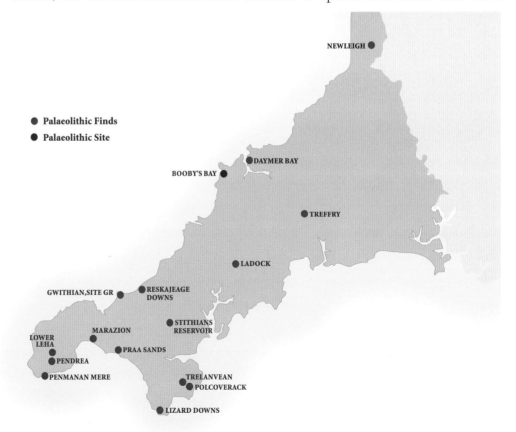

multi-purpose tools for hunter-gatherers on the move who wanted to travel light. The flint and chert they were made of came from the Devon-Dorset border, and from the Haig Frais sea-mounts beyond Scilly.[18] The latter may have been buried by glaciers in the ice ages, but these were unlikely to have been the direct source anyway: in warmer times when sea levels were high, the Haig Frais flints washed up on the Cornish coast as pebbles, and were there for the taking when the sea once more receded.

Though some stone tools from the Upper Palaeolithic are the same as, or similar to, those of the later Mesolithic, they are much more diverse. That archaeological sites can themselves be sources of flint means that a whole lot of tools found in one place need not all be the product of a single period; they can be the work of different people at successive times. Stratified sites do exist, though, and the one at Booby's Bay[19] makes interesting points about geology and climate. It shows what climate and the law of gravity can do to a hillside site. Its flints lie buried under deposits caused by alternate freezing and thawing, and by the frost-shattering conditions of the period. They have also slid downhill, re-deposited from a higher site where plain and uplands met in an ecology combining the resources of both – just as at Kent's cavern. Among those resources were the flint pebbles embedded in raised beaches that the high sea levels of the previous interglacial had left behind – pebbles not to be found in the plains below.

Mesolithic Europe (10,000–3500 BC)

When the last Ice Age came to an end and warmth returned, the sea levels rose and lives changed.[20] As trees grew and forests spread, the fauna and flora of the open plain retreated to the north and east of Europe and Asia, and people gave up following large animals from horizon to horizon. They could get all they needed from smaller territories, for something was always in season.

Stone Age periods (all ending in '-lithic') mark off nothing more than changes in the tools that people used: they are not labels for different economic phases or lifestyles. Even so, the tools that are distinctively Mesolithic exploit the new ecology,[21] and make possible a new economy. First among these are the microliths – these were little stone barbs that tipped an arrowhead. Arrows were ideal in forests, where leaves and branches put a premium on stealth and the capacity to kill at moderate distance. The stone tools of the Mesolithic people were much more alike in different regions than they had been in Upper Palaeolithic times. In spite of suggestions that good ideas could spread easily when Britain was part of the continent in the early Mesolithic, and then less easily when it became an island in the late Mesolithic, there is little evidence of any exotic goods and materials changing hands in the period.[22]

NATURAL AND HUMAN WORLDS

Two great changes, one environmental and one social and economic, transformed Europe in the Late Mesolithic. On the environmental side, there were high temperatures and such a rise in sea levels that the northern plain became the North Sea, and the plains of the west became the Atlantic continental shelf. The economic and social revolution was driven by incoming communities of farmers who were rooted in the land they occupied, and set about changing the landscape itself.

Agriculture began in the Near East and spread west into Europe along a moving frontier between farming and hunter-gatherer groups, until its final triumph.[23] But it was a slow, hesitant process. In fact it stalled for all of a thousand years, from 4500–3500 BC, on a line just short of the north-west coast of Europe.[24] The resulting north/south divide separated more than just rival economies using different kinds of skill. It was the fact that the farmers altered the physical landscape that put them into such different worlds, and new technologies alone did not force change. Hunter-gatherers could adopt these skills and still continue to hunt and gather.

Some hunter-gatherers along the coasts of the European continent, such as the people of the Ertebølle Culture of southern Scandinavia,[25] found enough for their needs in one place to form sedentary communities. They left large middens of shell-fish, other signs of seafood processing, pottery and evidence of dense and permanent settlement. In Britain (at Culverwell, on the Portland peninsula, Dorset) there were such permanent structures as a floor, paved with limestone slabs, and hearths.[26] There were dogs, too, in Mesolithic Europe – Britain included. They were a sort of domesticated wolf, kept to help with the hunting.[27]

In the Early Mesolithic period stone tool production was fairly uniform in style over wide areas. The increasing diversity of the Late Mesolithic period, revealed by these two maps, is perhaps greater when the settlement and funerary evidence is also considered.

Early Mesolithic

MAGLEMOSIAN

SAUVETERRIAN

BEURONIAN

SAUVETERRIAN

Late Mesolithic

LARNIAN OBANIAN

ERTEBØLLE

TARDENOISIAN

INCOMING NEOLITHIC CULTURES

ASTURIAN

TARDENOISIAN

INCOMING NEOLITHIC CULTURES

Early Mesolithic settlement and rising sea levels: Cornwall (10,000–6000 BC)

It used to be thought that seafood only came seriously into its own in the Late Mesolithic.[28] Chemical analysis of Mesolithic human bone has changed all that, and it is now clear that it was a vital part of diet from the start of the Mesolithic. A review of Mesolithic campsites on the Lizard shows that they were mostly on the coasts, and any temporary camps inland were near rivers.[29] These temporary camps yield little evidence of stone working, virtually all the finds being microliths from arrows.

Another study of the Mesolithic in Cornwall[30] shows that sites not only cluster along the coast but also at the edge of moorlands – as excellent 'ecotones'. An ecotone is an area lying where two or more ecological zones join, thus giving the hunter-gatherer the best of at least two worlds. Recent studies of Bodmin Moor show sites strung along river valleys up into the moor,[31] which suggests there was food to be found inland for part of the year at least. Not all the flint tools now on the moor were necessarily there in ancient times; they may have arrived in the last two centuries, when farmers used sand from the beach (and any flints in it) to improve the acidic moorland soil.[32] Apart from one possible Upper Palaeolithic find, the Early Mesolithic is the earliest period for which there is evidence of settlement in Scilly.[33]

Recent studies of Mesolithic society suggest that nature was at the heart of its beliefs. Mesolithic artefacts are little altered from their natural state.[34] Necklaces of animal teeth and antler head-dresses are identifiable as such. The people created no artificial materials, so that ceramic technology invented in Europe in the Upper Palaeolithic for making figurines was abandoned in the Mesolithic. Only in southern Scandinavia, under Neolithic influences, did Mesolithic people adopt ceramics.[35] So it may be significant that stone artefacts found in Cornwall not only look like and are stone, but that their size matches the nodule or pebble from which they were made. Chert pebbles are larger than flint pebbles, so they become axes. Smaller nodules of flint become smaller tools – awls, arrow barbs and scrapers. The nature of the original is respected too. Chert resists weathering and is hard, hence it is found as bigger pebbles and is suitable for axes.[36] A harder type of stone, quartzite, is made into bevelled shapes, pitted at the ends. What these are for is a mystery, but the stone itself, less brittle than either chert or flint, is certainly good material for pitting.[37]

It may seem obvious that the qualities and sizes of source materials should have a bearing on their choice. However, in later periods perfectly good local materials were ignored in favour of exotic ones, and the shape and size of an artefact reflected some idea entirely in the mind and had nothing to do with fidelity to raw material. What changed was people's attitudes to their own environment and its resources. Trading entails bringing objects in from someone else's environment, and there is little evidence of this in Cornwall. Once it was thought that chert axes, for example,

were too big to have come from stones on Cornish beaches, and must have come by trade from Devon and Dorset – but that was based on faulty beachcombing.

The campsites of the Early Mesolithic may also express an affinity with nature. They stand on what seem to be the migratory paths of animals and fish, for they are never far from water. There could also be a parallel between them and the spiritual pathways of the Australian aborigines,[38] which connected natural features like rivers and rock formations. It is also a theory[39] that the hilltop enclosures of the later Neolithic people continued the Mesolithic tradition of reverence for the tors of the high moorlands.[40] While tors were special to the Later Mesolithic people, there is no evidence that they were sacred to the Early Mesolithic in Cornwall, and the pathways past water and up rivers may just relate them to a particular ecology. There are good examples of societies of hunter-gatherers, now and in the past, that have expanded and retreated with certain kinds of ecology, such as tundra, as the ecologies themselves grew and shrank; examples include Palaeoeskimos and Palaeoindians in the Canadian Arctic.[41]

Funerary rites also connect with nature. There are no burial sites in Cornwall and few, indeed, in the British Isles at all. Those few are caves from the Early Mesolithic, and the remains may not be from burials as such but simply from the deposition of bodies.[42] From the Late Mesolithic burials are unknown, even in caves,[43] but this cannot be dismissed, as the lack of Palaeolithic campsites can be, as mere absence of evidence. Since Mesolithic campsites survive – consisting mainly of scattered flints and hearths – then any graves dug into the soil would have survived. Conceivably they might have preferred sites on the now submerged plain, but not everyone would have died conveniently close enough. It was much more likely that bodies

were left in the open to 'excarnate' – to be stripped of their flesh by wild animals and birds, the elements and natural decay. If so it could well explain what was to happen in the Neolithic. Excarnation fits in well with beliefs based on the natural cycles.

Meanwhile sea levels were rising. Along the coast of Cornwall now lie sunken woodlands, stretches of peat and other habitats.[44] Rich and diverse ecologies were shrinking. But whether human action made any difference is moot. There is evidence of what could possibly be the burning of woodlands on Dartmoor during the Mesolithic.[45] However, a pollen study from Dozmary Pool, to the south-east of the Jamaica Inn on Bodmin Moor, gave a similar result and proved to be unreliable.[46] Its radiocarbon dating showed levels in the soil were not trustworthy, and one sample was not necessarily older than another just because it lay deeper. A team looking at similar ground in the Peak District[47] suggested that people had deliberately cleared it to create grasslands for herd animals. People in Cornwall might have had the same motive to act in the same way, but if so they left no evidence of any great change.[48]

Late Mesolithic changes, and attitudes to nature (6000–3500 BC)

The Early Mesolithic was a long period that came to no abrupt end, but faded into the Late Mesolithic after many small and subtle changes. The Late Mesolithic world in Cornwall was smaller, with roughly today's coastline – but a warmer climate. The increased ratio of coastline to land meant that resources were concentrated. That may partly explain why campsites were larger; and the bands of people were presumably larger too. Whether it was the sea that helped to feed them all is not clear: recent work on prehistoric diet does not cover the period.[49] It could be that at sites like Poldowrian, close to deep water, people could catch deep-sea and inshore fish.

Late Mesolithic campsites in Cornwall were selected for their panoramic views. This is half of the view from the Trevose Head (TV1) site above Booby's Bay – headlands succeed one another into the distance.

The Trevose Head site, like others in Cornwall, has piles of flint marking the edge of the ridge. The large amount of gleaming white flint like this specimen suggests that these piles were meant to be highly visible.

PALAEOLITHIC
(400,000 years
ago–10,000 bc)
& MESOLITHIC
(10,000–3500 bc)

The sites of Late Mesolithic base camps seem to have been carefully selected. Here at Poldowrian the flat landscape is interrupted by a valley cutting through the cliffs. To the left of the farm buildings a spur juts out into the woodland. The Late Mesolithic site is at the end of this spur and but for the woodland would have a commanding view of this valley and the approach to the sea.

Larger and more settled campsites may also reflect changes on the continent. Although there are no cist cemeteries from this period as there are in Brittany or Denmark,[50] the new trends on the continent certainly left their mark, and are now suggested here as the first signs of a new attitude to the environment. Farmers on the continent were changing the landscape in order to raise exotic domesticated animals and plants. To an older way of thinking this was an affront to nature inviting terrible retribution. To those hunter-gatherers, the landscape was nothing but what nature had put there: there were no artificial monuments, no large permanent buildings, no field systems and no mounds. Most alien of all were the 'transported landscapes' brought in by the agriculturists, mimicking those from which the exotic animals and plants had come.[51] All this novelty called not only for an intellectual but also a spiritual response.

There are in fact signs of such a response. In Cornwall in the Late Mesolithic the campsites now stand on the edges of natural terraces or low ridges. Undramatic as that sounds, it is not as straightforward as it seems. From close up and below, the terrace itself is visible, but hard to see from far away. Anything happening there is not clearly visible from below and anyone on it has a clear view of the land below it. An observer from the hilltop above can see everything on the terrace. Now in spite of these terraces and ridges being entirely natural, their choice as campsites is entirely artificial. It has nothing to do with following herds or catching fish, and everything to do with a hierarchy of nature. Hills and high ridges are above the world of humans; the rivers with their associated game and vegetation are below. The occupant of the terraces looks down with a sense of possession – master of all he or she surveys. Intruding bands (and animals), following the river paths or coastline, had to approach with no clear line of sight, at a physical disadvantage and, in the case of the humans, at a psychological disadvantage too. The sites near Crowdy Reservoir on Bodmin Moor tell the whole story.[52] Crowdy Reservoir is on the north-western side of the moor near Davidstow. The Early Mesolithic sites simply line the edge of the old water course (before the reservoir engulfed it), whereas the single Late Mesolithic site is set well back on the terrace against the hillside.

The large base camps contain a wide range of tools, from microlithic barbs to scrapers, burins and awls.[53] Burins and some kinds of scraper were used in working wood and bone, other scrapers and awls in making clothes. A spotted skin slung over one shoulder makes a handy cartoon cliché, but hardly a garment that fits the facts. Clothing from ethnographically similar groups today and from Mesolithic sites elsewhere in Europe is more varied, and much more sophisticated. Skins are carefully cut and sewn, and fabrics are woven from plant fibres. Cloth of that sort found at sites in the Czech Republic dates right back to the Upper Palaeolithic.[54] A new type of tool is a pebble hammer with an hourglass-shaped central hole for hafting. These

hammers, probably for cracking nuts, were made by stone-grinding methods borrowed from farming communities across the Channel.[55]

Waste flakes of flint and chert and the diversity of tools found on Late Mesolithic sites show that tools were not only made but used there for a wide range of economic and domestic purposes.[56] The waste flakes do not look as if they lay where they fell from the tool maker's hands; instead, they are arranged, along with the tools themselves, as mixed, apparently unsorted collections in small mounds and ridges. Seen from one side these features seem to echo or accentuate the edge of the terrace, but from the opposite side they seem to mark, and perhaps even designate, the line of approach to the largest feature or features at the end of the terrace. There are surveyed or excavated examples at Site TV1 (Trevose Head) overlooking Booby's Bay, Penhale Point, Poldowrian and Beagle's Point.[57] The pattern at Poldowrian has perhaps been disturbed by later Neolithic pits, but probably not changed by them, given that the same pattern recurs at the other sites. The Poldowrian site, which is one of the most scenic, is open to visitors by appointment and has a small museum. The Windmill Farm site on the Lizard and Crooklet's Inlet, near Bude, are on the coast but are otherwise similar in topography and have yielded similar artefacts.[58]

The Stithians Reservoir site[59] seems, on the basis of topography and the flint finds, to be an example of an inland version. It sits on a low ridge, just north of the car park and leisure area by the reservoir dam. In the landscape of its time it had a commanding view over the Kennal Valley, which sloped away sharply to the south, as well as over the springs to the north from which the Kennal rises, and a tributary valley to the west. The view is impressive, and shows that Late Mesolithic people had an eye for drama, not just for practicality. The Croft Pascoe site[60] on the Lizard is close to a stream and on the edge of a scarp, and has both Early and Late Mesolithic material on it. Although right for a Late Mesolithic base camp, the finds

Mesolithic campsites are usually represented by scatters of flint and charcoal; where there is evidence of dwellings, they suggest round, tent-like structures. This illustration shows two different types of reconstruction. The tents may have been covered by skins or bark, and such campsites would have been occupied by extended families.

suggest it was a temporary, seasonal hunting camp. The closeness of the Poldowrian and Windmill Farm sites probably made another large base camp unnecessary.

All this signifies a new sense of separateness – that people were separate from nature and must therefore find the means to placate it. They may have done so through shamanistic ritual; camps set up in high places fit well with the out-of-body flying that shamans claim they do in states of trance. The Early Mesolithic people thought the opposite – that they were part and parcel of the environment. A parallel might be the Inuit belief that the spirits of people, animals and all things natural are alike tied to one place and never cease to exist.[61] The souls of the dead migrate into the bodies of their newborn kin, and the cycles of the seasons match life cycles in a world that is at once both matter and spirit.

Regional interaction and attitudes to the human world

There is as little evidence of traffic between regions for the Late Mesolithic as there was for the Early Mesolithic. Chert and flint occur locally, so do not need trade to explain their presence; but if objects stayed put, ideas and know-how spread across wide regions of Britain and north-west Europe. Across the whole area there was a trend away from microliths that were broad to narrower, lanceolate forms.[62] The move to larger campsites was a general trend too. It could even be that there was a whole south-western Mesolithic area with a common cycle of economic activity.[63] By this theory, spring and early summer were a time for fishing and seafood; in mid to late summer people hunted herd animals in the granite uplands; in autumn and early winter they went back to the beaches; and in late winter and early spring they hunted again, this time in inland woods. More than just a shared way of behaving, the theory entails a shared way of thinking about human beings and their place in the environment.

Once a people see themselves as separate from nature, it is a short step to seeing themselves as a group separate from others. The sense of their own identity may have emboldened groups to do things their own way, and thus led to the cultural diversity of the Neolithic. Believing themselves part of natural cycles, people would previously have had no reason to split into self-conscious groups. So – contrary to ideas that Mesolithic conformity was simply due to interaction,[64] which can just as easily drive people apart – Mesolithic 'groups' would have been happy to use each other's ideas unmodified because they they felt they were all birds of a feather. Growing Neolithic influence would have changed all that, and it was visibly there. Two examples are the pebble hammers with hourglass perforations for hafting, and the countersunk pebbles[65] shaped by grinding, a classic Neolithic technology.

Environment change may have hastened social change. Rising sea levels produced not only a high ratio of coast to land, but also many large creeks running deep

• **Mesolithic Sites and Finds**

Mesolithic settlement patterns are noticeable for their coastal concentration. This is likely to be linked to a greater reliance on seafood as sea level rose and the coastline grew over the course of the Mesolithic. The few moorland sites properly represent the supplementary hunting of migrating game animals such as red deer and roe deer during the summer.

inland. For Mesolithic people, with no animal transport, all this water made it temptingly easy to move about, because dugouts and canoes made of skin or bark were the fastest and simplest means of transport. That and the larger numbers of their bands may have accelerated social and religious change.

The large bands occupying sites like Poldowrian and Windmill farm imply that there was now, comparatively, plenty to eat. High sea levels brought fish, the Gulf Stream brought mild air. Maps of present day vegetation show wild ancestors of cabbage, turnips and beet growing on the Cornish coast.[66] Many members of the cabbage family, of the pea and vetch family, also grow on the coast, and so do edible common weeds like Goosefoot, Fat Hen and Good King Henry. All of these could have been either picked where they were or transplanted to more convenient places, or both. Unlike cereals, wild cabbage is hard to preserve so its earliest use cannot be dated archaeologically; but it is so abundant that it is safe to infer that it was eaten long before its first written mention in Roman times.[67]

The Palaeolithic and Mesolithic periods in Cornwall were, then, periods of great length, and as such saw major environmental changes. There were also other changes, from the following of herds across frozen landscapes to the exploitation of seasonal resources in the warmer times after the Ice Age. We can even detect how attitudes to nature changed – from identifying with it to respecting it as separate from human identity.

CHAPTER TWO

NEOLITHIC CULTURE IN CORNWALL: NEW TECHNOLOGIES AND EXCHANGE

Early & Middle Neolithic (3500–2700 BC)

THE LIFESTYLE IN CORNWALL at this period is a matter of hot debate. Until recently the Neolithic was seen as the period of the first farmers, but now it is seen more as a time of tentative agricultural development. Farming as the mainstay of the economy may well have come later.

The defining mark of the period – what makes it a new and different '-lithic' – was that its people ground stones into shape to make tools, instead of 'knapping' (or chipping) them. Pottery was another new technology that arose; and exotic materials appeared on a scale beyond anything seen in the nascent exchange systems at the end of the Mesolithic. The possible exchange of flint and chert has been mentioned in Chapter One. The adoption of all these new technologies also involved a major shift in ideological and religious thought.

Neolithic culture in north-western Europe

The northern European Neolithic began when the Linear Pottery culture brought the ideas of farming and its associated technologies to the Northern European Plain as far as the Paris Basin,[1] and they spread in modified form to near the coast. However, the line of advance halted for about a thousand years from 4,500 to 3,500 BC (see Chapter One), before taking in the north-west coast of Europe, the British Isles and Scandinavia.[2] In that time the Mesolithic cultures at and beyond its frontier had to confront new ideas and lifestyles.

Mesolithic communities had to cope with the radical changes that the Neolithic was bringing in – of which the most radical was the impact of farming peoples on the landscape.[3] One result of that cultural collision was 'megalithism' – the use of large stones for monuments. Apart from a small area of western Poland[4] they were non-existent in the original Neolithic territory, and only appeared in the Mesolithic areas that were beginning to digest Neolithic influence.

Megalithic tombs including Long barrows & Long cairns
Megalithic tombs
Long houses

This map shows the north and western distribution of megalithic tombs – in other words, where Late Mesolithic populations had been. It also shows that longhouses and long cairns only overlap in western Poland. The long barrows and long cairns were copies of ruined, deserted longhouses of Neolithic populations to the east created by their Late Mesolithic neighbours to the west when they took on Neolithic ideas.

The difficulty with the idea that the Neolithic economy was largely based on farming is that the landscape did not change enough for this to have been the case. Such farming would have needed the land to become an environment fit for such exotic crops as cereals and of animals originally from the Near East: that did not happen. Meanwhile, the old contract between humanity and nature faced the challenge of new, 'unnatural' ways of using raw materials – such as turning clay into ceramics. An alternative theory is that religion, rather than economics, is the key here.[5] This would suggest that the new artefacts are not purely functional, but give access to ritual knowledge. Ceramics, for example, appear to consist of an artificial material not found in nature – magical to the uninitiated. So it could be that the megaliths simply bear witness to mystery, and that changes in the landscape, such as the erection of stone monuments, were about society and religion, not production and consumption.[6]

Megaliths and earthen monuments included long barrows and causewayed enclosures typical of the lowland areas. One conjecture is that they copied the abandoned settlements of the Linear Pottery culture, and because they had funerary uses they represented the longhouses and settlements of the dead.[7] In some highland areas, structures such as portal dolmens that mimicked natural rocky outcrops became objects of veneration.[8] (Portal dolmens are commonly known in Cornwall as quoits.) Along the coasts of north-west Europe there are Late Mesolithic cist burials, such as at Téviec in Brittany and Vedbaek in Denmark,[9] and these could have been the precursors of the megalithic tombs in these areas. Indeed it could be that all such change to the landscape was for ritual, and that to alter it for economic reasons was taboo until much later – perhaps even as late as the Middle Bronze Age.[10] If you lived in a fully natural landscape, the idea of your woods or heathland being ploughed up would be shocking.

There was, however, a lot of regional variation at this time. Many archaeologists agree that even within the British Isles there could have been a patchwork of communities embracing the new technologies and ideas in very varying degrees and each with its own religious and social views.[11] Without a state to enforce uniformity one must expect such diversity.

Megalithic hunter-gatherers and herders

The hot debate on lifestyle has its parallel in the debate on the economy of the Neolithic, and it bears on how we are to interpret the arrival in Cornwall of Neolithic technologies. Until recently it was thought that the new farming technologies came into Europe from south-west Asia as part of a package that included pottery and ground stone tools.[12] Today the package has gone, and its place has been taken by a 'repertoire' from which different cultures picked the components that suited them.[13] Just because we find pottery and ground stone axes, for example, it does not follow that these are evidence of agriculture. There are no remains of Neolithic field systems in Cornwall, so the arguments about farming have focused first on settlements and secondly on artefacts.

Settlement sites of this period were generally seasonal campsites or hilltop enclosures.[14] The former include base camps, or camps for special purposes – fishing, gathering, hunting, even herding. They consisted of temporary seasonal shelters where people could cook their meals over an open fire, make flint tools and make clothing out of hides and plant fibres. Such sites leave traces of the fire and a scatter of flints on the surface. The hilltop enclosures, on the other hand, were probably sacred – for ceremonies related to exchange and rites for the dead. In the Isles of Scilly, terraces on hilltops and ridges are perhaps the local variant of the terraced hilltop enclosures of the mainland,[15] which are treated more fully here below.

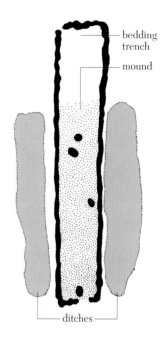

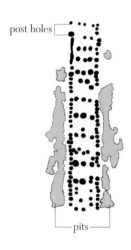

An example of a long barrow at Kilham (top) has a rectangular plan and ditches along both long sides. The longhouse (above) makes an interesting comparison with the barrow because it also has a rectangular plan, with similar ditches caused by extraction of clay to make the daub for the walls.

41

**NEOLITHIC
CULTURE IN
CORNWALL**

As in the Mesolithic, seasonal camps were still set up along coasts[16] and inland rivers.[17] One study of the Lizard,[18] suggesting that inland sites became steadily more important, supports the idea raised in Chapter One of a change in diet to land-based food,[19] such as nuts and berries, wild boar and deer. These seasonal camps differed in their siting from those of the Late Mesolithic. No longer does a commanding view matter; now – as long before – it is ecology that counts. The Early Neolithic camp on the Kennal River (where Stithians Reservoir now is) was at the edge of a marsh near a spring.[20] Probably the new hilltop enclosures, as sites of solemn significance, made it less necessary for the siting of camps to make a spiritual statement.

The annual cycle of the Mesolithic probably involved following the deer up onto the high moors.[21] The settlement pattern for the Neolithic suggests that those expeditions continued, but no animal bones survive, so whether the people drove domestic livestock too is moot. A clue to any possible hunting or herding may lie in the recent discovery of 'propped stones' on the Cornish moorlands,[22] such as the one on Twelve Men's Moor, on Bodmin Moor. These consist of a large elongated boulder propped up by smaller stones, and they seem to be pointers along a way. Aligning as they do on distant hilltops, perhaps they showed the course that animals took on their summer migrations, or perhaps the route to sacred hilltops.

'Propped stones' are perhaps the earliest type of megalith, alluding to natural features. They are easily missed and were discovered only through the diligence of amateur archaeologist Tony Blackman, who constantly walks the Cornish moors in search of new sites. This fine example is at Twelve Men's Moor, just below Kilmar Tor and on the way to Trewortha Farm.

As for farming, the analysis of human bone from this period suggests a shift towards land resources,[23] but not necessarily farmed resources. The absence of plough or ard marks on hilltop enclosures and the lack of real evidence for erosion only reinforce the suspicion that agriculture did not take place on the terraces.[24] (An ard is like a plough, but only cuts into the earth and does not turn it over; there were no true ploughs in British prehistory.)

My suggestion is that there was farming, but not arable farming. Cornwall (and Britain) were latecomers to the European Neolithic, and by then there had been a shift all over Europe from largely arable to more pastoral farming as the climate turned cooler.[25] Herding may have made better sense anyway on Cornwall's poor soils and marginal land. Some hunter-gatherer groups in Siberia provide an example of such practices; they used to supplement their economy by herding, and would domesticate a few deer to act as decoys to others, or even for milking.[26] Chemical analyses of residues left in pottery from elsewhere in southern Britain at this period have demonstrated the presence of dairy products.[27]

The Early Neolithic people kept animals for fewer uses than livestock farmers do today. The sheep were like the Soay sheep from the Hebrides, which are not fully domesticated and do not round up as easily as modern sheep. The Soay is essentially for meat; its wool does not lend itself to shearing, but it can be plucked when it moults. The Manx Loughton, on the other hand, is more like the proper wool-bearing sheep that came in during the Early Bronze Age.[28] In effect the Early Neolithic people used livestock as if they were game animals in captivity – not only sheep, but cows, pigs and goats. They kept sheep primarily for meat, but also used the bones as tools. The transition from having herds of wild animals to herds of domestic ones would have been a relatively small change. In the Isles of Scilly, however, with the sea all round them, people mainly lived on seafood instead.[29]

Prehistoric domestic livestock were different to today's breeds, but a primitive breed similar to Soay sheep (top) was introduced for meat during the Early Neolithic, and one similar to the Manx Loughton (above) was introduced for wool during the Early Bronze Age.

Arable farming is likely to have been a minor, but perhaps ritually significant, addition to the diet. Evidence of actual cereal produce, even in the Wessex chalk-lands, comes only from ritual sites.[30] Many archaeologists see the period from the Early Neolithic to Middle Bronze Age as one where agriculture is either only a minor extra means of livelihood, or just for ritual.[31] As for crops like wheat and barley, how were they stored? There are only a few shallow pits and relatively small pottery containers of Hembury Ware – enough to supply the odd ritual feast. Evidence for the processing of grain on the hilltop enclosures is the presence of saddle and bowl querns at Carn Brea, and associated rubbers at both Carn Brea and on Helman Tor. Grain was placed on the quern stone and the rubber was pressed down on the grain to grind it. Two querns at Carn Brea[32] hardly compare with the fifty from Windmill Hill[33] in Wiltshire, even allowing for the differences in the areas excavated.

The area cleared for arable farming is likely, therefore, to have been minimal – if any was cleared at all. The idea that tracts of land might have been cleared and then left to regrow on the slash-and-burn principle (that is, 'swidden agriculture') is not tenable: any clearances would have been on the same small scale as in the Mesolithic, and probably to serve the same purpose of encouraging the sort of plants that attract game. Neolithic people were still interested in hunting game; but good conditions for game also, and more rewardingly, meant good conditions for livestock. Cornish pollen sequences (at Redhill Marsh,[34] Bodmin Moor and on Crift Down)[35] and sequences of creatures like snails (Towan Head, Newquay) show evidence of greater clearance only later emerging over the course of the Bronze Age.[36]

As for the tools to achieve clearance, Neolithic people in the south-west, like their Mesolithic predecessors, had axes. The Late Mesolithic people, in the south-west at least, had used knapped chert axes.[37] It is true that some of the new Neolithic axes are functional; fine-grained igneous rock ground to shape is more stable and stronger than the chert used in the Mesolithic, and less likely to split. Even so, some of them were never meant for use, and all of them were exchange items. Perhaps they did duty as weapons, and thus they could have been power symbols. But they look special – not like mundane tools for cutting down trees.

That arrowheads changed in the Neolithic may also point towards a continued interest in hunting and away from any new interest in farming. A leaf-shaped, single-bladed arrowhead now replaces the Mesolithic barbed arrow. Examples mostly turn up on moorlands like Butterstor,[38] Bodmin Moor, and Trelanvean, Goonhilly Downs.[39] The arrows could have seen service in war, too. The most spectacular concentration of them was found at Carn Brea,[40] where they may have been used in an attack on the hilltop enclosure. Meanwhile other flint and chert artefacts such as scrapers and burins are still found, but they say nothing one way or the other about farming or hunting.

To sum up so far, environmental and settlement patterns show there was real change to the economy in Cornwall. The land becomes more important, the sea less so. Farming exists, perhaps as some herding alongside hunting and gathering.

Regional exchange and conflict

Exchange was now beginning to count in the economy, and even more in social and religious life. Luxuries were made, taken to hilltop enclosures for distribution, and given in return for exotics. This label need not mean – especially at first – that such goods came from enormously far away. In this period exchange was not for profit, but had more to do with prestige, power and religious belief.[41] Even so it could create conflict, and that is why hilltop enclosures must be seen both as sacred places and defensive positions. In the give-and-take of exchange Cornwall had some valu-

The spread of agriculture from the Near East was punctuated by long pauses. One such of up to a thousand years (4500–3500 BC) was at the boundary of north-west Europe, and meant that coastal communities of Mesolithic hunter-gatherers were able to coexist with these agricultural communities. The Mesolithic people began to change culturally, perhaps under the influence of their neighbours, though environmental changes such as sea level rise may have contributed too.

able assets, which included a number of hard, fine-grained igneous rocks and a particular clay that produced good pottery, even with the unpredictable bonfire-and-clamp technology available in Britain at that time. Its lacks included good-quality flint, chert and jadeite.[42]

There appear to have been three main phases of exchange. The first started in the Late Mesolithic and involved the local exchange of pebble hammers with hourglass perforations from the north coast between St Ives and Gwithian, possibly for exchange against good-quality Beer flint and Portland chert.[43] This phase saw the development of local exchange in exotic goods. The next two phases widened the networks.[44] The combination of axes in their first rough shaping alongside finished ones is found only in Cornwall, so the clear inference is that axe-production was local. Control of the exchange system, however, became ever more dispersed – especially in the third phase.

Phase two[45] (around 3000–2700 BC) involved ground stone axes from Carn Brea, the St Ives area, Balstone Down, near Callington, and an axe which could either have come from near St Austell, or possibly from near St Erth, West Penwith: all of these were traded north as far as the central Wessex Chalklands. During this second phase other groups of Cornish axes, such as in Mount's Bay, were only traded locally. Pottery of the Hembury Ware type travelled by water from 3000 BC onwards to the central Wessex Chalklands, where it is found in causewayed enclosures.

Phase three[46] (after 2700 BC) saw stone axes from the Mount's Bay and St Ives Bay carried by sea to entrepôts in Wessex, Essex and even Yorkshire. From these entrepôts the axes then became part of local exchange systems. The exchange of axes made of non-local materials, and sometimes from places never seen by the recipients, would have made the axes objects of wonder and awe in a world where objects had previously come from local sources.

The exotic goods that entered Cornwall included mostly Beer flint, a little Portland chert and, in eastern Cornwall, axes from the Lake District, North Wales and the Shropshire-Montgomeryshire border. Four possible jadeite axes have been found, three definitely in the Falmouth, Hayle and Newquay areas. The issue of the source of jadeite has not yet been resolved, and Switzerland[47] and Brittany[48] (though the Breton material is the wrong sort of jadeite) have been suggested. Switzerland seems at present the most likely source, though it is exceptional in being an overseas source of imported stone. For example, groups of Breton are found as far as the Low Countries to the east and Provence to the south, but only four have been found in southern Britain and none in Cornwall.[49]

Artefacts like axes and pottery, including those from Cornwall, were exchanged widely across Britain. But some archaeologists have tried to suggest links with Brittany, Ireland and the Continent[50] – perhaps looking too optimistically for the roots of what was later the case. The boats of the time were small – paddled rafts, dugout canoes and skin boats – and hardly ocean-going, so Channel crossings would have taken place at its narrowest point at the Dover Straits, where the cliffs can see each other on a clear day. Every shipment would have gone in small and special packages – like the 'Le Moustier hoard' of high-quality imported flint scrapers and elongated blades found at Camborne.[51] Although the tools found have built up over hundreds of years to an impressive total, they represent a minute traffic in any year – each a cargo of modest size, but enormous value.

So it should be no surprise that such exchange could occasion conflict. The old Neolithic ground surface at Carn Brea was burnt and covered with 703 leaf-shaped

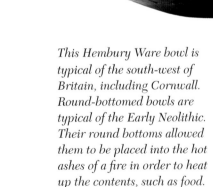

This Hembury Ware bowl is typical of the south-west of Britain, including Cornwall. Round-bottomed bowls are typical of the Early Neolithic. Their round bottoms allowed them to be placed into the hot ashes of a fire in order to heat up the contents, such as food.

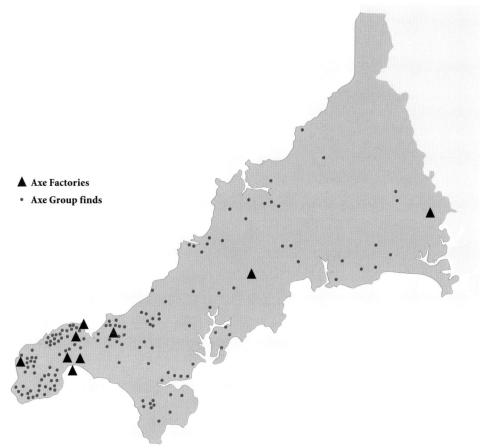

The map shows the distribution of axe factories in Cornwall. These were places where particularly fine hardstone was found near the surface. Neolithic people fashioned it into polished stone axes, which were exchanged both locally and to regions as far away as East Anglia and east Yorkshire. Stones such as the Cornish greenstones were prized not just for their quality but no doubt also for their colour.

▲ Axe Factories

• Axe Group finds

arrowheads (also showing signs of fire damage) at the edge of the eastern summit enclosure.[52] Their presence in the enclosure wall rules out any idea that they might simply have been concentrated at the edge of the enclosure by erosion. From the same period elsewhere in southern Britain there are signs of violent attack on causewayed enclosures, which are also set on impressive hills, indicating that Carn Brea was part of a wider pattern. There were the same concentrations of leaf-shaped arrowheads, and the same signs of burning, at Crickley Hill[53] in Gloucestershire and Hembury[54] in Devon. Also at Hambledon Hill[55] in Dorset a man and a child were killed and left in a ditch. Their design and commanding position gave these enclosures an impregnability that is nowhere more obvious than at St Michael's Mount[56] – which then rose out of a flat, dry plain. At Helman Tor[57] there was marsh on three sides, a lower ridge on the fourth. Attackers with bows and arrows would have found it difficult to aim over the low walls that defined the terraces along the steep slopes. And if the occupants preferred to run rather than fight, their view – at any rate in daylight – gave them plenty of time to escape while the approaching threat was still miles away.

Given the changing patterns of exchange there must have been enormous competition between the rival groups and their hilltop enclosures. These extend into Dartmoor;[58] then causewayed enclosures take their place. These were also set on hilltops, but with segmented ditches with causeways between them, instead of stone walls as the boundary feature. Few of the hilltop enclosures have been investigated. Carn Brea, which has been excavated, has low stone walls, linking the natural tors of the hill, constructed with boulders and filled in with smaller fist-size stones and earth. Behind are terraces dug into the hillside, which had lean-to shelters with hearths or fireplaces. Finds of exotic goods are uneven, so they may not have been cause for rivalry everywhere. Roughtor and Stowe's Pound on Bodmin Moor,[59] and the apparent enclosures in the south-east of Cornwall,[60] do not necessarily point to conflict; and excavations at Helman Tor[61] show no sign that it came to a violent end.

Monuments and nature

Archaeologists have recently begun to appreciate that not all societies see a clear distinction between the animate and inanimate:[62] in Greek legend, anyone who set eyes on the Gorgon would turn to stone. To some ancient societies natural things might possess souls and even divinity, and the archaeological evidence of such a belief is the clear association between what they built and what is there in the landscape. Only recently have archaeologists begun to put the two side by side in a systematic way, so much here reinterprets old knowledge in the light of new ways of looking at it.

The two main ways in which the Neolithic expressed its attitude to nature were, first, the

Prominent landscape features were enhanced by earlier Neolithic monumental architecture. This photograph reveals a thick enclosure wall made of stone rubble around the hilltop at Stowe's Pound near the Minions on Bodmin Moor. There is no entrance and the main rock formations have been enclosed – except for the Cheesewring, which is just outside the enclosure wall to the right. The sudden drop to the right is the 19th-century Cheesewring quarry.

way it treated natural features and, second, the way its monuments imitated or emphasised them. In the earlier Neolithic era, people saw themselves as separate from nature but still intimately bound to it. This is the first period of monument building – the first time people made major changes to the landscape, by placing conspicuous artificial elements within it. Perhaps they imitated nature, in fear of hubris. Meanwhile, as the identification with nature was gone, communities newly aware of their regional identity began to differ culturally from one another quite quickly, no longer evolving in unison, smoothly and gradually, across great territories. Never again would artefacts look so alike in such wide distribution.

How might Neolithic people have looked at what was around them – at the prominent rock formations, the large trees and groves, the unusual but smaller features? In an experiment[63] at Leskernick, on Bodmin Moor, a mixed group were given cameras and asked to photograph whatever interested them: the result was that the men on the whole were interested in wider landscapes and the women on the whole in smaller, more personal subjects. So perhaps men are drawn to the spectacular and women to the intimate in the way they look at space.[64] Equally, it may be that there are individual and group ways of looking at landscape.[65]

A study of Bodmin Moor by Christopher Tilley shows that the change from Mesolithic to Neolithic sites is a change from riversides to hilltops.[66] My own research shows that the Late Mesolithic people were already choosing prominent natural locations below the hilltops (see Chapter One), perhaps acknowledging the sacredness of the hills. So putting sites actually on the hilltops in the Neolithic may imply more than simply worshipping the tors,[67] but placating them too. Building low walls abutting and linking tors and cutting terraces into hillsides are fairly drastic actions. The results seem to mimic the natural terraces overlooking the sea or river valleys used as campsites in the Late Mesolithic. People in the Neolithic, in awe of nature, used the symbolism of nature to make sure of divine help.

Besides hilltop enclosures, other Neolithic monuments consisted of arrangements of stone: propped stones, portal dolmens and entrance graves. Archaeological books sometimes call portal dolmens 'Penwith Chambered Tombs', though they also occur outside Penwith and are not necessarily tombs.[68] The mistake arose from reading a residue of cairn material around their bases as the remains of mounds of earth and stone that had supposedly once covered them. Subsequent dating shows that this material came later, in the Late Neolithic and Early Bronze Age; and everyone now agrees that they were bold and naked from the first, built to strike the eye. What is their message? To echo nature seems the likely answer. One idea is that their cap-stones were purposely slanted to reflect the slant of tors.[69] Another is that cup-marked stones imitated the basin-shaped hollows left by weathering on the surface of tor rock. (See also Chapter Three for discussion.) The propped stones could have imitated nature too. They seem like other rock that lies at random, and it needs a purposeful eye to pick them out from the clitter of the moors. The entrance graves are a complete contrast. Sited on the lower slopes of hills, and away from the tors and clitter near the coast,[70] they are covered to blend in with the earth and stone of low-lying ground. Their cap-stones lie prosaically flat and foursquare on their stone uprights, and they are built to do a self-effacing job.

Monuments are the most visible aspect of the new relationship with the natural world, but unusual raw materials can reveal more detail about the beliefs that accompanied this relationship. There is not much evidence from Cornwall on this score, but elsewhere it is obvious that there was ritual attached to mining. It has been shown, for example, that winning flint from mines ranging from the north-east of Scotland to East Anglia and Sussex was much more than a business enterprise.[71] Apart from the small amounts they produced annually of what was a luxury, not just an everyday, commodity, the miners most carefully sealed shafts and galleries when they were worked out. They buried the bodies of the dead and left offerings underground and then, when the mines were abandoned, continued to do so at the surface. Richard Bradley[72] has investigated rock formations over upland Britain and found unusual offerings and human remains. It is likely that the behaviour of the people that resulted in these remains had its counterpart in Cornwall too, but unfortunately the acid soil of Cornwall dissolves human bones and none survives. Even so there are indications that the stone and clay resources of Cornwall were treated with ritual respect.

Greenstone is an example, though it has been hard to find its source. Roughly where the outcrops were situated is known, but no actual quarries have been discovered. The axe quarry near Carn Brea[73] may be buried under tailings and waste from later mines; others like the Mount's Bay sites may be under water in the bay itself. For all the lack of identified quarries, greenstone axes have been found in ritual contexts both in Cornwall and elsewhere in Britain. At Carn Brea, for instance, greenstone was placed in cairn material round a large torstone, and was also deposited in the enclosure wall.[74]

Equally, a number of studies[75] of the gabbroic clay from the St Keverne area of the Lizard cover its history from the Neolithic up to and into the Iron Age. The advantage of gabbroic clay is that it fires hard and properly even in a bonfire or clamp;[76] other clays in those conditions would fire incompletely and yield poor results. In many societies and many parts of the world (for example, Siberia[77]) fire has ritual meaning, so a material perfectly transformed by fire may have been endowed with magical or divine properties. Archaeologists think that is why pottery from the Lizard is found so far afield, though it could be that other deposits of gabbroic clay were available near Start Point in Devon.[78] Recently archaeologists such as Lucy Harrad of Cambridge University have begun to examine how this pottery was disposed of, to see if that also involved ritual.[79]

In making these first, daring changes to the natural environment – by setting up architectural monuments in it and dispersing unusual materials taken from it across great distances – Early Neolithic people needed to be circumspect. So they built their monuments in a way that imitated nature, in order to make them subservient to the landscape; and (on the basis of studies made of other areas of Britain) they apparently disposed of unusual raw materials ritually – for example, in rock formations, long barrows and mines. At least the idea of terracing hilltop enclosures was not new in this period but rather an idea inspired by the form of local Late Mesolithic campsites.

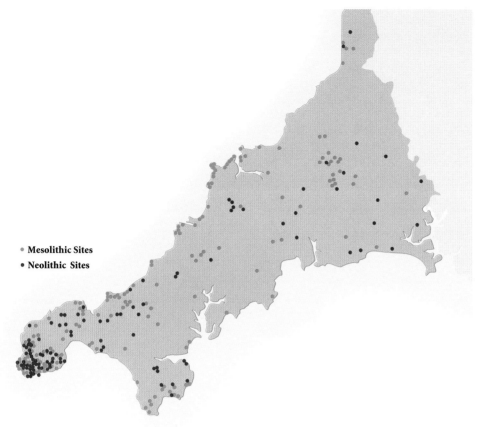

- Mesolithic Sites
- Neolithic Sites

Neolithic settlements are concentrated inland, reflecting a change towards such land produce as deer and wild plants. This change is likely to have included domestic animals such as sheep and cattle and some limited experimentation with crops. The Mesolithic campsites were concentrated mainly along the coast, where a diet with much seafood sustained their populations.

Communities of the living and the dead

The treatment of the dead in this period in Cornwall is a particularly troublesome problem. Portal dolmens are not necessarily sepulchres, particularly as any human remains at these sites are associated with later cairn material. Some long or oval barrows and cairns like Woolley Barrow[80] have revealed no cists or other signs that human remains might have been buried there; others, like Catshole Tor long cairn[81] and the long barrows in the Wessex chalklands, were used as tombs. It could be therefore that these two types of monument were not made specifically as tombs, but more generally as shrines or places of worship.

East of Dartmoor, where causewayed enclosures and long barrows predominate, the evidence suggests that human corpses were laid out for excarnation in the cause-wayed enclosures.[82] Similar enclosures to hilltop enclosures[83] occur across large areas of north-western Europe: minor differences aside, they were all places where dispersed and semi-mobile people could meet for ritual purposes – including funeral rites. Excarnation meant the practice of leaving corpses in the open for birds, wild animals and microbes to reduce them to bones. Those bones were then deposited as ancestral relics in passages and chambers in long barrows, where they would be accessible for ever. Many cultures preserve bones and other relics of ancestors and important figures in their community, so that they can be revered and consulted for inspiration and advice. In the Sepik valley of New Guinea, men's meeting houses contain decorated skulls of ancestors that continue to preside over proceedings after their death.[84] In Europe, saints' relics are kept in churches and (if the stories are true) still work miracles.

From Dartmoor westwards, the causewayed enclosures are replaced by hilltop enclosures. As for the storage of human relics, in West Penwith and the Isles of Scilly the long barrows with passages and galleries (side chambers) are replaced by entrance graves. From the outside and above they are round, but still contain passages like those in central Wessex.[85] East of West Penwith to Dartmoor, there are long barrows and cairns – and these seem not to symbolise the same idea of death in a different way, but to stand for a different idea. The openable entrance grave suggests continued access to, and communion with, the dead but not departed; the closed chambers of cairns and barrows suggest the end of a one-way journey.[86] It may be that, in the latter case, those who were physically gone could still be spiritually recycled. The portal dolmens of West Penwith are from the same period so they must have had a separate role from the entrance graves. It seems likely that the hilltop enclosures, being analogous to the causewayed enclosures as they were similarly proportioned and occupied similar locations, served the same purpose.[87] That purpose was the excarnation of the dead, and all the rites and ceremonies of death. These would have included wakes, feasts when the bones of the dead were collected and regular feasts in their memory.

On the Isles of Scilly there are no terraced hilltop enclosures. Instead the people constructed simple hillside terraces imitating natural ridges of unweathered granite with entrance graves on them – showing how closely they were linked.[88] In West Penwith entrance graves are close to terraces but not visually tied to them. In view of what was happening at the time in the long barrows of central Wessex, and their later use for funerary purposes by the Beaker culture, it seems likely that entrance graves were long-term reliquaries for ancestral bones.

Within hilltop enclosures the evidence for ritual use is robust. On Carn Brea and Helman Tor the ground surfaces of the lean-to structures by the terrace walls were covered in shallow pits full of charcoal. The pottery taken from it was covered on the outside and part of the inside with some sort of black carbon paint.[89] This treatment of pottery has so far been found only in the hilltop enclosures of Carn Brea and Helman Tor, never in any domestic site.

The ritual associated with hilltop enclosures, long and oval barrows and cairns, and entrance graves more than merely states that mankind and nature are separate. It claims a destination for the dead. Their placing in these monuments removes them from the open-air cycle of life and death in which dead bodies simply decompose. The artificial stone monuments and the tors would have been associated with ancestry, or with death and rebirth. That elvan, gneiss (for querns and rubbers) and greenstone (for axes) all come out of the moorland ground makes one more link with ritual and death. If the tors at the top of the moorlands received the dead, then the living received the precious stone, which in turn was redeposited on hilltop enclosures or other sacred sites in southern Britain. Julian Thomas has suggested[90] that, in the Late Neolithic, the sheer plurality of artefacts meant they formed a multitude of different connections with a natural world which was '... rationalised in the form of spirits or deities embodied in raw materials'. It may be that raw materials in the Early Neolithic period in Cornwall and Dartmoor had already acquired this hallowed character.

The Neolithic thus saw a new relationship with nature, new cycles of life and death and the beginnings of more marked regional diversity. Cornwall and Dartmoor had different monuments from those to the east and north. West Penwith and the Isles of Scilly were an especially distinctive region within the upland area of south-west Britain. However, the patterns of behaviour in Cornwall do seem to mirror, economically and in ritual, the new cultural influences of true farming societies to the East.

In the Isles of Scilly, entrance graves are found in proximity to ridges of granite. Here, Lower Innisidgen entrance grave (foreground) was found along a ridge of granite that stretches out into the sea near the north end of St Mary's (background). Such monuments would have been among the earliest human rather than natural constructions on the islands and would have seemed more impressive than they appear to us today.

CHAPTER THREE
THE AGE OF THE MEGALITHS

Late Neolithic & Early Bronze Age (2700–1500 BC)

THE BRONZE AGE no longer seems a useful term to archaeologists, as the only thing its different segments share is that each had bronze but no iron. The period I deal with in this chapter straddles the Late Neolithic and Early Bronze Age – known by its acronym LANEBA.[1]

In most of Britain during the LANEBA old ways persisted. Hunting and gathering went on as before, and livestock were still driven between their summer and winter grazing grounds. But more and more people made monuments that rose up among the already sacred features of the natural landscape; new technologies created new kinds of artefact that were traded across Britain and Europe, and some of them ended up in ritual sites in Cornwall. That does not mean, however, that the whole trading region had a common culture. Elsewhere societies were rooted in status rather than age and experience, but in Cornwall there is little evidence of such hierarchies, and people continued to worship nature rather than their ancestors.

While Cornwall was still Neolithic, the north-east Balkans and the steppes were developing new technologies and new societies.[2] These changes spread piecemeal and patchily, neighbouring groups adopting what suited them and grafting them onto their existing way of life.[3] They used copper, gold and later tin and bronze – though not yet iron or silver. They tamed the horse. They buried their chieftainly families, including children, in the round barrows which became the most prominent monument of the 'Bell Beaker' culture.[4] This culture had its rise in the early third millennium BC in the north European plain, where it stretched from Belgium to Poland and later spread into Britain. If a prosperous society is one that produces and trades in surpluses, then the Bell Beaker people knew prosperity.

The evidence lay in those barrows – in the shape of pottery, amber, ceramic beads with a glassy paste called faïence, gold, metalwork and jewellery.[5] It includes pots so fine that archaeologists once took them for wheel-thrown work, and flint daggers so thin as to be translucent. Some of the material was traded (amber comes from the Baltic shores, faïence originated in the eastern Mediterranean); and societies that struggle to subsist have no hands to spare for crafts as exquisite as these. So this was a society that was able to support the producers of luxuries – and specialists in their

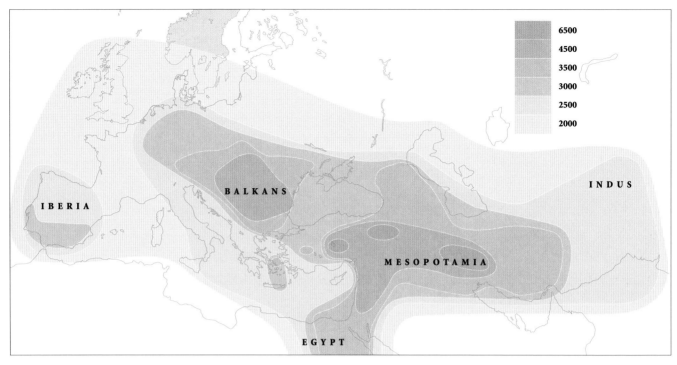

Legend:
6500
4500
3500
3000
2500
2000

IBERIA BALKANS INDUS MESOPOTAMIA EGYPT

Copper was independently discovered and worked in different parts of the world. In the area of the Mediterranean, there were separate traditions of metal working in Turkey, Mesopotamia, Iberia and the Balkans. The introduction of metallurgy into the British Isles, along with associated cultural elements, was largely influenced by the metalwork of the Balkans.

trades at that, for these grave goods were not just the trappings of manhood. A chief might take his masculine regalia and weapons with him when he died – an archer's wristguards, for example, or arrows with barbed stone points – but his wife would be buried with her distinctively feminine jewels. Some types of jewellery were designed for men.[6] From barrows in the Wessex chalk, for example, has come jewellery made from Whitby jet and Kimmeridge shale.[7] All this points to a society that honoured women as well as men – a complex, stratified society with chieftains, priests, armourers, jewellers, craft workers of all kinds, and traders and labourers. In Britain the Bell Beaker culture landed in two waves. The first left scattered shipments of objects at coastal sites, but a later, stronger wave swept deep into Wessex and thence to Cornwall.[8] Then Britain and Brittany produced something all their own – the stone circle, as well as the henge in Britain.[9]

Stone circles,[10] as their name suggests, are rings of upright stones set at roughly regular intervals. Although the sizes of stones and of circles can vary, and the 'circles' are often ellipses, a well preserved stone circle is hard to mistake. Henges[11] are less obvious, especially if they enclose large stones or stone circles that catch and hold the eye; they are simply rings of earth shaped by an outer bank and an inner ditch. The great exception is the site that supplies the name – Stonehenge itself, which unusually has its ditch outside the bank, and has impressive trilithons (two upright stones supporting a lintel stone).

Where do they stand, and what did they signify? Some made alignments, three or four circles in a row – either lining up with each other, or with older Early Neolithic monuments like long barrows and long cairns. People in the Late Neolithic and Early Bronze Age often altered these older monuments. They sealed

56

West Kennet long barrow in Wiltshire, for instance, and turned it into a closed mound like a round barrow.[12] In effect they rewrote their past in terms of their present, in symbols that all could read.

Larger and more impressive circles stand not on the crowns of hills but even more conspicuously on their slopes, or on plains surrounded by hills – as if to make powerful architectural statements. The only puzzle is where people stayed during festivals. Outside the Orkneys, all the known Late Neolithic houses in Britain are either in, under or near ritual monuments,[13] and a recently discovered feature near two small henges in Dorset may help with the answer.[14] It has has yet to be fully surveyed, let alone fully excavated, but a house with its hearth has come to light, as well as many post holes, stake holes and pits – all the signs of a settlement. Could this be lodging for devotees? Finds include exotic and luxurious objects, and as the henges flank a cursus (a long earthen monument stretching over miles) it could be that the hierarchy controlled access to the cursus, as well as commerce with incomers. Certainly some henges had high banks and even walls and roofs, so nobody could just walk in.[15]

As to what they signified, it could well be that the LANEBA eventually transformed the old ideas of time and space. Gradually the idea that time moves in circles matching the cycle of the seasons seems to have yielded to the sense that time is linear, an arrow flying forever forward.[16] By setting up monuments along pathways or in relation to one another, people could picture the passage of time: each successive monument marked another step in time. Cemeteries for people of rank, with grave goods from faraway places, came to be set out in lines that traced the ancestry of chiefs. At first the barrows fringed, then encroached upon and even covered, the earlier stone circles.[17] Like the private chapels of the wealthy in a church, these trespasses upon old and sacred spaces look like assertions of power, and as they were visible for miles around, they were very loud assertions indeed. As time passed burial practices changed, and by the middle of this period British society had embraced a custom of cremation, so that later barrows are found to contain more urns than skeletons.[18] Cremations were placed in urns, and the urns were then put into pits or cists under barrows – a cist being a chamber constructed for the dead made by lining a pit with large stone slabs.

Mostly Stone circles
Mostly Henge zone

The distribution of henges and stone circles looks at first sight to be linked to local availability of stone, but culture must have played a part too, as stone is found in many areas on either side of the dividing line.

PRECIOUS OBJECTS

The colours of gold and amber are suggestive of the sun. Both materials came from overseas, and their origins were not likely to have been known by people in Cornwall or indeed anywhere else in Britain, which would have contributed to the allure of objects made from them. People of this period were the first to experience such objects, and they could have imagined mythical origins for the gold and amber, mysterious materials that gleamed and glistened. That gold and amber were highly valued is evidenced by the fact that they are found in high prestige burials. The golden armilla (*centre below*) from Ropley, near Winchester, was found in a round barrow. The gold lunulae (*left below*); the Rillaton Cup from Bodmin Moor, Cornwall, made in imitation of a coil pot (*right below*); and necklaces of amber beads and plates (*bottom*) are rare finds. Gold found in Cornwall came from Ireland and was probably exchanged for passage around Cornwall to get to the continent.

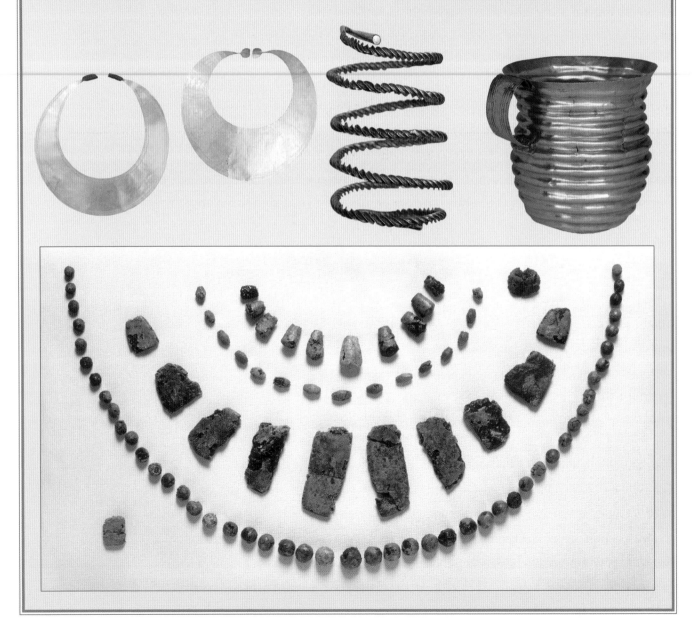

But all this threatens to become too tidy, for LANEBA people were a broad church, with rituals and ideas that varied from place to place and group to group. Across the upland sweep of moors and downs, monuments ranged from the intimate shrine around an unusual natural feature through small henges and barrow cemeteries to the splendours of Stonehenge or Arbor Low.[19] Avenues of stone uprights and ceremonial pathways (which are also of this period) no doubt got people used to a linear view of space; and the sense that all these new exotic things must have travelled from out there to here on some extended route is also a linear idea. The origins of these mysterious goods from lands beyond their ken must have provoked speculation. From Denmark comes a golden artefact depicting cattle pulling a cart bearing the sun's disc.[20] From one part of Poland comes an amber disc with sun symbols; from elsewhere in Poland the Bronocice bowl has a four-wheeled wagon with a sun symbol on it.[21] The colours of gold and amber speak of sunlight, and stone circles and henges like Stonehenge were probably connected with cycles of the sun and moon. But people can absorb new ideas that they can give no real account of; they can even invent myths to explain them; they can certainly use new technologies that they do not even understand.[22] So we must remember that new cultures do not always quickly sweep all before them, and old ways of thought and behaviour modify the new ones that eventually prevail.

Finally, what was the impact of metal in Britain in this era – copper, tin, lead and gold? The LANEBA was an enormous span of time, and any finds made of these metals and their alloys at the beginning of the period were certainly exotic. They came into the hands of a population rather like the Khanty-Mansi people of Siberia mentioned in Chapter One, who lived on the margins of a richer, more technological and strongly agricultural society.[23] By the end of the period copper and tin were mined, smelted and cast in Britain[24] and Ireland; while tin was exploited in Cornwall, copper was not – it was mined at Great Orme in Wales, and Ross Island and Mount Gabriel in Ireland. Odd as it may seem that anyone should bother to go underground for metal when it was there for the taking in Cornish streams, that is only true of tin:[25] copper oxidises quickly once it separates from its lode and little of it gets into alluvial deposits.[26]

The Beaker culture, and trade

The people of Cornwall were in the right place at the right time for the arrival of early Beaker influences in Britain. New technologies and new specialist crafts had created new products in surplus across northern Europe and up the Irish Sea[27] – supply looking for demand. Cornwall was there at a pivotal point on the sea routes, with raw material of its own to trade in exchange. Sea routes made sense twice over: not only was it quicker by sea (even though sails did not appear until the Late Iron

Age) but cheaper, because unlike overlanders the seamen did not have to hand out gifts to every tribe on the way. Where Cornish ores were won and smelted are questions with no apparent answers,[28] but metallurgical tests show that Cornwall and (especially) Dartmoor were the likely sources of tin in British bronze.[29] The southwest also supplied raw materials for faïence beads, and tin was so prized that it went far afield indeed. In the form of beads it has turned up in Holland and Bavaria; and tinned Migdale axes and inlaid tin in a jet button have been dug up in Fife.[30] Nor was Cornwall's contribution to the exchange system limited to metal, because Trevisker urns from Cornwall have been found in graves in Wessex and south-east England.[31]

Given the importance of the sea routes, it is not surprising that Penwith and Scilly have the sites touched by early Beaker culture. The Penwith entrance graves in Bosiliack and Tregiffian are two of them.[32] These were graves built above ground – passages leading to large round chambers – and had been the tombs in Neolithic times of excarnated ancestors. Now they held food vessels and beakers, which also

This map shows the extent of Bell Beaker production in Europe by cultures that were part of a growing network of exchange. The beakers are not necessarily important in themselves but are illustrations of shared ideas across wide areas.

Bell Beaker distribution

went into satellite cists. Similar and better preserved Penwith/Scillonian entrance graves at Bant's Carn and Innisidgen tell the same story.[33] Later in this period the entrance graves at Ballowal and Chapel Carn Brea in West Penwith were turned into cairns large to the point of sumptuousness.[34] That all this was going on between, in effect, two island communities suggests that it had to do with sea traffic, because the Penwith peninsula was then very much an almost-island – barely attached to the rest of Cornwall by a narrow, swampy isthmus flanked by sand dunes.[35] West Penwith and Scilly, being isolated from the mainland, were safer for mariners to visit, and one can imagine the people in charge of the boats leaving exotic gifts in local shrines as offerings for peace and a safe journey.

Later Beaker influences came overland through Wessex and, again, older monuments were co-opted into the new religion. Finds include gold and amber objects in Woolley Barrow,[36] near the source of the Tamar in North Cornwall, and a single-handled beaker in Try Cairn, Gulval.[37] Occasional examples of other Wessex influences have come to light in the shape of Food Vessels and Grooved Ware, as well as all manner of gold from Ireland, especially Northern Ireland – such as the *lunulae* found at St Juliot, Harlyn Bay, and Gwithian and the cup from Rillaton Barrow on Bodmin Moor[38] (A *lunula* is a piece of sheet gold cut in the shape of a crescent moon. *Lunulae* were probably worn round the neck – by someone of noble or priestly rank. They were often embellished with punched zigzags and hatched triangles.[39])

Bell Beakers (above left and below) are usually well represented on archaeological sites and help us to understand the movement of ideas such as chieftainship and the development of long-distance trade in exotic items such as amber. The name of the vessels comes from their bell-like shapes.

Economists feel no need to explain demand. They take it as a given that human beings are acquisitive and love possessions, particularly beautiful possessions that excite envy. So an older school of archaeology rooted in economics saw it as obvious that anyone would covet the kind of thing traded in the LANEBA, and left it at that. Why confuse a simple story? But that is only to say that treasures are always desirable; it does not explain what they mean when they cease to be possessions and become sacred objects in tombs and holy places. One suggestion is that as these artefacts multiplied, became more various and more variously decorated, they served to refocus reverence from the ancestors to powers inherent in the objects themselves and the materials from which they were made.[40] This view is part of the debate already touched on that surrounds the flint mines of the Neolithic and the contemporary copper mines. My own conjecture is that new exchange systems working over longer distances may have reinforced the power of emergent hierarchies.[41] If the pathways unrelated to farming and foraging – and running between barrows and other monuments – were (as is likely) not simply for ritual but also for the traffic in exotic gifts, then every exchange of gifts would strengthen an alliance. If amber were the emblem of the sun, for example, then hierarchies controlling the supply of amber might have claimed descent from a sun-deity, and therefore kinship and common cause with one another.

Unfortunately, on that theory, Cornwall is an anomaly because monuments that ought to be the resting places of the powerful often contain no human remains. Cairns and barrows frequently cover natural features or natural objects, and though monuments in Beaker and Wessex style are there, they are not the mausoleums they should be. How did people at the time resolve the dissonance between old and new gods, old and new customs? Perhaps they told themselves mythic stories about pathways – on the lines of the Dreamtime of the Australian aborigines.[42] Mythology would have linked the old and the new as if they were part of the same story.

Over the Early Bronze Age items of exchange became steadily more artificial and magical-looking – translucent flint knives, flat and low-flanged axes, daggers fastened by rivets to handles, collared urns, pygmy vessels and faïence.[43] The inspiration came mostly from Wessex, but from right across Europe too. Faience beads are a case in point. It used to be assumed that they must have been imported from the Mediterranean if they were dug up in Britain,[44] but it is now known that some were made in

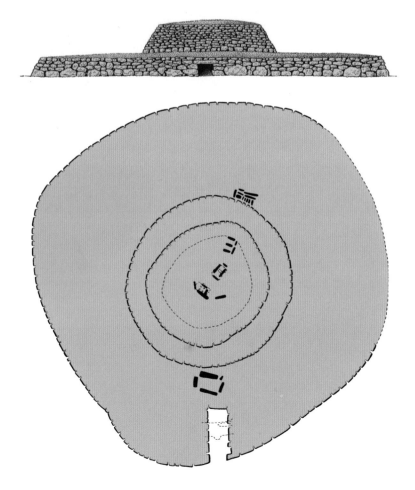

Some cairns were effectively redesigned and extended Neolithic entrance graves. Ballowall (pronounced 'bah-low-wall' and sometimes known instead as 'Carn Gluze'), just west of St Just near the cliffs, is the largest of these cairns. Within the cairn are a number of cists or burial chambers, as the plan on the left shows, containing cremated bones and pottery. Unlike the earlier Neolithic monuments, the chambers are not accessible. This exclusion, together with the overall size of the monument, is meant to convey power and mystery.

Britain – including grey-coloured beads that were made in Cornwall itself – on the evidence of chemical analysis.[45] An outside influence can simply be a matter of style, and just as there is an 'art deco' look that applies to many things, so there was a Wessex look, or a Beaker look. Two-grooved biconical beads from Boscregan seem to be in the Wessex idiom because they are like the biconical shale beads with inlaid gold wire that have been found in some wealthy Wessex burials.[46]

How might the new culture have been generally explained? It could be that fire was the key to the story. Pottery, metal, faïence, cremation – all of these need fire. In Cornwall, however, signs of cremation and human remains are rare and it may be that excarnation was still the rule. So the majority might still have turned to the gods of nature and natural features, and have viewed the minority steeped in the new culture as a powerful class apart. They may have been powerful because they could make fire work for them (craftspeople using fire have a priestly role in many societies), powerful in the wealth that they alone controlled and traded and powerful because cremation reunited them to the source of their power.

Some of the new exotic material may have been talismanic.[47] Rub amber and jet and they produce static electricity – to the innocent eye uncanny; and there is ample written record going back to Roman times that people saw them as magical. (Judging by how worn they became some amber and jade objects were prized enough to be handed down as heirlooms for 200 to 300 years.) Similarly, segments of lily-shaped fossils left by ancient relatives of the sea-urchins were used in necklaces, no doubt as charms, because they looked like faïence beads, and may have been taken for otherworldly kinds of faïence. It seems likely because no such necklaces predate the arrival of faience itself.[48]

Cornwall was not a great exporter of finished goods, but there is evidence of exported raw material, and there was some local interchange. The gabbroic clays of the Lizard made excellent pottery, notably the early Trevisker Ware, but it was not always the only clay used in every kind of Beaker pottery.[49] It was mixed with local clays to make the pottery found in North Cornwall at Treligga and Davidstow Moor, so perhaps that area lay at the limit of the local trading system.[50] Food Vessels and Collared Urns traded across Penwith and Kerrier (like the ones found at Poldowrian and Gwithian) are made of nothing but gabbro – no doubt because the source was hard by.[51] Some small items did travel far though. A button from the jacket of a man buried in a cist at Rameldry Farm in Fife was made of a soft stone from the Lizard, unsurprisingly named Lizardite; it was inlaid with tin and, unusually, glazed.[52]

Wider trends in monument building

Like its artefacts and exchange systems, the monuments of the LANEBA reflect a collision between revolution and inertia. New ideas from the outside world sweep in

LUXURY GOODS

With chieftainship came the demand for specialist craft workers. There were improvements in flint working for finely knapped knives (*below left*) and new barbed and tanged arrowheads (*below centre left*). The barbs are the two projections at the bottom corners of the triangle and the tang is the projection in the middle, which fixed to the arrow shaft. The new metalworking skills saw polished stone axes replaced gradually by bronze flat axes (*below centre right*) and flint knives by bronze daggers (*below right*). In a reconstruction (*bottom*) a smith pours molten bronze into a one-piece mould to create a flat axe, its form partly in imitation of an earlier polished stone axe.

– and then, locally, nothing much happens. Continuity continues – as long as one bears in mind that continuity is not as simple as it looks. The word suggests that new generations, cherishing folk memory, carried on just as their forebears had done over centuries. But in real life memory is continuously corrected by the visible traces of the past. An analogy might be our experience of remembering the dead. Gradually our memory fixes the picture: *he did this, she looked like that*. Then we see an old photograph or letter, or hear a new story about them. At once, for better or worse, the picture changes. The older the memory, the younger you were when they died, the sharper the revision. In an age without writing or photographs, monuments would have been the most powerful record of the past. Moreover, at the dawn of the LANEBA, past and present were indistinct and 'memory' must have been a more fluid concept.

The new monuments – stone circles, a few henges and standing stones – brought conspicuous change to a landscape of hilltop enclosures, dolmens, long barrows and entrance graves. They are where they are most visible – on crests or apparent crests, on hillsides facing open landscapes, on plateaus or low-lying ground ringed by hills. In Cornwall and on Dartmoor the circles are mostly of quite small stones. The henges, too, have low banks, and look more like landmarks than barriers, and an inference from this openness is that they belong to an open society of equals with no lofty hierarchy.[53] Different as they were from the existing monuments (and younger), they literally lined up with them, so as to look like a part rather than a contradiction of timeless antiquity.

It seems likely that the monuments lined up with one another along pathways, and were probably designed individually to mark movements of the sun and of the moon.[54] Standing stones by themselves do not work as astronomical sight lines but they do line up with other monuments, including earlier monuments, possibly as landmarks.[55] In West Penwith, for example, they seem to follow contours and so could have been there not only for ritual purposes, but also to mark the boundary between one way of using the land and another.

The idea of pathways was already there in the Late Neolithic, but it becomes stronger and clearer with the aligned barrows of the Early Bronze Age, and there are several lines of triple stone circles – like Tregaseal (West Penwith), the Nine Maidens near Wendron, the Hurlers (Bodmin Moor) and King Arthur's Down (Bodmin Moor).[56] Indeed the entrances of circles and henges can form lines with other monuments: for example, one of the entrances to the Stripple Stones henge is aligned on the Trippet Stone Circle.[57] There is nothing peculiarly Cornish about these circles. The central Hurlers circle and the Stripple Stones have imposing central monoliths, and so do stones in Ireland.[58] The bank of the Stripple Stones henge extends in obedience to the same geometry that rules the massive Wessex henge at Durrington

OPPOSITE

Stone circles are often found in alignments, demonstrating that, just like barrows and stone rows, they are meant to be seen as part of a wider sacred landscape. The Hurlers here form a line of three (formerly four) stone circles. To the left and above the stone circles is the source of the Witheybrook; springs are often associated with stone circles.

Walls in Wiltshire.[59] Even the smaller isolated stone circles point to a wide tradition stretching across Devon and Dorset.[60]

As well as lining up with features in a generally sacred landscape, some LANEBA monuments may actually mark them. It is quite a coincidence that the Trippet Stones and the Stripple Stones are near the southern headwaters of the De Lank River; that the Hurlers and Craddock Moor are near the source of the Lynher; that the Goodaver and Leskernick circles are near the source of the Fowey; and that the Leaze and King Arthur's Down circles are near the northern headwaters of the De Lank.[61] This seemingly deliberate siting fits in neatly with the way the Dorset cursus – a long enclosure with two long, straightish sides curving to join at the end – links a number of seasonal springs, and its associated henges cluster round them. Perhaps the circles and henges were shrines to the miracle of water issuing from the earth.[62]

Their precise site, their place in the landscape and the very way they were made are all clues to the ideology of circles and henges. Among the clues from construction are the acoustics of stone circles and the unusual stones that some of them contain. Recent research from outside Cornwall suggests that rings of tall stone are a battle to sound waves.[63] Individual stones such as large central monoliths can play interesting tricks, as indeed can the whole circle, by containing the sound and bouncing it back and forth. The shorter stones typical of Cornwall no doubt limit the effect, but if so more people could take part in ceremonies, or at any rate hear what was going on.

The unusual stones, though certainly clues, are cryptic. Were they allusions to the places from which they came and, if so, did that have some special significance? Instances include the large, shining, quartz-white stone of the Boscawen-Ûn circle in West Penwith, and the large quartz uprights in the small circle at Duloe, near Looe.[64] Other examples are holed stones like the ring-shaped Men-an-Tol (West Penwith), and the freestanding Tolvan at Gweek (Lizard) – a variant presumably on the ordinary menhir,[65] a menhir being a long, upright stone, often taller than a person. One suggestion is that they may have been made to mimic the natural rock basins formed on granite tors;[66] a rock basin matching the size and shape of the Men-an-Tol is still to be found on Zennor Carn.[67] Then too, for whatever reason, there are circles with stones of uniform size apart from one that is exceptionally large – as in the Stripple Stones, Boskednan and King Arthur's Down.[68]

As time passed and ideology changed, so the dialogue between the living, the dead and the landscape expressed itself in changes in the older monuments, just as in the new. The later stone circles, as well as more ancient monuments and sacred natural features, were modified by cairns, cists and offerings placed inside them.[69] Cists and cairns intrude on the edges of stone circles like the Men-an-Tol,[70] or straddle the ring as at Leskernick,[71] or go right in the middle – as in the western circle of the King Arthur's Down group.[72] Menhirs frequently had cists or cairns at their feet,[73] like those at Try, near Gulval[74] in West Penwith and Longstone Down near St Stephen-in-Brannel.[75] The alteration denied that anything was altered. Just as Squealer – the propaganda pig in Orwell's *Animal Farm*[76] – changed a few slogans to rewrite history, so every modified ancient monument confirmed the message of the contemporary world.

New and old were not always side by side. Cairns and round barrows also stood at a distance from the circles but still within sight of them, on ridges and hills. The reason, on one reading, is that the new elites could annexe as their own what had once belonged to all.[77] Previously holy ground was still holy ground, still visible to everyone, but it was now dominated by the graves of a new dominant class. In Cornwall, however, because there were so few actual human remains in any of them, the explanation may have to be the opposite – that people refused to bow to the kind of hierarchies taking charge in Wessex. By making their stone circles subordinate to natural monuments like tors, by using numinous rocks like quartz

Stone circles are varied in design. At Boscawen-Ûn, there is a central stone upright (above). At Men-an-Tol, there is a holed stone in the stone ring (left), although its present position between two uprights represents a post-medieval rearrangement when the other stones of the circle had fallen over.

- **Barrows**
- Cairns

Barrows and cairns are widespread throughout Cornwall. They are found along ridges and on hills where they could be well seen. Cairns made of stone instead of turf and earth are, not surprisingly, usually found in areas like Bodmin Moor and West Penwith where there are scatters of loose rock to be found on the ground surface.

and by placing exotic goods in the nearby barrows and cairns they could keep their circles sacred to the old, natural cosmologies. This might also be the place to mention a rare and rather inscrutable example of a statue menhir – a combined standing stone and effigy – on Chapel Down on St Martin's, Scilly and next to it a later Bronze Age cairn.[78] It seems reasonable to think of it as having been set up in reverence to some local deity rather than as a relic of ancestor worship. Smaller cairns and barrows are commonest in less conspicuous low-lying areas[79] and may have served as shrines to local physical features, or to some local event.

As well as impinging on monuments constructed by people, cairns and cists also cluster round tors and rock formations as if in spiritual deference to them. A spectacular example of a tor cairn crowns Showery Tor on the north-eastern side of the Roughtor ridge.[80] A wide, flat cairn surrounds the tor, highlighting it against the otherwise clitter-strewn hillside. Some portal dolmens like Lanyon Quoit and Sperris Quoit also have cairn material round them, and cists or cremation pits,[81] emphasising their continued religious significance. Occasionally barrows and cairns incorporate torstones in their construction, as at Caerloggas I[82] and Watch Croft.[83] Cup-marked stones like those found at Stithians Reservoir[84] may imitate the natural basin-like weathering on granite tors, in line with the resemblance[85] between the Men-an-Tol and a natural hollow on Zennor Carn. Some of these cup-marked stones crop up in cairns and barrows like the one at Starapark,[86] near Camelford – just as they are there in early Neolithic monuments, though much more frequently. It could be that there are cup-marks from both eras at the Tregiffian entrance in St Buryan at West Penwith. One of the cap-stones has a cup-mark, and so do the blocking stones, but the latter might have been added as an afterthought in the LANEBA.[87] The consensus is that putting holed stones into barrows is another example of the new culture paying tribute to the old, but it could also be argued that the very act of burying them is evidence of a break from nature worship.[88]

Although both cairns and barrows often look alike from the outside, there were big differences in the ritual that attended them – all of them, however, identifying powerfully with the landscape. Even externally they are by no means uniform, and there is quite a lexicon of bowl barrows, plate barrows, bell barrows, disc barrows and platform barrows.[89] Internal differences are just as great, but often masked by successive phases of building, for what started as a ring of stakes or posts could be replaced by an earthen barrow or cairn. In the same way, menhirs sometimes replaced wooden posts: the two standing stones at Longstone Downs,[90] St Stephen-in-Brannel are just such replacements.

Evidence of the rituals that took place inside barrows is rich, complicated and not easy to construe. What is clear is that inside are pits and graves to take whatever the ritual may have prescribed, including cremations. There are hearths. There are kerbs of stone or small stakes. There are platforms or mounds of earth, stone and turf. There are ditches outside the mound or platform. As well as artificial structures, there are sometimes loose torstones; or living rock can be part of the fabric. However, that may be only what is obvious to a modern Western eye. At other times and to other cultures there may be no gap between art and nature.[91] A torstone in a pit may have been not a stone, but the living presence of someone dead; charcoal in a hearth might be the spirit of a revered and fallen tree. Holed and chipped stones, carefully positioned in the Tichbarrow and Davidstow barrows, might have turned them into houses for the dead;[92] for these were stones that had probably once

Earlier monuments such as portal dolmens (known as quoits in Cornwall), like Trethevy Quoit situated on a knoll below Caradon Hill on Bodmin Moor, frequently have later cairns built around their base in the Late Neolithic and Early Bronze Age. For this reason the dolmens themselves were often wrongly dated to this later period.

weighted down a roof of thatch. There is a slate disc associated with a ring from Davidstow Moor Barrow I that bears the image of a human face.[93]

Digging often exposes earlier rings of stakes or posts in round barrows. Davidstow Moor I[94] and Trelan 2[95] are cases in point. In neither case do the stake holes go further than the ancient soil surface, with no traces actually cutting through the covering mound. In other words, there were rituals involving a timber circle that were required before the construction of the mound – harking back to henges and stone circles. In the same way, it could be that some cairns were built where stone rings once stood, the rings consisting not of individual uprights but of stone walling – cairn 3 at Stannon Down[96] on Bodmin Moor being one such site. If so it is fair to suppose that the rings of stakes or posts supported a low fence made of hurdling. In time barrows came to be covered by mounds and surrounded by ditches. A dig at Nancekuke Barrow turned up a burnt wooden shovel that may have been used in the building.[97] It might then have needed ritual burial, having become taboo for ordinary work – it is after all unlikely to have been burnt as a result of digging or deposited far from a settlement. In some cases, like Trelan 2, the mound was made of carefully laid turfs,[98] and at Crig-a-mennis the lie of the turfs suggests that the mound had been conical.[99] That may also have been the case at Tregulland, where the slate revetment had collapsed because the mound was so steep.[100] The roundness of barrow mounds might suggest that these were houses of the dead,[101] but permanent houses do not appear till the Middle Bronze Age. Their builders, however, did live in tent-like structures, so perhaps these conical mounds were tents for the dead.

Once the mound was built, paved areas such as forecourts or the stakes themselves provided a focus for worship; a posthole, still with the impression of its post, was found on a site[102] at Colliford Reservoir, Bodmin Moor. Sometimes small pits in or near mounds contain offerings of charcoal, chert or quartz (for example, at Davidstow Moor site IV, Trevellas Down). The Stannon Down 3 site had what has been described as a wall enclosing the barrow and attached to it; but was it in the usual sense a wall, and was its purpose to enclose? It does close off an apparent entrance, so to that extent it is enclosed; but it was two metres wide, flat and lower than the cairn, and as the paved 'forecourt' was actually on it, the wall can be described as a ritual embanked avenue for initiates to process along while everyone else gathered in the enclosed area.

That paths traced out the ritual landscape from one shrine or temple to the next, marking the cycle of the year, is an idea that has grown from the convergence of a lot of different evidence. This includes, for example, the way monuments line up along paths that may be straight, or may follow the natural contours of hills and ridges; the ubiquity of stone rows; the way some monuments imitate natural features – like the oddly shaped cairn on Brown Gelly, a cameo of Roughtor and Brown Willy

*The idea that there were once
processions between
monuments is supported by
'embanked avenues' – low
and broad raised walkways of
stone. This one on Bodmin
Moor aligns with one tor of
Roughtor, only to change to
face another tor as it goes
further up the slope.*

in the distance; the existence of at least seven stone rows on Bodmin Moor; the fact
that they all draw the eye to features in the landscape that could be overlooked; and
the recent recognition of raised ceremonial walkways known as 'embanked avenues'
and typified by one on the side of Roughtor which first aligns on Showery Tor, then
curves to face a tor now missing. All these observations point to what might nowa-
days be called a joined-up cosmology, literally joined by clear, well-trodden paths.
The monuments that punctuate them, whether natural or built, fall into a hierarchy
of size. Great features like Roughtor or Chapel Carn Brea commanded the alignment of other monuments within their wide horizons, and embodied public religion.
The shrines of private religion were in smaller sites, but no less important to those
who tended them.

The monuments were all that was constant about the LANEBA – a permanent
focus of religious and social activity to a people of no fixed address, usually staying
nowhere longer than a season. About life in their encampments little is known,
although archaeologists have combed a number of sites yielding flints scattered over
thousands of years from the Mesolithic to the Early Bronze Age. One of the best of
the known Beaker settlements is at Poldowrian, on the Lizard. A mound of burnt
clay, burnt black earth, stones and charcoal, along with shards from Beaker pots, may
be the remains of a 'burnt mound' left as waste from cooking. The cooking in question meant digging a hole in waterlogged ground, lining it with leather or basketry,
and bringing the resulting ooze of water to the boil by dropping very hot stones into
it. Stones heated up in this way bear characteristic cracks. Another Lizard site, at
Polcoverack, produced a range of flint tools and Beaker pottery, as well as more

73

burnt mounds. Polcoverack was possibly a base camp, for among the pieces of daub that came to light there was one that had an impression of wattle – so there could have been huts nearby.

The Early Bronze Age was little different from the Earlier Neolithic in the nature of its impact on the land – which reveals a patchwork of temporary clearances and regrowth. There were temporary camps in the valleys, and anything worth calling settlements at higher levels.[103] There the more open landscape meant easier clearance, and if there was any arable farming, the thinner and poorer soil at least made lighter work. For example, a study of soils and pollen at Colliford Reservoir shows that what had been relatively open grassland with only scrubby local oak and hazel was replaced by heathland. Early Bronze Age land management improved this state of affairs so that grasses eventually replaced the heather – partly, perhaps, because cereals were grown, but mainly as a result of grazing.

In summary, the LANEBA was an age in which ritual landscapes formed on growing, long-distance exchange routes that opened Britain to new ideas at odds with the old nature worship. In Cornwall the collision led to a synthesis: the new *things* – monuments and artefacts – were accepted, but not the ideas that informed them or the uses proper to them. In effect the new monuments slipped into the sacred landscape as if they had been always there. The religious landscape, with its increasing numbers and kinds of monuments, was mentally mapped in ever-greater detail. The new exotic artefacts and new trading contacts were proof of an outside world, but that world was still a mystery, explained in magical terms.

LATE NEOLITHIC
& EARLY
BRONZE AGE
(2700–1500 BC)

OPPOSITE
The best known stone circle in Cornwall, the Merry Maidens in West Penwith, near St Buryan, illustrates the fact that stone circles are not always on hilltops but can be found in equally conspicuous low-lying locations.

CHAPTER FOUR

SETTLED FARMING COMMUNITIES IN THE ANCESTRAL LANDSCAPE

Middle Bronze Age to Middle Iron Age (1500–200 BC)

AFTER THE FIRST IMPACT of farming technologies, people became more territorial and settled. Settlements tied by definite farms to their adjacent field systems are now the focus of community efforts – whether as small hut circles, or large enclosures, or even hillforts. In the Middle Bronze Age (MBA: 1500–1200 BC)[1] monuments became part and parcel of settlements, not structures set apart in sacred isolation. There is some evidence of ritual around the settlements, including the burial of human remains. Even so the monuments from previous periods still filled the landscape and were left largely intact. Prized artefacts were ritually consigned to water – to lakes, rivers and bogs. Meanwhile the exchange networks of the Early Bronze Age (EBA) became busier, then waned and were replaced in the Early Iron Age by more far-reaching networks connecting those of northern Europe with the Mediterranean.

Northern Europe and the Mediterranean

In the MBA and the Late Bronze Age (LBA: 1200–700 BC), northern European exchange routes reached the Mediterranean, but were not really integrated with the Mediterranean trade and exchange systems. However, changes in agriculture, warfare and social organisation led to more traffic across greater distances in the Iron Age, and the networks joined.

At first the exchange networks of the EBA were as active, if not more active, in the MBA. Gold, amber and tin were distributed widely. Thanks to new technologies[2] in Cornwall as in the rest of Europe, the range of artefacts increased. Among the innovations of the MBA was *cire perdue*[3] – the lost wax process – by which a finished metal object takes its shape from its own model in wax. Round the wax model a clay mould is made and then heated: the wax runs off, and molten metal replaces it. The result, when it cools and the mould is removed, is a perfect copy of the wax original.

The new technologies ran right through the period. In the MBA flat axes gave way to 'palstaves' – axes attached to split wooden shafts by grooves in their sides; these in turn gave way in the LBA to socketed axes, hollowed inside to take their shafts. Similarly the daggers of the EBA were replaced by rapiers – long, narrow and thin – in the MBA, superseded in turn by the leaf-shaped swords of the LBA. The weight and shape of these swords made them unwieldy for stabbing, but ideal for slashing. The LBA also produced the first forgings,[4] and the first sheet copper and bronze (sheet gold had already been achieved); from the sheet bronze came cauldrons, and chest armour and helmets for battle. Yet in spite of such manufactured objects, and especially metal ones, becoming ever more various and sophisticated, trade in the LBA generally declined, as the decreasing number of exotic items dating from this time demonstrates.

This reconstruction of a Middle Bronze Age settlement at Trewortha on Bodmin Moor gives an impression of life there during that period. The thatched-roofed roundhouses in their field systems and sheep grazing on the rough pasture illustrate the scene, though the conifer plantations would not have been there then.

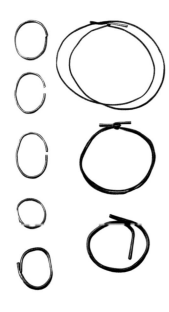

Irish gold made its way to Cornwall as part of the long-distance trade networks established by the Late Bronze Age. The Towednack hoard here is an example of the wealth that passed along these routes. The hoard includes two bar-torcs with a twisted design and five bracelets. The technique of manufacture was to produce ringed jewellery by hammering a pre-prepared gold bar into shape.

On the trade routes from Ireland to south-east Britain and the continent, Cornwall was pivotally placed.[5] For instance, a hoard (or more likely a ritual deposition) of objects found at Morvah included two types of bracelet – of the broken-ring, Irish type and the British 'carp's-tongue' type. They show how it is that comparable material from Ireland comes to light in north-west Iberia.[6]

Much debate surrounds the eventual decline of the exchange systems in the LBA.[7] Some archaeologists argue that advances in metallurgy meant better arms and armour, and that war was the new priority. They see the new types of hilltop enclosures as hillforts, and land divided by walls, fences and ditches as land to be defended. They even see the previous growth in trade as harbouring the seeds of its own decline. The greater the traffic, the more people it would employ and the more pressing the need of surpluses to feed and clothe them: so more land would come into cultivation and good land would be worth fighting for. The counter-argument is that the paraphernalia of war were signs of rank paraded for display, not signs of an especially warlike society. The hillforts[8] – so-called – often contain little actual settlement and large areas devoid of huts, so they were probably either to confine stock or to serve as public, ceremonial space. Perhaps the truth lies in the middle: war as a feature of the LBA can be overstated, but there is no denying that weapons were used and that conflict could have helped to slow down trade.

The Iron Age introduced enough changes to some parts of northern Europe and the Mediterranean to reverse the trends of the LBA. In some areas, like Bavaria and the south-east of Britain, larger and stronger fortified hillforts became the principal settlements, and the 'markets' for exchange. Occupied all year round, and commanding lower-lying ground, they could dominate an area well beyond the land from which they drew immediate support. Some authors link their appearance to the rise of new and larger political entities,[9] each with an active internal exchange system, and all involved in frequent long-distance dealings. Meanwhile change was afoot in the well-established trade networks of the eastern Mediterranean. The collapse of the Hittite Empire in Anatolia and the Levant left a power and trade vacuum, but it also spelt the end of the Bronze Age: iron-working was no longer a Hittite monopoly.[10] Successor states, especially those of the Greeks and Phoenicians, spread the trade and craft technologies of the eastern Mediterranean to Italy, Spain and North Africa.[11] They also spread statehood itself: in northern Italy, under Greek influence, the civilisation of the Etruscans represented a local response to the new concept of the state.[12]

With the arrival of states in the western Mediterranean, and therefore of cities that could support industries, crafts were now the product of workshops and not just of individual pairs of hands.[13] Luxuries multiplied – their attraction being less the mystic value of the intrinsic materials and more the magic in their making. The great

A PREHISTORIC ARMS RACE?

These swords and a spearhead are the sorts of weaponry increasingly produced during this period. Some scholars believe they represent a prehistoric arms race spiralling out of control, and that this led to a decline in trade. Others suggest that this was rather a heroic society in which flashy military imagery was important for prestige and ritual.

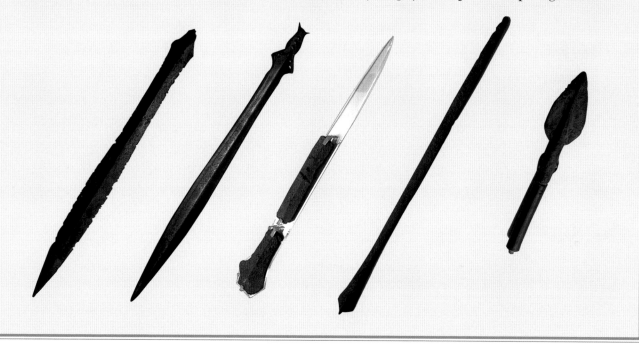

rivers of Europe – the Rhine, the Rhône and the Danube in particular – were important in their distribution. The products and influences of northern Europe and the Mediterranean richly intersect in the Alpine region; but a wealth (in both senses) of the products of Mediterranean craftsmanship spread far into northern Europe, some of it into Britain.

Iron may have played a role in shifting the spell from exotic materials to magical skills. Iron is found more or less anywhere; tin, copper and lead are not. As the fourth commonest element in the earth's crust[14] – after oxygen, silicon and aluminium – iron is widespread in soils and subsoils, in bogs and in rocky outcrops. So, unlike those other metals, its distribution could not be easily controlled. However, the technologies needed to win it from the ore and turn it into product are harder to master, especially as they demand higher temperatures and proper kilns – not just clamps and bonfires.

Seen as a whole, the growing output of increasingly sophisticated artefacts stimulated rivalry between social and political units that were ever extending in size. The competition was sharpest where farming was most productive and society was most hierarchical. Hierarchy in this context is not chiefly about rank, but about status based on tasks, roles and chains of responsibility. The state-organised urban societies

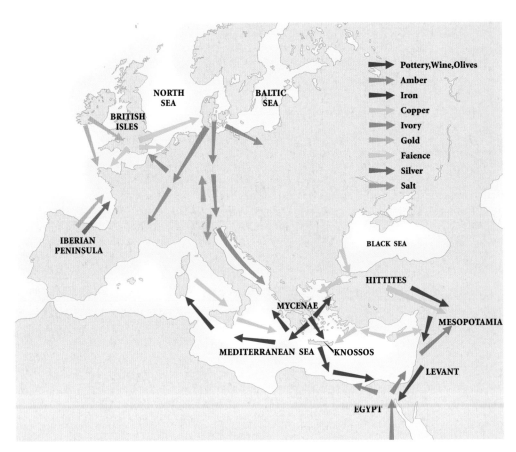

The trade in gold from Ireland continued during this period. The three copper and gold arm rings (above) were found together at Rosemorran. The map (above right), showing a selection of the important trade routes, demonstrates that by the Late Bronze Age trade networks extended beyond regions like the British Isles or the Eastern Mediterranean to encompass the breadth of Europe and the Mediterranean.

of the Mediterranean were the most hierarchic in this sense. In northern Europe, the conspicuous consumption of luxury goods and the hostility it engendered have been compared to the 'potlach' of the north-west coast of North America. This involved great chiefs ceremonially piling up gifts to each other to advertise their wealth and standing, and to keep face by matching munificence with its equal.[15]

The significance of agriculture and exchange

Between about 1500 and 1200 BC, field systems appeared across the moorlands and lowlands of Cornwall, as they did over much of the British Isles. The fields are usually dated (by radio-carbon dating) from pottery and charcoal found under their boundary walls. In Cornwall the field boundaries were usually built from stones. Though these stones were just cleared from the surface (they are rounded, therefore not quarried) there was nothing haphazard about where they were put into place. Earlier fields such as those on Brown Gelly,[16] Bodmin Moor, were curvilinear, arranged in clusters that grew by accretion, and associated with roundhouses.[17] Roundhouses had low walls of stone or of panels of woven wooden rods daubed with clay. The roof was supported by a ring of posts with wooden beams across them. Inside, excavation shows that there would have been a stamped earth floor. ('Roundhouse' has replaced 'hut circle' – not to be any more precise, but to line up with terminology that describes Late Medieval buildings of similar size as 'longhouses'.[18]) The regularity of later rectilinear fields like those on Carne Downs[19] suggests that areas were enclosed in a single act by boundary banks, and were then subdivided. Any irregularities are the result of later rearrangement, or the meeting of one system with another. Though perhaps less impressive than cairns and hilltop enclosures, the field systems of the MBA meant moving a lot of stone in a relatively short time. Most of the field systems in lowland areas have been obliterated by later generations, but one of the few that survive hints at how extensive these lowland systems were: a roundhouse settlement with its fields, it is at Trethellan Farm, near Newquay.[20] The flood plains of river valleys were not cultivated, and were only occupied before the MBA by temporary camps.

Because these field systems hindered movement, and not merely dominated but occupied the land, they made a greater visual impact than the earlier ritual monuments. The walls were low from the first; they have not been stripped to their present height because people needed the stone. They were hardly walls at all, obviously no good for penning animals, but boundaries for crops. With their exotic food plants they would have stood out against the surrounding rough grasses and heath of the moors, exotic here including not only wheat and barley, but rye and oats – none of them native to the British Isles. Legumes increasingly joined the arable list as well: peas and the newly arrived broad bean were both important to crop rotation.[21]

Moorland locations like Brown Gelly on Bodmin Moor began to be transformed by permanent settlement and field boundaries in the Middle Bronze Age. No longer were hillsides characterised just by plain vegetation and the occasional rock.

In the Neolithic and the EBA, slash-and-burn farming had allowed people simply to move on when the soil was exhausted. The fixed field systems of the MBA and later prehistory made it essential to rotate crops to keep the soil in good heart.[22] Nutrient-hungry cereals were followed by legumes, which help fix nitrogen in the soil, followed by a year of fallow – and then the cycle began again. Livestock may have grazed the land left unenclosed, but it is not clear how they were kept off the crops. An idea that farming on Dartmoor became specialist might apply to Cornwall too; some areas with smaller settlements, fewer roundhouses and more unenclosed land specialised in livestock, while others concentrated on cultivation.[23] Certainly new breeds of sheep that gave better wool were introduced, and from some settlements like Trethellan have come related finds – loom weights and spindle whorls. Other finds include querns – artefacts associated with the processing of grain.

During the MBA the exchange networks of the EBA became more active, and growing exotic foods on farms instead of foraging in the wild may have been part of the reason. Surplus grain would require larger and better storage jars. Gabbroic clay in Trevisker Ware would be the very thing – protective and endowed with magical properties, which may account for its wide distribution.[24] When trade fell off it was perhaps not only because of wars for land, but also because farming had been all too successful. It could have stimulated production of metal goods to the point that they lost value and therefore the power to symbolise status. Alternatively it may have been due not to agricultural success, but failure. The drop in temperature at the time,[25] along with shrinking harvests from over-exploited upland soil, may have led to the desertion of the upland fields.[26]

Finds of saddle querns like this one from Tredarvah, Penzance, became common. The rider stone would have been pressed down on the grain placed in the trough of the quern and then rubbed up and down. After some hard effort, this ground the cereal grains into flour.

Be that as it may, the LBA and the Early Iron Age (EIA: 700–400 BC) saw a major reorganisation of the landscape. The lowland settlements with their field systems continued; their productivity would have easily eclipsed that of the upland fields in any case. The upland fields were abandoned except as seasonal pasture, as permanent settlements were abandoned. Animals would be driven in summer to graze there when the fields were at their most lush and bountiful, and to take the pressure off the grazing round the lowland farms. There is an example of what could be an upland camp for just such summer use on Louden Hill, Bodmin Moor, where remains of roundhouses cut through an earlier boundary bank.[27] Still later, hillforts and rounds in the EIA and Middle Iron Age (MIA: 400–200 BC) like Bury Castle (Bodmin Moor), Warbstow Bury (North Cornwall) and Tregonning Hill (Kerrier) were built on the edge of moorland.[28] 'Rounds' are smaller, less defensible enclosures with a bank and ditch – better suited to keep out livestock, wild animals and thieves than to defy full frontal attack. Though not actually on the deep moorland, hillforts and rounds were close enough to suggest they had a role at the end of summer when the beasts were rounded up. Equally, as they were on the edge of the lowlands, they may have been useful for storing the grain and legume harvests. That could be why Killibury Hillfort,[29] dating to the 3rd and 4th centuries BC, contained deposits with charred grain. Malting is part of the storage process, and charred grain indicates the slow burning that can accidentally occur in malting.

Meanwhile, as part of the reorganisation, hillforts and cliff castles went up on the existing field systems – but not necessarily as rude intrusions. For instance, Maen Castle, on the footpath from Sennen Cove to Land's End, neatly fits into an earlier field system with a kink in its rampart to absorb an earlier field wall.[30] The material removed to create the ditch outside (which follows the kink) was therefore not needed to create this length of the rampart, and was used to make an outer wall instead. So the castle did not negate the previous set-up, it just modified it. Field systems now served fewer, larger centres of storage (and possibly redistribution), instead of widely scattered settlements of all sizes. Channel Four television's 'Time-team' recently undertook a geophysical survey of Gear Hillfort, near Gweek on the Helford River; it emerged that Gear replaced a former settlement and many of its fields. Field systems emerged from the MBA, and the land needed to create hillforts meant sacrificing some of the fields and their valuable crops. Hillforts provided in recompense an impressive community monument that could be used for ceremonies and trade. Given its size and its position overlooking a large tributary creek where it meets the main Helford River, Gear Hillfort was likely to have played an important role in the exchange network.

● Trevisker Pottery

Trevisker pottery was made of gabbroic clay, which meant that it did not require sophisticated kiln technology to fire well. Its distribution locally was largely coastal from the Camel estuary to south Devon, which could mean that it was used to carry materials to exchange.

The changing and varied nature of enclosure

Since the abandonment of the Early Neolithic hilltop ritual enclosures (which had huts in them), enclosures had been strictly for ritual. The MBA marked a return to the idea of enclosure for settlement – and for more permanent settlement than in the Neolithic. However, the apparent correspondence between MBA enclosures and LBA and Iron Age hillforts can create a false impression of continuity. There are walls, albeit not particularly impressive ones, around enclosures like Stowe's Pound[31] and Berry Castle,[32] and they possess no ditches. As for any settlement they might be protecting, there are roundhouses outside as well inside the wall, and large open spaces in the enclosures that are empty of anything, let alone houses. In the EIA and MIA also, hillforts and cliff castles such as Rough Tor and Treryn Dinas had large pen areas within them, though there are other sites like Carn Brea and Castle Pencaire with more convincing evidence of having been fortified settlements. For instance, there were more roundhouses – evidence of actual settlement enclosed within defensible ramparts and ditches.

As stone circles and henges were enclosures, and religious enclosures at that, it would not be surprising if these later enclosures had religious purposes too.[33] Indeed, they often incorporate earlier monuments – round barrows, cairns, long barrows. However, the traces of Neolithic hilltop enclosures seem not to have much respect in the Iron Age and, in the case of Trencrom, near St Ives, were obliterated in part by MIA fortifications. Human remains and offerings were left in ritual hollows in parts of the site at Trethellan Farm, near Newquay; but if there were any in the upland areas they could not have survived the acid soil.

Cliff castles and hillforts may have come into being in the Iron Age in response to competition for land, and the access to exchange goods that control of land conferred. In the EIA these sites lay behind a single bank or ditch, but from about the beginning of the MIA multiple banks and ditches appeared.[34] That we call them cliff castles and hillforts begs the question though, because their bank-and-ditch 'defences' may have had more to do with managing livestock. Some of these hillforts with wide space between the banks and ditches (known as 'multiple enclosure forts') could have used that space to pen animals – a possibility reinforced by the fact that their builders in Cornwall, Devon and Somerset often avoid the upland areas entirely.[35] From the MIA smaller enclosures called 'rounds', usually with a single bank and ditch, became the commonest type of settlement. They were hamlet-sized, for farming not defence, and far commoner than used to be thought. Cornwall's Historic Environment Service has shown that there could have been as many as a thousand in the county,[36] two per square kilometre in some areas; but as their existence spans about a thousand years, they would not all have been occupied at once. A round was essentially a small farmstead and probably represents the home of an extended family. Within the enclosure would have been storage pits for grain, and running round the houses would have been chickens – a later Iron Age introduction. The roundhouses would not have had windows as the walls were low, and light would have come in through the entrance. Most activities would have taken place outside anyway, in the enclosure and out in the fields.

Perhaps the most impressive feats of building were the linear earthworks. In south-east Britain in the Late Iron Age they defined major tribal centres complete with settlement, fields and cemeteries; but in other areas and earlier periods (the LBA to the MIA) they seem to have been boundaries between major tribal units. On Salisbury Plain they were created in the LBA but still used in the Iron Age.[37] Cornwall in later prehistory was probably a patchwork of local settlements organised as small, politically equal tribal units, as there is no compelling evidence of a hierarchy of sites. Each therefore was probably the social and religious focus of a single tribal group. A still visible linear earthwork in Cornwall is the Giant's Hedge, running between Lerryn and West Looe. The surviving parts show that it consisted of a large ditch, mostly though not always accompanied by a large bank.[38] It cuts off all the land south of it between the Fowey and Looe rivers – which, with its many settlements, probably equates to a tribal unit.[39] Another less well-preserved earthwork once crossed West Penwith. There is a reasonably well-preserved section near Varfell, Ludgvan;[40] I have seen and confirmed it, and think that it too was a tribal boundary.

The Bolster Bank, by St Agnes, probably had a different role because it encloses a rather smaller area – of upland heath with rich tin lodes but little settlement.[41] Other equally rich tin grounds have no earthworks to define them, however, so the tin was probably not the main factor, but the absence of any real settlement is curious. It encloses a particularly prominent hill, St Agnes beacon, which can be seen for many miles around. The hill overlooks the sea on one side, and a wide area of lower ground on the landward side. As linear earthworks can call attention to a space at the same time as denying access to it, perhaps it was a warning that here was ground too holy to tread. Parallels are everywhere: at Ayres Rock in Australia, in Beijing with its Forbidden (to ordinary people) City, on Mount Olympus – forbidden to all but gods. It could hardly have been used for large public ceremonies as there would have been more evidence of buildings, but a ridge with a barrow cemetery and the unusually rich tin deposits could have lent it magical significance.

The settlement as monument

In this period settlement itself becomes settled. As hunting and gathering declined and farming grew, people became more geographically tied, and their homes more permanent. Hitherto the fixed points had all been ritual monuments, while people and their settlements moved: now the settlements were themselves fixed points at

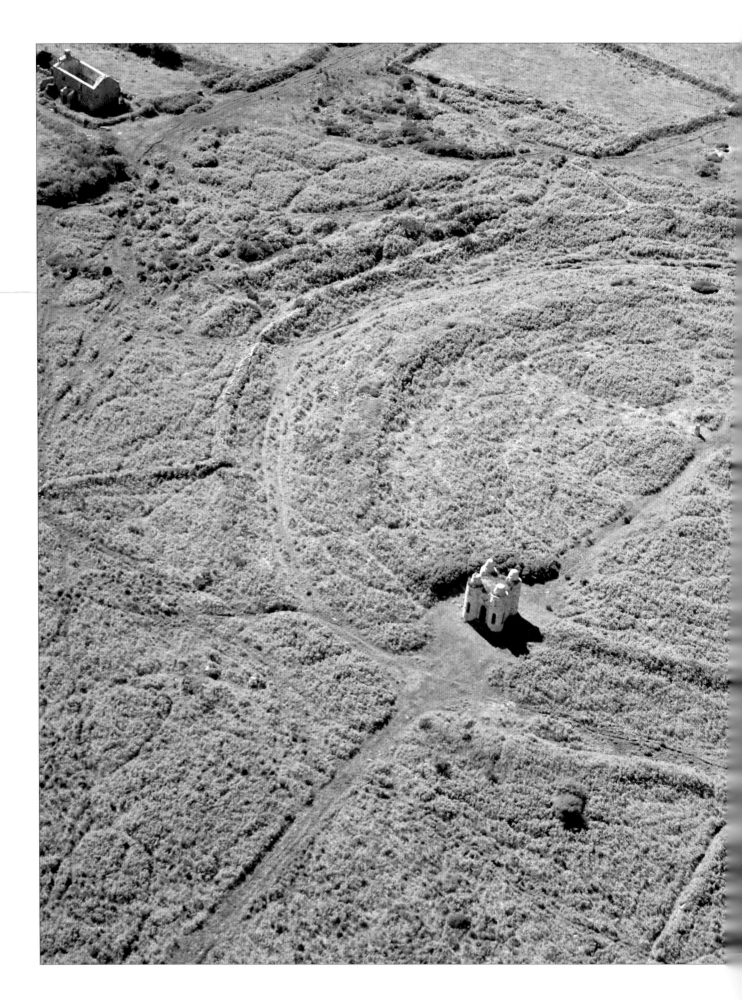

*Castle-an-Dinas in West
Penwith is an Iron Age
hillfort (post-400 BC) with
few roundhouses inside it. It
was probably a central place
for economic and religious
assembly. The 19th-century
imitation of a castle, 'Roger's
folly', represents the older
view that hillforts were
largely defensive. To the right
of the folly, and within the
double rampart and ditch
construction, are traces of the
original single rampart from
the Early Iron Age.*

which social, religious and exchange activities could all take place. Most of the holiness of the old shrines attached itself to the still older works of nature, but some literally came home.

The earliest roundhouses appeared in the MBA. In the MBA and LBA they occurred sometimes singly, sometimes in small villages. This suggests that the basic social unit could have varied from families to extended families to a wider kinship group. For example, the roundhouse at Poldowrian occupied the upper slope of a small sheltered valley on the Lizard, and lived off a system of small irregular fields.[42] This little valley on the edge of the Lizard moorlands perhaps represented the resource base for one family group. Trethellan, near Newquay, consisted of three residential houses and four ancillary buildings within a richer lowland field system,[43] and looks like the hamlet of a much more extended family. The family must have had access to meadows in the valleys and upland pastures for cows or sheep too, as milk products have been discovered in residues from pottery at the site.[44] Larger still was Stowe's Pound – a whole village of many roundhouses within a stone-walled enclosure.[45] Here lived a wider kin group of connected families, probably engaged in rearing livestock. No two settlements are quite the same. On Nornour, in Scilly, there seems to have been an extended family, in a small group of roundhouses sheltered in the lee of a hill, that lived both from agriculture and what it could win from the sea – which included seals.[46] As for religion, a single roundhouse at Callestick, Perranzabuloe, had ritual deposits and quartz blocking stones in the entrance, set in a way that recalls the ritual sealing of the earlier round barrows.[47]

In the EIA and MIA there was just as much variety in the way settlements were organised. At Bodrifty[48] in West Penwith and Kynance Gate[49] on the Lizard, open settlements of roundhouses and outbuildings, unenclosed, stood among fields. In some upland areas like Bodmin, graziers in summer improvised their housing by reusing MBA roundhouses at Garrow and even a ring cairn at Stannon Downs.[50] They needed only temporary shelters to last the summer, so these older structures saved them a lot of work. Hillforts and cliff castles, which might seem to rank at the top of the settlement scale, varied a lot in their roles and the population they sustained. As the main settlement type was the round, cliff castles and hillforts – if they

MULTIPLE ENCLOSURE FORTS

These examples of multiple enclosure forts in Cornwall show the wide spaces between ramparts, which suggest that they contained areas for corralling livestock. Such forts are found in highly visible locations with poor defensive positions. As for dwellings, they have few, if any, roundhouses within them. The three enclosure forts here are Hall Rings (*right*), Round Wood, Feock (*below left*) and Helsbury Castle (*below right*).

Geographic location is helpful in interpreting multiple enclosure forts. This distribution map shows how they are located to avoid the poorer soils on the granitic moors and Culm measures, which gives weight to the impression that they were agricultural in nature.

were not for war – probably did have a socially lofty role within the general settlement pattern, as well as being important ceremonially and as stations on the exchange network.

The cliff castle at Treryn Dinas, with its magnificent and haunting rock formations, is especially interesting from this point of view. At the top of these formations the Logan Rock, which could easily be tipped on its point of balance till the 19th century, probably formed the focal point. Two very small roundhouses near the western edge of the Logan Rock are the whole settlement; its ramparts lie below a slope and it would be hard to defend; but a Bronze Age cremation urn found eroding out of a crevice[51] hints at what the headland may have signified spiritually.[52] The Irish archaeologist Gabriel Cooney[53] has described Irish Sea promontories and islands as having a liminal quality – as if, like cloud-capped mountains in many mythologies, they were the threshold of the spiritual domain.[54] Treryn Dinas is an especially atmospheric example, even without the Logan Rock. The rock formations look like the turrets of a castle from a Gothic romance.

Religious or at least ritual activity is also found in the ordinary lowland settlements. At Trethellan one of the roundhouses had a young adult male burial at its centre, placed in the former hearth, and covered over with ash and burnt lumps of quartz.[55] The hearth was then reconstructed and put back into use. A number of other ritual finds at the settlement included hollows with layers of pottery, animal

BELOW

Funerary urns such as these Cornish ribbon-handled urns (Trevisker Ware) from Liskey Hill, Perranporth could have been suspended on cords from the ceilings of roundhouses prior to their end use amongst the dead.

89

bones and snail shells capped by slates, all in a rich covering of organic material – some of it burnt.[56] An enigmatic stone building at Trethellan may also have had a ritual use.[57] Similar ritual evidence has come to light elsewhere – in the Gwithian settlement,[58] for instance, where the burial of a child and several cremation mounds were found close to the roundhouses.[59] Clearly people were linking fire, heat and death. Perhaps fire was seen as cleansing or life-giving, restoring vitality to the dead.

The *fogou* could certainly have had ritual significance, too. Derived from the Cornish for 'cave',[60] and pronounced 'foo-goo', it is a type of passageway with a side chamber. As a rule, but not always, *fogous* were dug into the ground with stone uprights as wall panels and large stone roofing slabs to prevent subsidence. The most plausible explanation for their use is that they were for storage related to ritual, and for ritual itself. That many *fogous* are hidden behind buildings or in stone hedges may mean that valuable cult objects were hidden in them; and the presence of cremated bones – possibly though not definitely human – adds credence to this view. They would not have been good for storing food, except perhaps milk and beer.[61] As for the idea that they might have had some defensive use, they have been found in settlements that are weakly defended – as at Carn Euny[62] and Chysauster, which are on the slopes of low-lying hills. Most of the known sites have no defences at all, and where they exist they are a simple bank and ditch, at best fit only to deter thieves and trespassers. Besides, some side chambers are too small to take more than three or four people, and some entrances are too narrow for adults – as at Pendeen Vau.[63]

Finally, it is interesting to notice the similar architecture of roundhouses, and the round barrows and cairns. Some of the cairns and roundhouses at Stannon Down are alike in having walls revetted inside and out with rubble in the centre. The entrances

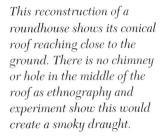

This reconstruction of a roundhouse shows its conical roof reaching close to the ground. There is no chimney or hole in the middle of the roof as ethnography and experiment show this would create a smoky draught.

in roundhouses are like cairn forecourts; some have central pits – a hearth corresponding to a ritual/cremation pit. Roundhouses and round barrows both leave the impressions of post or stake holes. The transition from the MBA to the LBA and the Iron Age produces similar correspondences in Wessex and south-east Britain.[64] The similarities between roundhouses and barrows, including their use as repositories for burials and cremations, suggest both that a technique for putting up a religious building transfers to secular use and that domestic buildings are now seen as holy.

Landscape of nature, landscape of ancestors

Although there is a general move away from building ritual monuments (including monuments that celebrate natural rock formations), there is still much in this period that testifies to a reverence for ancestors and nature. The old Neolithic enclosure at Stowe's Pound, which includes the Cheesewring rock formation, was incorporated into the MBA enclosure, while hillforts and cliff castles incorporate rock formations within their ramparts. In addition, metal ware was consigned to water as offerings – to river or sea. There was a trend from domestic to military items in these offer-

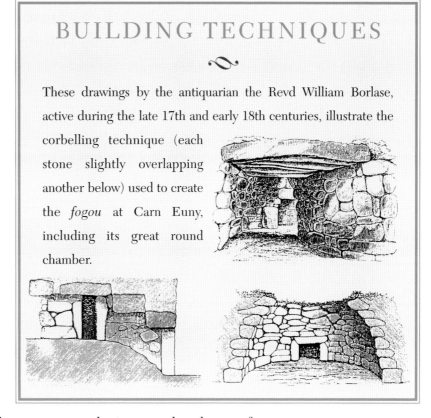

BUILDING TECHNIQUES

∾

These drawings by the antiquarian the Revd William Borlase, active during the late 17th and early 18th centuries, illustrate the corbelling technique (each stone slightly overlapping another below) used to create the *fogou* at Carn Euny, including its great round chamber.

ings, and the usual inference has been that war was on the increase, but the act of deposition suggests that they were votive or sacred offerings to water gods. As for ancestral features, round barrows, long barrows and cairns often remain untouched when hillforts and cliff castles go up around them. On the other hand, Neolithic enclosure walls are often ignored, slighted or removed – as at Trencrom, near St Ives – which reinforces the idea that the immunity of long barrows and cairns was an act of conscious choice.

Most of the evidence of how people disposed of the dead comes in the form of individual bones found in and around the settlements. At Trethellan there was a full burial under the hearth, and at Gwithian, under a house wall, was an entire skeleton of a child. The individual bones, however, suggest that the tradition of excarnation continued and bodies were left in the open to decompose. Everything points to a strong association of land and community – the human remains placed within the settlements, the field systems, the dividing and enclosing of land; and community included ancestors. MBA fields enclosed not only good land, but also areas of barren rock and stone, and these barren patches in the MBA settlements at Leskernick on Bodmin Moor may have been fields for the dead.[65] In striking contrast to earlier periods, monuments set in the landscape do not mimic it in any way. An Iron Age settlement at Bodrifty confirms this by making respectful, but nevertheless practical, use of the granite boulders found there. For instance, one roundhouse has a flat boulder as its floor. The land thus belongs to a community of ancestors and living relatives, not to the gods of nature.[66]

This period was one in which the permanent settlement became the main focus of the community, not just for economic purposes, but also for social and religious ends. It is almost as if people permanently settled the ritual location, so that houses could contain both the living and the dead. That people, rather than nature, were increasingly the main ideological concern is illustrated most dramatically by the landscape. The natural look of the landscape, enclosed by field systems, was radically altered – far more so than it was by the ritual monuments of the previous period.

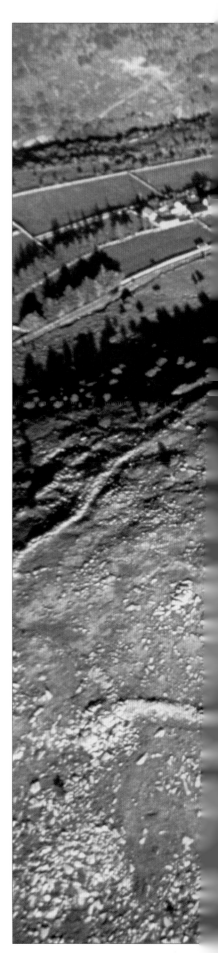

CHAPTER FIVE

CITIZENS OF THE EMPIRE: *ROMANITAS* IN CORNWALL

Late Iron Age & Roman Period (200 BC–AD 400)

THE ROMAN EMPIRE was extremely diverse in culture, economy, and social and religious outlook,[1] and the many signs of acculturation are plain to see. Instead of Roman towns, aqueducts, bathhouses and villas, Roman ideas and influences were adopted into more local ethnic traditions. It was in this way that Cornwall achieved a clear sense of *Romanitas* or Roman-ness. Influences came from provincial Roman developments, and only in a weaker fashion from the toga-wearing metropolitan Romans, evidenced from classical texts of the 1st centuries BC and AD.[2] These wider imperial influences themselves changed: for most of the 4th and 5th centuries the rulers of the Empire were a tunic-wearing[3] Christian elite,[4] brought up on Neo-Platonism and a rejection of urban life.[5]

Roman civilisation certainly influenced Cornwall, especially West Cornwall – because it was the pivot of sea routes around the province and over to Ireland, without being much of a trading destination in itself. The first influences probably came indirectly via Wessex. Later, as part of the *civitas* of the Dumnonii,[6] within the Province of Britannia, it formed the westernmost hinterland of the Roman city of Isca Dumnoniorum, present-day Exeter. Roman provinces were subdivided into *civitates* – a *civitas* translating as a city state on the classical Mediterranean model of an autonomous, or semi-autonomous city with dependent territory around it. The *civitas* of the Dumnonii included Cornwall, Devon and parts of western Somerset.[7] The tribe of the Dumnonii was probably something of a fiction, as there is precious little evidence of political consolidation before the Roman conquest.

The advance of the Mediterranean: trade and warfare

During the last two centuries BC, the Roman Empire grew to take in the whole of the Mediterranean, and Gaul as far as the Channel. The trade networks of the Classical world now interlocked with those of the British Isles, but the first wine and olive oil arriving in Cornwall came indirectly – through internal British networks. Julius Caesar (who only raided Britain in the mid-1st century BC, and came, saw, but

did not conquer)[8] was aware of its tin, but knew only that it came from somewhere in its interior.[9] In fact the main trading post in south-western Britain was at Hengist-bury Head in Dorset, not in Cornwall.[10] Up trade routes running from the eastern Mediterranean, through southern Gaul and to Britain came amphorae of wine and olive oil; cattle, grain, slaves and tin went the other way. (If we are to believe Quin-tus, the brother of the great orator and writer Marcus Cicero,[11] slaves were the only significant commodity.) The first sailing ships in the archaeological record appeared at around this time;[12] examples from elsewhere in Britain, such as the Blackfriars shipwreck,[13] show that they were about the size of a modest yacht.

Such was the competition for access to these Mediterranean goods in parts of Britain that trade war was no figure of speech. Cunliffe's studies of the Danebury region[14] in Hampshire show that hillforts became fewer but larger, more complex in design, more redoubtable; and from the distribution of Iron Age coins it seems that tribal areas, too, became fewer and larger. But outside the south and east of Britain, where hilltops were giving way to *oppida*,[15] there was still much diversity in the pat-terns of settlement, and the evidence of competition was weaker. *Oppida* were large settlements of almost urban character. The tribal territory of the Dumnonii, includ-ing Cornwall, was by contrast full of small hillforts, rounds and small undefended settlements. In the north and west of Britain generally there was little or no consol-idation of political and economic power before the Roman conquest was begun by the Emperor Claudius in AD 43.[16]

In Cornwall complex fortification may have served no martial purpose. Cliff cas-tles like the Rumps,[17] Treryn Dinas (the Logan Rock)[18] and Gurnard's Head[19] added on some impressive banks and ditches, but these may have related to particular rock formations. Other clues point to ritual use. On Gurnard's Head, part of a child's skull was found in a midden behind a rampart, and the roundhouses on the site are too small for the normal living conditions of the period.[20] At the Rumps, near St Minver (north of Padstow and the Camel River), a triple bank and defence system closely encloses two rocks stacks, each with a roundhouse at its foot.[21] Beyond the stacks, which are still part of the peninsula, lies a tall island in the form of an even larger stack. At Treryn Dinas,[22] behind the inner rampart that also tightly encloses its rock formations, two ovalhouses of Roman date (see page 111) show that these cliff cas-tles continued in use after the conquest.

Cornwall or Dumnonia: views from antiquity and now

Cornwall in the Roman period formed part of the *civitas* of Dumnonii, and must be seen through its role as part of both a *civitas* and a province. As far as material evi-dence goes, Cornwall at this period was no isolated place. Some of the artefacts that have survived belong to parts of Cornwall alone; but others straddle Cornwall and

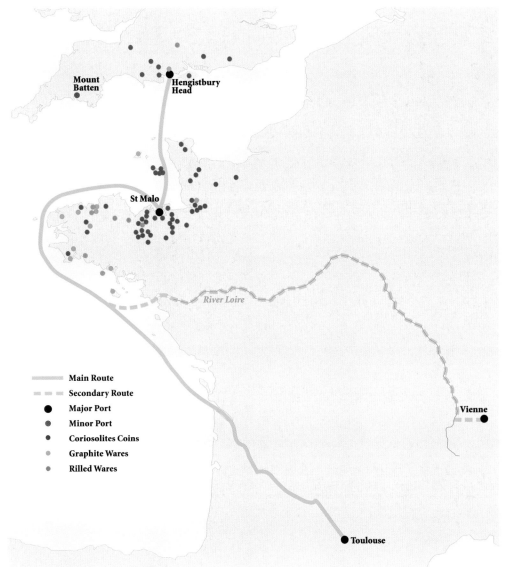

This map strongly suggests that Dorset, not Cornwall, was the main British trading partner for Brittany during the Late Iron Age. Amphorae containing wine and olive oil were traded up from the Mediterranean to Brittany and on to Dorset. Note that coins and pottery from Brittany are also found in Dorset and some neighbouring areas. The connection between Cornwall and Brittany belongs to the next period.

Devon, others are found all over the south-west and indeed Britain, others again across the whole Empire. Vessels of gneiss and elvan (a soft granite) are concentrated in West Cornwall, with a few found further east as far as Kent.[23] South Devon Ware is distributed through eastern and northern Cornwall.[24] South West Decorated Ware spreads over the south-west up to Gloucestershire and Dorset;[25] although it was made of different local clays that produced minor local variants, the general similarity is what counts and a recognisable look or fashion caught on over a great area. Finally, in Cornwall as all over Britain, had Roman pottery from other parts of Britain – like the utilitarian Oxford Ware; or from other parts of the Empire – like Terra Sigillata, a glossy red luxury tableware from Southern Gaul, and North African amphorae, the tall, handled jars for wine and olive oil.[26] These have all been found on local native settlements of the Roman period.

It is difficult to imagine why there should be a particular Cornish identity at this period. People on both sides of the Tamar would have spoken the same Celtic language, and there was no political consolidation to create large regions in the south-west before the Romans came. The Tamar itself, as a major waterway, was likely to have united the communities on either bank through trade, as movement was then easier and quicker by water than by land. Dartmoor's economy and landscape made it more akin to the moorlands of Cornwall than to the rest of the south-west; and the South Hams and Torbay have more in common with the creeks and coastline of the Fowey, Fal and Helford than with coastal areas to the east. Finally, the high cliffs of Cornwall's north coast look much like north Devon and the cliffscapes of Somerset and Exmoor. It is not hard to see why the Romans would have seen Dumnonia as opposed to Cornwall as a logical area of administration.[27]

Yet its name – Cornubia – could date from this time. Oliver Padel suggests, in his *Cornish Place Names*, that it comes from a tribal name derived from the Latin *cornu*, meaning 'horn', the tribe in question living at the end of a long horn-shaped peninsula.[28] However, its first occurrence in a document (shortly before AD 705) labels the place, not a tribe. Despite its distance from the capital of the *civitas* at Exeter, west Cornwall – Penwith and Kerrier – has a marked concentration of Roman finds and influences after a gap in the rest of the county. It may be that the name was given to the helm-turning point in sea journeys from southern Britain to Ireland and western Britain round the horns of Land's End and the Lizard. The Romans left their mark on Scilly, too – including what may be a seafarer's shrine on the island of Nornour.[29] Cornubia could be the sort of name given to defining headlands by Ancient Greek seafarers like Pytheas,[30] who described Britain in terms of three points – one at Cape Wrath in Scotland, the second at Dover and the third at Land's End, *Belerion*. Later European explorers thought in the same way about the Cape of Good Hope and Cape Horn.

Large Cordoned Ware jars like this example from Probus (below left) show how designs could spread across the Empire. Such jars are influenced by a Gaulish style, and could be used for holding liquids. South West Decorated Ware (below centre and right) illustrates the different shapes and sizes of vessel that were available during this period.

Acculturation and participation: material culture and customs

Roman influence pervaded everything, down to the remotest settlements, and changed everything: technology first, then social life, economic activity, perhaps even religion. It was a process (in academic parlance) of acculturation – whereby one culture gradually becomes like another by contact and osmosis. Some of the Roman influences were seaborne, coming in on the long-distance trade networks. Some were due to being part of the Empire, in particular the province of Britain and the *civitas* of the Dumnonii.

The earlier developments in the Late Iron Age (LIA: 200 BC–AD 43) were mostly technological. For example, wheel-thrown pottery from northern Gaul and the Mediterranean reached settlements in Cornwall from Hengistbury Head in Dorset.[31] These wares were impressive enough to inspire imitations, like the Cordoned Ware that copied northern Gaulish jars. In fact much of the pottery in Cornwall at this time used to be thought of as wheel-thrown, but has turned out just to have been extremely well made – perhaps trying to emulate thrown pots. It could be that trade in material of this quality helped to revive ritual activity at cliff castles, for here were highly desirable goods, exotic and local, crying out to be given and received in showy competition. Eventually, however, demand for Roman pottery went beyond a mere urge for display: people used it. Ranges of individual tablewares and *mortaria* (as in pestles and mortars) demonstrate that Roman cooking and dining customs did in some degree arrive, especially in the west of Cornwall. A *mortarium* was used to turn herbs and spices, or nuts and berries, into pastes that could go into sauces and condiments. The inference from individual tableware is that people now had their own plates at table, instead of sharing from a common bowl or

cauldron. It was a great symbolic change. Although people no doubt still ate together, the fact of having an assigned portion of food redefined them as individuals within the group. As well as crockery, fashion accessories went Roman too, as witness the brooches, such as *fibulae*, and glass beads; what happened to actual dress styles is harder to say.

During the Roman period itself a more commercial type of trade, probably barter, began to replace the potlach kind of socially competitive exchange. Settlement sites begin to yield Roman-style weights of standard size made of elvan and gneiss – which are relatively soft and easy to carve. A lead weight, possibly from a Roman steelyard, was found at Treryn Dinas in West Penwith – which again suggests that measurement was now an important aspect of trade, and that commercial values now counted. True, the weights as physical objects could have been something that only the Romans demanded and meant little to anyone else, but their local production from local stone makes that unlikely. Confirmation that 'trade' was now closer to its modern meaning is to be seen in a society changed by the existence of barter, which allows wealth and status to be the reward of personal effort instead of being the emblem of divine will or providence. Trade meant that wealth was no longer exclusive and that social mobility was possible.

In the Late Iron Age, penannular brooches did not simply represent jewellery, but were a means to fasten clothing like cloaks. This 1st-century AD example is from Castle Gotha, near St Austell. Later, penannular brooches were supplemented by Roman fibulae *as some elements of Roman fashion were adopted.*

The Romans also introduced their coinage into the province of Britannia. In the LIA, parts of southern Britain had minted their own coins, the nearest to Cornwall being Dorset – the territory of the Durotriges. It was not till the Roman period itself, however, that coins came to Cornwall, and it is not certain that they amounted to currency in the true sense.[32] Quantities of coins are only found in so-called 'hoards', which may have been ritual offerings like the deposits of valuable metal items in the LBA and Iron Age. The likely scenario in Cornwall is that trade was carried out by the whole community, not individuals. Coins may have played a subsidiary role since there were not enough of them; they would be given *in lieu* of goods that did not materialise in time, and kept to buy other goods later or to pay taxes. Indeed, taxes may be the main reason for the spread of weights and measures, because if officials levy tax on the basis of exact measures everyone subject to tax will want to buy in exact measures too, for their own protection. Tax may also lie behind the production of salt at Gwithian, Trebarveth and Carngoon Bank, near the entrance to today's Lizard village. The industry may have been set up to cure surplus meat for delivery to the *civitas* headquarters at Exeter as a way of paying taxes in kind; or it may simply have been to provision passing traders. The same alternative explanations apply to the use of corn driers at Halangy Down in the Isles of Scilly (see page 104).

Actual villas and towns on the Roman pattern are absent. So far only one fort has been found – at Nanstallon near Bodmin,[33] overlooking the Camel valley, but also close to the Fowey valley, at a commanding position near the ridgeway running through the central spine of Cornwall. It was built for a mixed infantry and cavalry regiment, and – judging from pottery and coins from the site – lasted from about AD 55 to the 80s. Although there were no villas, there was a residence for visiting officials at Magor,[34] near Illogan – the only one of its kind in Cornwall.[35] It had mosaic floors and frescoes but they are plain and unexciting. It also lacked outbuildings associated with agriculture or craft workshops, and it stood right by a major area of placer deposits of tin in the Red River. All this suggests it was probably a *mansio* or official guesthouse. The rooms in this guesthouse were more or less of equal size, except some smaller rooms added later to one side and this, too, suggests its official nature. Its regular straight sides, uncompromising in their rejection of the natural forms of stone and wood, and even the smooth flat plasterwork inside would have been astonishing to those versed only in local architectural and landscape aesthetics. In fact, as the only such representation of metropolitan architectural norms in Cornwall in the 3rd century AD, the *mansio* would surely have attained a fame locally beyond the scale expected of such a building.

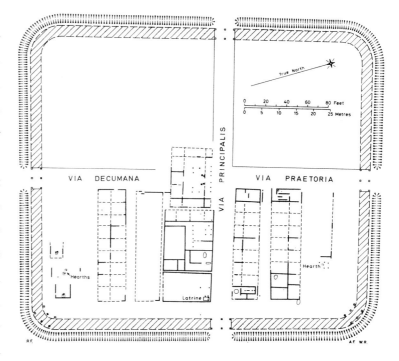

Although only one Roman fort has been discovered in Cornwall, at Nanstallon, near Bodmin, it may well have contributed to local architectural change. It has the typical regular layout of Roman forts, with four entrances, two main streets meeting at a crossroads, a commander's residence in the centre and barrack blocks. The overall shape is rectangular.

Major changes took place in the local settlements. Some hillforts like St Mawgan-in-Pydar[36] continued into the Roman period but were abandoned by the second century. On the other hand, rounds like those at Shortlanesend,[37] near Truro, and Castle Gotha,[38] near St Austell, continued to be erected and occupied throughout the Roman period. Additionally, a new type of enclosure appeared all over Cornwall – and Devon: the rectilinear enclosure. In the past some of these, like the enclosures at Merthen,[39] near Gweek, have been confused with Roman marching camps. The latter, however, have parallel sides whereas rectilinear enclosures take on a variety of polygonous shapes.[40] It seems most probable that buildings like the Roman 1st-century fort at Nanstallon, near Bodmin, and others in Devon were the inspiration for its architecture.[41] The gates, banks and ditches of rectilinear enclosures were more like those of the Iron Age rounds (see Chapter Four) than of Roman forts, though the enclosure at Golden, a little south of Carvossa, is the size of a hillfort. The Roman fort at Nanstallon, in contrast, relied on a substantial timber stockade with towers at the corners.

Within rectilinear enclosures there were further changes: ovalhouses replaced roundhouses. In roundhouses an internal circle of posts supported a conical roof

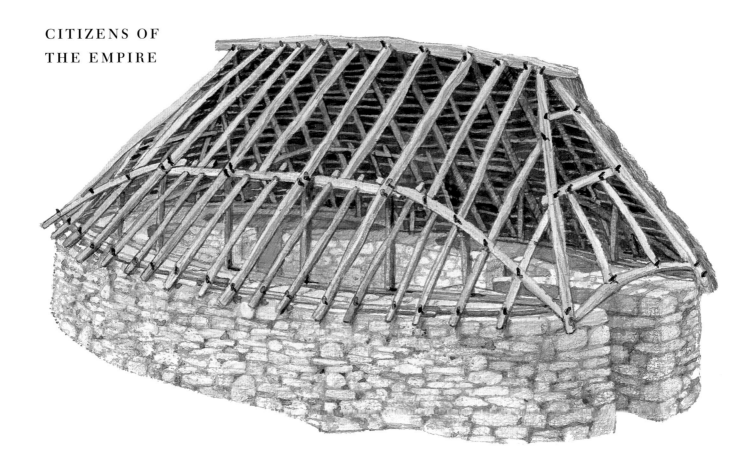

This courtyard house reconstruction shows an up-turned boat design, with the roof height slightly exaggerated to reveal more detail. The ridgepole is the 'keel' and the 'gunwales' lie over the stone walls, all fixed with wooden pegs. Struts resting on the walls derive from supports for a ship's deck. Thatching around the overhanging 'keel' leaves a triangular smoke vent – as found in folk architecture in Jutland, Denmark. The aerodynamic design deflects high winds, while the corridor entrance prevents incoming draughts.

(see reconstruction of one of the Trethellan roundhouses on page 90). Ovalhouses adopted the Roman idea of the ridge-pole, where two lines of posts or drystone side walls supported a triangular-section frame holding a pole or beam running length-wise, which in turn supported a roof with a central ridge and gables at either end. Unlike the barracks or the commander's residence at Nanstallon fort, however, the side walls of local ovalhouses were not parallel but curved inwards at the end. Anyone visiting the *civitas* capital of Isca (Exeter), for example, could have seen Roman buildings with rounded ends, but the handling of the gable ends of oval-houses suggests no debt to the Roman apse, but seems more like an awkward com-promise with the earlier roundhouse. It could be that it borrows from boat-building – the ridge pole on this theory bent like the keel of an upturned boat. Roman influ-ence comes out in other ways though. Trethurgy house A1[42] and Trebarveth house 3[43] had culverts in them; they were dug into the soil, sometimes covered by stone slabs, and perhaps lined with wood. Trethurgy house T4 also had a paved area out-side it, which may be a relic of Iron Age ritual practice, whereas Trethurgy house Z2 had paving inside the house. On balance it seems that people in Cornwall were trying to produce the new Roman look using the old building methods.

Domestic building in West Penwith and the Isles of Scilly took a line of its own, and unenclosed settlements of 'courtyard houses' replaced the earlier systems of hill-forts and rounds.[44] They vary from the larger groups of Chysauster[45] and Carn Euny[46]

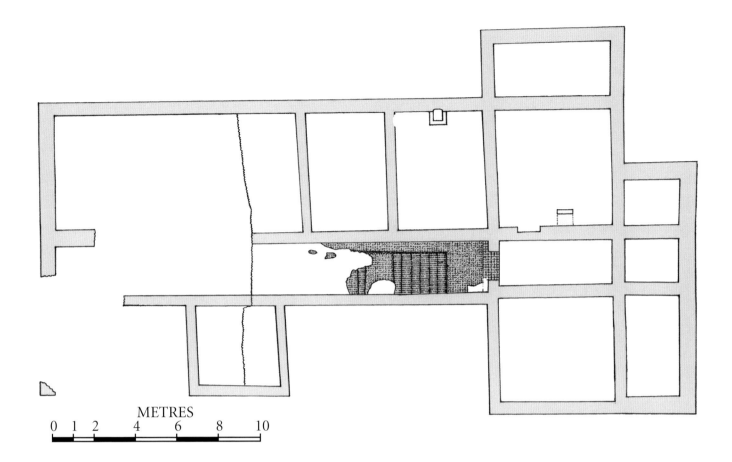

METRES

0 1 2   4   6   8   10

to the single courtyard house at Goldherring,[47] and are tied into the existing Iron Age field systems. Low walls often connect houses to each other, and seem to enclose communal spaces and level areas that could have been gardens. These houses were unlikely to have had open courtyards despite their name because rain from the roof would have flooded the interior.[48] The houses were actually oval as in the rest of Cornwall, and are likely to have had ridge-pole roofs. Courtyard houses may well have had roofs like upturned boats too. The only difference was that a courtyard house had an internal partition.

Courtyard houses are peculiarly interesting because the many Roman influences in their structure reveal a lot of social and economic change among the local people who built them and lived in them. Aside from the roofs possibly reflecting the architecture of the deeper-keeled sailing ships of the period, like the Blackfriars and County Hall ships found in London, there are so many other striking points of comparison. The very fact that they were split up into rooms is new and significant, because rooms of different sizes and for different purposes are a feature of the Roman house. For example, the commander's residence in the fort at Nanstallon had a large public room with smaller private rooms round three of its sides. More significantly though, Roman villas and townhouses generally in Britain seem to have been modelled on military structures such as *mansiones* and barracks. They have large dining rooms with hearths and a series of smaller rooms used as antechambers

Apart from the Roman fort at Nanstallon, the only classically Roman building in Cornwall is that at Magor, near Illogan. The lack of outbuildings and the relative lack of difference in room sizes (apart from three small rooms tacked on later to the right-hand side) suggest a military building, such as an official guesthouse or mansio.

103

and bedrooms.[49] Principal bedrooms also possessed hearths. This arrangement mirrors that in the courtyard houses. Additionally there were narrow rooms in Roman houses that were used as places to keep household gods,[50] which may suggest such rooms in courtyard houses had similar uses. Courtyard houses had culverts for drainage, lined and covered with stone, just as in Roman forts and towns. Pivot stones on one side of a doorway allowed doors to swivel open on a pole. The pole forming the inner edge of the door would have had the lower end in the pivot stone and the upper end probably in a socket carved into the timber superstructure. There were paved areas: at entrances to houses – though these could be the vestige of Iron Age ritual; within enclosed areas between houses, such as passages and open courtyards; and sometimes within the houses themselves. Some rooms contained basins carved from blocks of granite. Hearths were lined with stones and pottery sherds. At Halangy (pronounced 'Linjy') Down on St Mary's, Scilly[51] the courtyard houses eventually came to have special corn-driers like the ones that became common in Late Roman (4th to early 5th centuries) villas in Britain.

These features, especially the internal partitions, suggest not only strong Roman cultural influences but also major changes in family life. Iron Age houses had just been one big room where everyone slept, and where economic activity like weaving and sewing went on in the same space as cooking and eating. In courtyard houses different activities and indeed different people could each have space of their own. If the idea of a single roof[52] is right, then there may well have been extra room for storage on an upper floor supported on the internal partitions. It could also be that the family – albeit larger than the modern nuclear family, and including grandparents, aunts, uncles and cousins – could have had at least some privacy and physical separation. Romano-British villas had separate suites of rooms for the high-born lady and gentleman of the house, but here there is only one suite. It therefore looks much more like the separation of senior couples from their children and lesser relations. That arrangement could well account for a particular house at Chysauster where a second half-dwelling with a new main chamber, small room and large private room was later nestled on to the side of the original. Perhaps older offspring had reached maturity and had offspring of their own to support.

There is no need to infer that extended families lived together from any fear of their neighbours. If anything, the houses in rounds, rectilinear enclosures and especially courtyard villages huddled steadily closer together. What seems more likely is that people found it made economic sense to work together as coherent, well-regulated communities. Some such regulation may be implicit in the now divided courtyard houses, signalling who did what, where they did it and who in the family had status. Status and role in most non-urban societies (and many urban ones) are governed partly by age, partly by gender. Individual differences such as some special

skill can weigh heavily – but probably not among people like these with their communal view of property. An interesting comparison with this society is that of 19th-century New Caledonia in the South Pacific where French peasants with their individual holdings could not, despite the best efforts of the French colonial régime, compete with the communally run agriculture of the native Kanaks.[53] Their pooled land gave the Kanaks an economic advantage from sheer economies of scale.

It was not only in the dwellings of the living that Roman and Mediterranean influences took root. In the Iron Age, burial of the dead gradually became standard practice in all of Cornwall (bar the northern part) and southern Devon; notable long-cist cemeteries are at Harlyn Bay, Trelan Bahow, Stamford Hill outside Plymouth and many sites on the Isles of Scilly.[54] Long cists are rectangular or coffin-shaped burial chambers lined along the sides with stone slabs, and their use lasted through the Roman period right into the Late Medieval. The LBA and the Iron Age celebrated community in its monuments, and the long cist continues the tradition with a subtle difference, for the presence of the dead in shared space with the living (described in Chapter Four) was now a thing of the past. The Roman way was to have separate communities for the living and the dead: the living kept to their *polis* (or town), and the dead kept to theirs – the *necropolis*. What continued, in life and death, was social equality. In the largest and most centralised chiefdoms in the south-east of Britain it is difficult to identify any building or structure used by an elite in life. Without mounds or other surface features, the cemeteries that were the communities of the dead in Cornwall were even more egalitarian. The bodies were placed in a crouched position with their heads to the north, perhaps signifying night time and eternal rest, as the sun is in the south of the sky. The cemeteries overlook agricultural land on the slopes of hills.

Pax Romana and changing settlement

The Romans saw their role as civilisers and bringers of peace. Their objective was not to annihilate or to enslave the populations of their provinces, but to turn them into model citizens who would help the Empire grow and flourish. On occasion they could certainly be cruel and barbarous, but where they ruled they attempted to maintain an orderly society. In Cornwall hillforts and castles were abandoned over the course of Roman rule, and rounds, rectilinear enclosures and courtyard houses were set among their fields in low-lying areas. Many of them were at a positive military disadvantage – this was the case with Chysauster's courtyard village, the settlement below Castle-an-Dinas in West Penwith, and the round below Tregonning Hill.[55] If Roman authority put an end to cattle-raiding and blood feuds the ensuing peace would allow economics to dictate how settlement patterns would subsequently change.

Law and order may be intangible but they leave tangible traces: stone weights, the fort at Nanstallon, the possible *mansio* at Magor all point to the smack of firm Roman government. These and the eventual abandonment of fortified sites (possibly linked to the abandonment of Nanstallon at the same time) are good grounds for arguing that, at the end of the 1st century, a civil society existed that could prosper in peace. The hillforts and cliff castles may have been abandoned for more reasons than no longer having a military use. Changes in religion – mentioned above and in the last chapter – could be part of the reason. Elsewhere in Britain it was Roman policy to bring religion into the new Roman towns and settlements, in a formal Romanised setting – giving due honour to each tutelary spirit. To some gods a temple would be built; the patron deity of the town would watch over the basilica and guide the civil power; baths would be dedicated to water nymphs and amphitheatres to the gods of war. The idea was to associate a native cult with a Roman, so that native populations would continue to worship their gods but in a Roman way. For instance, Sulis, goddess of the hot springs at Bath, was associated with Minerva, the Roman goddess of wisdom. Having no towns or major public settings, the people of Cornwall could only abandon worship at fortified sites and intensify worship within their low-lying settlements. Given the impact of Roman culture in other ways, we should expect signs of Roman religious observance too. *Fogous* and specially paved areas may be two of them. Paving around entrances had been a long-term trend with religious associations (see Chapters Three and Four) though it no doubt served a practical purpose too; but now it gathers pace and literally covers more ground – in courtyard house settlements, and in the Trethurgy houses.

Settlements are where they are, not only because that is where the farming was good, but sometimes also – continuing a trend from the LIA – for reasons of trade. Quantities of imported Roman pottery have been found at Carvossa, overlooking the Fal valley, which was ideally placed for access to a great tidal river and streams rich in tin. The Fal Historic Audit maps all the local settlements and shows how much they depend for their siting on the river Fal. Jacqui Wood has suggested that courtyard settlements in West Penwith may have had a role in the tin trade because stones and boulders from the beach are found in them.[56] Passing traders needing provisions and safe haven were probably the major factors in the economy of many settlements, especially in West Cornwall. The settlement on the islet of Nornour[57] (then part of one large island joining up most of the modern Isles of Scilly) contained a rich variety of brooches, rings, bracelets, coins and beads, vessels which may have been votive offerings, as well as figurines of a fertility goddess. She may have been Venus,[58] or a local deity identified with Venus, a sea-goddess in one of her guises. Three prominent rocky eminences behind the site are reminiscent of the LIA cliff castles of the Rumps and Treryn Dinas, and may have influenced the settlement's siting.

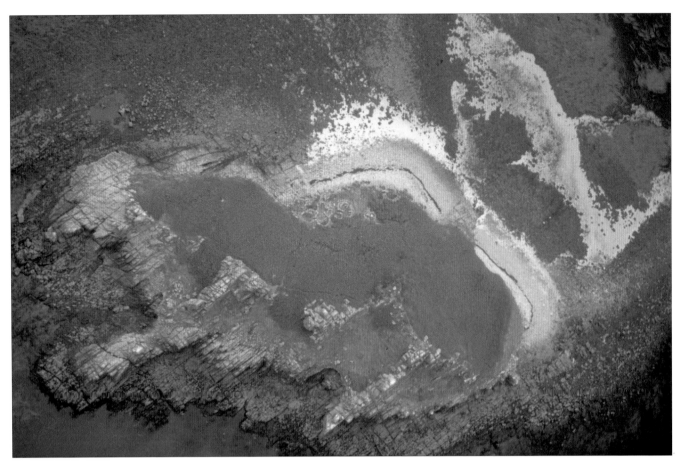

Spectacular rock formations attracted religious and ritual activity during the Late Iron Age and Roman period. The settlement of Nornour (which has subsequently become a separate island) contained what may have been a seafarers' shrine. The site is sheltered behind the rocks. To the right here, where the water gets deeper, would have been a deep harbour, perhaps the main port of Roman Scilly.

The rock formation and a hill behind the site also provided shelter against the winds and sea spray for the stone-walled huts of the settlement. Further west stretched a low windswept plain beyond the hills of what are now known as the Eastern Isles.

There may be still more to Nornour. The Latin name of Land's End, *Antivasteum Promontorium*, hints at its being opposite (*anti-*) a shrine or beacon on an opposite shore – presumably Scilly.[59] There are other such pairs of beacons, such as those at Dover and Boulogne. The eastern summit of St Martin's, then attached to Nornour as part of the larger island of Ennor, overlooked a deep harbour to the north of the Nornour settlement. (Ennor was substantial, comparable in area to West Penwith – itself almost an island at the time.) The barrow by the statue menhir on Chapel Down would have made a convenient base for a beacon, and such a beacon could have been one of a pair, its companion perhaps on the prominence of Great Ganilly or on high ground on St Mary's. Beacons such as the pair at Dover and Boulogne were part of the infrastructure of Roman navigation, and a corresponding pair on West Penwith and the Isles of Scilly is a fair conjecture. They stood, as in previous periods, at a crucial junction of seaways from the Channel westward to Ireland and north to the Irish sea. It is not surprising that stone *mortaria* from western Cornwall made from local stone have been found as far away as at Richborough in Kent.

Away from West Cornwall and Scilly were lesser stations engaged in general passing trade. From Duckpool, near Morwenstow in North Cornwall, come finds suggesting a limited business in imports, like South Devon Ware and reworked copper,[60] whilst Kilhallon, near Tywardreath, produced a selection of grey wares and black burnished ware from Dorset.[61]

The Late Empire: mining and the Pagan Revival

In the 3rd century many provincial armies rebelled to install their generals as Emperor. In the late 3rd century some regions had had enough of this turmoil and set up their own breakaway empires. Britain was part of two of them – the first was a Gallo-Roman Empire, the second a British Empire. All this fracturing caused trade to be interrupted and shortages of things like tin in the smaller empires – so Cornwall and Dartmoor became important in possessing this scarce resource. Stability and a semblance of unity were restored by two strong Emperors in succession, Diocletian and Constantine the Great; the legacy of their reforms, at the end of the 3rd century and the beginning of the 4th, divided the Empire in two under two partner Emperors. Provincial armies were also divided into static frontier forces and a mobile field army, and so were civilian and military authority – to prevent conspiracies to seize power. The new military structure meant diverting resources from large towns to a host of fixed fortifications by such means as the *annona* or grain tax. The new-found unity of the Empire was reinforced by a unitary religion, Christianity. Not universally popular, it provoked a reaction – especially in country areas scarcely touched by the new tradition. Cornwall and Dumnonia in general were ripe for what historians have labelled the Pagan Revival – revival in the sense of a reawakened zeal for beliefs that had never died.

Official interest in tin mining may be found in the possible *mansio* at Magor, together with a number of 'milestones' of the 3rd and 4th centuries such as those at St Martin-in-Meneague and Breage. 'Milestones' did not indicate distances, but were set up by detachments of troops dedicating a finished road to the reigning Emperor or Emperors. Romans placed commemorative plaques by a range of engineering projects much as people do today. The political difficulties in obtaining tin from northern Spain and the Mediterranean, and the apparent rise in the demand for tableware made of pewter – a lead and tin alloy, combined with debasement of the coinage, probably with lead and tin – meant that Cornish tin would have been in greater demand. Pewter vessels have been found in Cornwall,[62] such as the one from Hallivick near Grampound, while the stone bowls from Trethurgy imitate pewter bowls with handles. A tin ingot from Carnanton near St Columb Major was originally thought to bear official Roman stamps on it,[63] but still, together with another Roman plano-convex ingot from St Mawgan-in-Pydar, it is proof of the local tin trade.

The salt works at Carngoon Bank and Trebarveth were at their busiest during the 3rd and 4th centuries; they used natural evaporation and applied heat to separate

The Roman authorities' interest in mining Cornish tin is indicated by the creation and repair of roads. These activities were recorded as milestones with dedications to the reigning emperor. This example from Breage (now in the church) honoured the emperor Marcus Cassianus Latinius Postumus (AD 258–68).

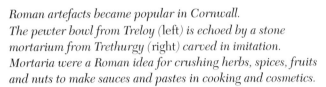

Roman artefacts became popular in Cornwall.
The pewter bowl from Treloy (left) is echoed by a stone
mortarium from Trethurgy (right) carved in imitation.
Mortaria were a Roman idea for crushing herbs, spices, fruits
and nuts to make sauces and pastes in cooking and cosmetics.

salt from seawater. The remains of workshops with shallow depressions, hearths and sherds from ceramic heating pans indicate the former presence of this industry. Like the corn-driers at Halangy Down,[64] they may have helped to provision the troops involved in securing supplies of tin and protecting seaborne supplies, as salt preserves meat and dairy products. A system of military watchtowers on the north coast of Somerset monitoring the Bristol Channel – like the well-preserved site at Martinhoe[65] – may have extended into Cornwall. At St Agnes, for example, a small, square embanked structure recorded in 1733 by the antiquarian Thomas Tonkin may be the remains of a protective enclosure round such a watchtower.[66] During the 4th and 5th centuries raiders from Ireland troubled western Britain, and an early warning system was therefore essential to the safe flow of trade.

The unity of the province was to be strengthened by its adopting Christianity – like the rest of the Empire – but there were obstacles in the way. Christian communities existed in Britain before Constantine made Christianity the religion of the Empire, but they were in towns. In the south-west generally the evidence suggests religious division. A Late Roman cemetery outside Roman Dorchester at Poundbury shows that Christianity thrived there. Evidence from mosaics in the villas at Frampton and Hinton St Mary suggests that the Dorset version of Christianity was probably Gnostic,[67] and so anathema to the official church; meanwhile other people were even setting up a pagan temple in Maiden Castle,[68] the nearby hillfort. If Exeter, Dorchester and their surrounding villa estates had become – as urban areas – largely Christian, there was an equal and opposite reaction in Dumnonia's rural west. There seems to have been an increase in the depositing of hoards alongside rivers like the Camel – evidence of a renewed interest in the earlier ritual practices.[69] Several sep-

*So-called 'hoards' of Roman
coins found in Cornwall may
simply be a continuation of
Iron Age ritual deposits of
metalware, particularly when
they are found near rivers or
strange rock formations.*

arate coins and a hoard found within the Bolster Bank[70] at St Agnes all date to the
Late Roman – as do most of the coins in the votive deposit at Nornour. The ovalhouses at Treryn Dinas,[71] too, may bear witness to the Pagan Revival.

The influence of the Romans was great, despite the lack of stereotypical features
such as villas, aqueducts and forts. Architecture and artefactual evidence reveal
major changes that go deeper than material culture into the realm of economic and
social life. These changes went beyond slavish copying, because they were also the
fruit of a vibrant regional culture. It is important to recognise that Cornwall was for
the first time part of a state, and was unified as part of the *civitas* of a new and large
tribal unit, the Dumnonii, which became the basis of the Early Medieval Kingdom
of Dumnonia.

CHAPTER SIX

THE AGE OF SAINTS IN A FRONTIER LAND

Early Medieval Period (AD 400–AD 1000)

WHILE THE OUTSIDE WORLD was in total turmoil, Early Medieval Cornwall went through gradual change. Still connected economically and culturally with the Mediterranean, Cornwall was untouched by much of eastern Britain and northern Europe. The gulf between Germanic and British societies had far-reaching consequences for Cornwall's future affinities overseas. Alienated from its neighbours to the east, Cornwall bonded with Brittany by migration, and with Celtic speakers in the British Isles – for instance, in Wales and Ireland. Christianity survived and the process of conversion was completed. Monasteries were places not only of prayer but of work; they were culturally important, centres of administration. The Anglo-Saxon conquest at the end of the period brought Cornwall back into political but not cultural union with its neighbours. It had become, and remained, different.

Late Antiquity: Christianity, Paganism and Islam

Until recently Late Antiquity (AD 300–700) was considered to be a period when the classical traditions of Greece and Rome went into decline and were overthrown by a degenerate barbarism, with only a few Christian priests to nurture the now dim light of civilisation. In fact it was a time of major economic and political renewal. This had begun under Roman rule, and it was rooted in a Neo-Platonic and Christian preoccupation with the nature of the Soul and what happened to the Soul after death.[1] Cities were despised as worldly and materialistic, and the return to the country was compared to Jesus going into the desert. The Desert Fathers of the Near East, ascetics like St Anthony of Egypt and St Pachomius, withdrew into the desert in imitation of Christ, and set up the first monasteries.[2] The monastic movement then spread across the Mediterranean, north to western Britain and eventually much further – its leading lights in Britain being St Patrick of Ireland, St Columba of Iona, and St Piran of Cornwall.[3] These missionaries – for Christ and against the city – made an impact on country areas like Cornwall beyond anything the Romans could achieve.

A result of abandoning urban life, particularly in the northern part of the Empire, was that resources could be diverted to security at a time when Germanic tribes

went marauding across the frontiers. To that end the late Roman Emperors had created a system by which the smaller territories were guarded by fewer troops deployed efficiently from strongholds.[4] The system was paid for in kind, thus trimming a once complex and costly bureaucracy. The local populace could be requisitioned for food, and the soldiers given land *in lieu* of pay. Small kingdoms in the Early Medieval continued to subsist round similar groupings of strongholds. Dumnonia, for instance, had one stronghold at Tintagel and three others in north Somerset at Cadbury Congresbury, Glastonbury Tor and South Cadbury.[5] As well as providing security, these strongholds were bastions of culture and religion. British elites were often champions of Christianity – against Anglo-Saxons, who were first pagans and later (in their eyes) Christian heretics.

The partition of Britain into separate British and Anglo-Saxons domains was stable as long as there was still some vestige of the Roman Empire across the Mediterranean. Its centre of gravity had shifted to the wealthier and more secure Greek-speaking city of Byzantium (or Constantinople), but its control of North Africa and parts of Spain meant that sea routes stayed open beyond Gibraltar; Cornwall and western Britain could therefore still feel part of the Classical world. Islam changed all that. A new Arab Empire swept all before it, and by the early 8th century Spain and North Africa were under its control. The old trade links were broken, and with them the cultural and religious links, so that increasingly Britain's outside contacts were with the neighbouring Anglo-Saxons, and later with the Vikings. The latter had set up new trade routes to Byzantium and beyond, tried to dominate trade in the British Isles and made their influence (if not their actual presence) felt in Cornwall. Against the threat of Viking incursion, King Alfred of Wessex (AD 871–899) strengthened the system of fortified towns or 'burhs' in Wessex.[6] These were set on raised rectangles of land surrounded by earth ramparts with some timber reinforcement, and inside they were divided into strips, with plots for houses and their land. The three westernmost burhs were at Pilton (near Barnstaple), Lydford (on Dartmoor)[7] and Halwell (near Totnes), and perhaps they formed an anti-Danish frontier, as the Anglo-Saxon Chronicle records that the Cornish had allied themselves with a Danish army in AD 835.

Elite sites, Romanitas and Mediterranean trade

In the Early Medieval period the Kingdom of Dumnonia emerged as the main counterweight to the Kingdom of Wessex, and was probably larger than the Roman *civitas Dumnoniorum*. Three major strongholds probably guarded the frontier along the northern border of Somerset – Cadbury Congresbury, Glastonbury Tor and South Cadbury – whilst Tintagel, deep in Dumnonia, was the wealthiest stronghold. The first two were old Iron Age fortifications, strengthened and renewed. Glastonbury,

114

which has yielded Romano-British pottery, glassware and coins, had possibly been used for pagan ritual during the Roman period – perhaps Tintagel, too, given its similarity to other Cornish sites on spectacular rocky headlands.[8] There were many minor strongholds scattered across Dumnonia, and in Cornwall they included modified Iron Age hilltops like Chun Castle (West Penwith) and Lestowder (the Lizard), as well as rounds like Trethurgy (near St Austell) and rectilinear enclosures like Grambla (near Helston). Chun Castle was a reoccupied Iron Age hillfort, which had dwellings with walls radiating inwards from its perimeter wall like the spokes of a wheel. It dominates the landscape, in contrast to the earlier Romano-British settlement of Bosullow Trehyllys in the saddle below Chun Castle. As for the old capital of the Dumnonii, Exeter, it had already dwindled in the Late Roman period and by now was a mere settlement with a cemetery.[9]

West Cornwall and Scilly were the most Romanised parts of Cornwall during the Roman period. Their pivotal position on the main trade routes was reinforced in the Early Medieval period. As everything from the Mediterranean to the western side of the British Isles had to pass by, they became the main points of contact with Mediterranean culture. Ships of the time needed sight of land to navigate, so they would have to pass west Cornwall even on the way to Ireland. Mediterranean imports have been found in greater concentration in Scilly and Cornwall than anywhere else in Britain. In mainland Cornwall the largest find is at Tintagel, the others being in Penwith and Kerrier. Scilly was an entrepôt for Mediterranean cargoes,[10] where they would be broken down and taken on in smaller vessels throughout the Irish Sea – especially the Kingdom of Dumnonia. Mediterranean goods can be traced as far north as the stronghold of Dumbarton on the Clyde, as far west as Cork and the west coast of Ireland and in various places on the south coast of Wales.[11]

These Mediterranean imports included amphorae of olive oil from North Africa and wine[12] from the Aegean and the Levant; luxury tableware from North Africa and the Aegean; glassware and mortaria from southern Spain; and some coarse ware from the Bordeaux area, which may have been containers of something unknown. Later arrivals were E-ware pots from the west coast of Gaul (then part of the Kingdom of the Franks[13]) containing a deep red dye from Dyer's madder (*Rubia tinctorum*) plants, as analyses of residues in the pots has demonstrated;[14] it was the closest thing to the dye from eastern Mediterranean seashells that produces 'imperial purple'. Purple was famously the highest badge of rank in the Roman and Byzantine world, and is still worn by European royalty, including Queen Elizabeth II, on state occasions. All this paints a picture of an elite preserving at least a show of *Romanitas* for public ceremonies and feasts. Dressed in sumptuous robes, eating food prepared in the Roman manner (with sauces, pastes and olive oil), and served in the Roman manner (in individual ceramic and glass vessels), and drinking wine poured from glass flagons, the Dumnonian kings, chiefs and their retinue enjoyed all the trappings of authority. They could show that Dumnonia was still a stable and authentically Roman state, nurturing Roman values and civilisation.

In Cornwall nothing matches the status of Tintagel.[15] Its size of 400 x 400 m (1312 x 1312 ft), the number of its dwellings and the wealth of its imports classify it as one of the most important sites in the whole south-west and beyond. The original rectangular buildings, made of timber, were replaced with rectangular houses with drystone walls. There were at least 120 houses, possibly more. Many were built on artificial terraces on the eastern, leeward side of the peninsula. (Today, erosion and slate quarrying have turned it into an island.) As well as inscriptions in a religious context there were secular inscriptions in Tintagel, so we know that people were at least to some degree literate. The Cornish archaeologist Charles Thomas has translated one of them – 'Artogonou, father of ... a descendant of Coll, has had this made/built/constructed' – and it has led to some popular speculation that it might have been to do with King Arthur, particularly as the medieval chronicler Geoffrey of Monmouth had claimed Tintagel as Arthur's birthplace. The name, however, is not Arthur and the element 'Arto' (meaning bear) is common in Celtic languages.[16] Even without Arthur, Tintagel was clearly a major stronghold of the Dumnonian kings. Tintagel and its counterparts in north Somerset might have provided seasonal headquarters for the Dumnonian kings and their retinue. Early Medieval rulers in Britain had to move seasonally from one stronghold to another, because no single place could afford their upkeep all year round. Since the Kingdom did not issue coins or have a monetary system, each place would provide resources such as food, raw materials and services. Even the powerful Frankish Kings, ruling the whole of modern-day France, part of Germany and the Low Countries, had to be peripatetic.

To pay for these rich imports from the Mediterranean, the Dumnonian elite had to organise the balancing exports. These included tin from Cornwall and Dartmoor, lead from the Mendips and items such as woollen clothes and hunting dogs. A supplement to the 7th-century account of an Egyptian saint, St John the Almsgiver,[17] mentions a voyage to Britain by a merchant of Alexandria whose cargo of corn averted a famine, and he received tin in return. As some imports to Dumnonia found their way to other strongholds in the western British Isles, what came back to pay for them? Perhaps their distribution had nothing to do with trade at all. Ewan Campbell has shown that, just as in Cornwall finds of luxury goods dwindle as the distance from Tintagel increases, so it is in Dumnonia as a whole: the further from the great strongholds, the fewer the finds. The same applies even outside Dumnonia, where some of these items went to major strongholds, from which a few trickled out into the hinterlands. The inference is that imported luxuries were commanded by the Dumnonian elites, who then rewarded faithful subjects with the occasional gift.

Commodities like tin, lead and wool were no doubt taken as tax: there was no need to buy them. Perhaps the materials found in other kingdoms were sent to cement treaties, or to be tokens of friendship or marriage gifts. Gifts in return could have taken the form of military help, or hunting dogs, or woollen garments.

The lesser elites held smaller strongholds in Cornwall like Chun Castle and Trethurgy. Chun Castle (West Penwith) was reoccupied in this period, having been abandoned at the end of the Iron Age for the courtyard house settlement of Bosullow Trehyllys. The new occupation involved 14 or 15 dwellings with their walls arranged like the spokes of a wheel backing onto the circular enclosure wall. Local pottery dominates the finds, and the discovery of a lump of tin slag weighing over 5 kg (11 lb) and a smelting furnace is evidence of tin production. This occupation may also have had a hand in collecting tin locally for shipment to more important strongholds. Further up the valley below Chun Castle is a contemporary memorial stone to Rialobranus, son of Cunovalus. The element 'Rialo' means 'kingly', which again hints that here was a minor centre of power. Trethurgy (near St Austell) continued to be occupied from the Roman period, and a tin ingot was also found there. Radio-carbon dating shows that a shovel at Boscarne (near Bodmin) and peats associated with tin ingots at Praa Sands also belong to this time, and reveal the wider network of sites delivering tin to these centres. Tin was extracted from deposits in streams. The deposits would have been dug out and washed, to separate the heavier tin from the light sand and clay that would flow away, suspended in the water. There is no evidence of deep mines with shafts from this time.

Early Christian Cornwall: monasteries and the countryside

As in other parts of the western British Isles, the Early Medieval period is also known as the Early Christian period by historians and archaeologists. The Late Roman state's efforts to convert its citizens to Christianity had been largely confined to towns, and whereas towns in the Mediterranean continued to thrive, they had given way in northern Europe to rural settlement based on villa estates in the former urban areas. Cornwall had anyhow been entirely rural in the Roman period, and reaffirmed its paganism (if it had ever been under threat) at the time of the Pagan Revival. So not only was there no Christianity, but there was also no administrative mechanism to introduce it. The answer came – via the trade networks – out of Egyptian monasticism: small communities of monks with very basic resources but first-rate minds could transform the remotest areas. Indeed the Life of St John the

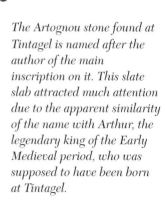

The Artognou stone found at Tintagel is named after the author of the main inscription on it. This slate slab attracted much attention due to the apparent similarity of the name with Arthur, the legendary king of the Early Medieval period, who was supposed to have been born at Tintagel.

117

*Inscribed stones were
memorials to elite people
during the Early Medieval
period. They were not all
Christian monuments, though
the two presented here were.*

Almsgiver shows that anything might be possible. The saint (who was Patriarch of Alexandria) directed some sea captain to sail to Britain, giving him both a ship and the gold to buy a cargo. As a divine reward for his endeavours and for mending his previously dissolute ways, his return cargo of tin miraculously turned into silver.

Overt symbols of Christianity appear in Dumnonia from the 5th century onwards.[18] At Tintagel, for instance, the base of a fine red-slip dish from the Aegean bore stamp decoration in the form of crosses, though their appeal might have been more aesthetic than spiritual. Not all memorial inscriptions in Latin include Christian symbols, but there are enough to suggest that Christianity was gaining ground. At Stourton, in south Devon, a cross-shaped stone bears a memorial dedication to 'Prince [or chief] Iuriucus, son of Audetus'.[19] In St Just church a memorial stone reads 'Selus lies here', a typically Christian formula, and there is a Chi-Rho symbol on another face (that being a monogram of X (Chi) and P (Rho), the first two letters of Christos, the Greek for Christ). The symbol has its origins in Christian communities in Egypt, and was an adaptation of an ancient hieroglyph which it closely resembles: this was the 'Ankh', representing the life-giving power of the Egyptian gods. Judging by its style, the earliest Christian symbol in Cornwall is the Chi-Rho on a stone in Phillack church.[20] Another version of a cross appears on the so-called Tristan stone found near an Iron Age hillfort at Castle Dore, near Fowey. On one side it bears the inscription 'Drustanus lies here, son of Cunomorus'; on the back of the cross is a Tau, or Greek T cross. Inscribed stones at Lewannick, Slaughter Bridge (near Camelford), and St Kew also bear inscriptions in Ogham (an Irish script based on straight lines engraved at the edges of stones) alongside Roman letters.[21]

As for monastic settlements, contrary to the impression given by the Cornish saints' lives in the archives of the Diocese of Exeter (which used to include Cornwall), the saints did not typically live like hermits in remote places but settled at the very heart of the most populous farming land. Nor is it any longer possible to accept the picture implicit in Canon Doble's *Lives of the Saints* that a tide of holy invaders, mostly from Ireland, washed up on Cornwall's shores. Who, then, were the saints, and what did they do?

Some were indeed incomers. Many of the saints settling along the north coasts of Cornwall and Brittany had come from Wales. Theirs was an organised missionary movement to spread a form of regional monasticism that had earlier struck root in Wales. The few examples of Ogham (five cases in three locations), together with some place-name evidence and instances of saints with Irish names, could mean that this monastic movement came with a migration of Welsh settlers of Irish descent.[22] Certainly south-west Wales was strongly influenced by Ireland – in fact St David, patron saint of Wales, was himself Irish. Even so the migration theory must not be pushed too far.

It is striking that the 'lanns', settlements of the monastic communities, are made exactly like the local rounds and rectilinear enclosures – indeed some are the old enclosures put to new use. Away from the north coast some saints' names are Welsh, some Breton, but most are plain Cornish. The material culture of these settlements is equally local and needs no mass migration of Irish people to explain it. It also used to be claimed that Northern Irish Souterrain Ware was the inspiration for Cornish grass-marked wares, but we now know that the Cornish wares ante-date the Irish. Finally, there is nothing especially Welsh or Irish about using earlier native enclo-

The Doniert stone, near St Cleer, consists of a plaited cord decoration with an inscription 'Doniert Rogavit Pro Anima'. This translates as 'Doniert requested this for his soul'. A suggestion that Doniert might be the same as Dungarth, the last recorded King of Dumnonia, is still a strong possibility.

sures or native traditions of enclosure and fortification: that is how they did it in the Eastern Mediterranean. Even so there is an interesting difference between the north-coast lanns with Welsh dedications and the others. The Welsh are larger and sub-rectangular (the strange name for rectangles with curved corners). This difference may support the idea that these monasteries are in some way special. The likeliest explanation, therefore, is that the connection with Wales was at royal level, and that Dumnonian kings granted prominent Welsh clerics the right to set up monasteries in Cornwall as part of their system of alliances.

Most of the lann sites are now parish churches with cemeteries round them, so little remains of their internal arrangements. Some of the best surviving evidence comes from the Isles of Scilly where, on the island of St Helen's, a lann site still retains its oratory or small church, a graveyard and living quarters in the shape of a single round cell. A stone-lined cavity within the altar of the oratory was probably made to hold holy relics. Excavations on the nearby island of Tean hint at the presence of a timber building that was a forerunner to the drystone oratory; some neighbouring graves lie under the stone oratory, but the overall plan of the graves leaves

St Piran's Oratory seen during a visit to the 1910 excavations by Thurstan Peter (above). The site generated enormous interest locally and among Cornish people elsewhere, and still does because of the association with Cornwall's *patron saint. The Oratory dates to the 10th century, probably succeeding an earlier wooden church. The nearby cross (left), though possibly associated with the Oratory, cannot be dated with confidence to the Early Medieval period.*

a rectangular space slightly to the west of it. An important mainland site is St Piran's Oratory at Perranzabuloe. Sadly it can no longer be seen because it lies under a protective concrete dome, but its enclosure earthwork is still faintly visible. The rectangular oratory or chapel was built of drystone walling, and would have had a timber roof, probably thatched. Its simplicity was typical of monastic oratories of the time. Monks were ultimately inspired by Jesus's example of resisting temptation in the desert. The main significance of this oratory lies in the later cult of St Piran himself, who became Cornwall's patron saint.

The Christianity of the native Britons and Irish had come largely from the Byzantine Empire, with its strong Greek and Egyptian influences. However, having been

part of the old western Empire ruled from Rome, Latin remained the language of learning and religious instruction. Yet their version of Latin was now old-fashioned and out of touch with the latest western thinking, including that of Rome.[23] So when Pope Gregory the Great sent St Augustine to convert the Anglo-Saxons at the end of the 6th century, he came with a Christianity rather different in form to that of western and northern Britain, and of Cornwall. The British Church was basically monastic, led by abbots rather than bishops. The dates for Easter were differently calculated, so the entire liturgical calendars were different. British rites were more Eastern or Greek than Roman, and some British ideas had no parallel even in the Eastern Church; the bells carried by priests, for example, were treated like crosses as

Early Medieval oratories of the native British church were rectangular in shape, with a ridgepole and pitched roof, as the east wall here at St Piran's demonstrates. The deep sand dunes preserved the structure well, including the walls, whereas elsewhere similar oratories have been replaced by later churches or remain with little more than foundations.

121

holy, as the evidence of bell-shrines and literary sources demonstrate.[24] In all this there was no question of theological schism – either between the British and Latin churches or the Latin and Greek; that was to come in the 11th century. The only differences were of ritual, administration and precedence. Precedence was about authority – whether churches might be independent or not, and if not and one church was beholden to another, what its obedience entailed. Those questions were settled in principle at the synod of Whitby in AD 664, when a joint decision by the British and Augustine missions agreed that the rules and traditions of the Latin Church would prevail. The reality on the ground was less tidy. The physical structure of the lann sites continued (though new ones were not constructed), sometimes beyond even the Norman conquest.

Lanns were important not just as centres of local elites but for the general management of the countryside. Some had an outer enclosure or enclosures, and at St Mawgan-in-Meneague an inscribed stone of possibly the 7th century sits on the outer boundary, with the church and its enclosure to the north-east near another edge of the same boundary. Similarly at Padstow (this example is actually mentioned in the life of St Petrock), the multiple outer enclosures can be picked out from the pattern of hedgerows into which they were later absorbed. The enclosures proclaimed status, though they also enclosed farmland for the monks.

Beyond the lanns and their privileged enclosures lay the ordinary settlements that had continued from the Roman period with only slow and gradual change. Houses at Gwithian, for example, were of the sub-square or sub-rectangular plan that replaced the ovalhouses of the Roman period, and were perhaps influenced by the design of oratories, or even of Anglo-Saxons buildings. Place-names have provided further confirmation of this pattern.[25] Where later building has erased surface evidence of Early Medieval occupation, place-names of this period in the east of Cornwall show a broadly similar pattern to Iron Age and Roman period settlements.[26] Settlements in both periods take the same richer ground and leave the poorer, presumably for summer pasture. However, Anglo-Saxon place-names in the south-east of Cornwall appear where there had been little previous settlement, and so they may represent fresh colonisation – round Hingston Down and the Greena/Ogbeare Moors, for example. Only in the far north of Cornwall round Bude, Kilkhampton and Stratton are Anglo-Saxon names a significant proportion of the total. This must mean a very early arrival either of the English language or even of the people who spoke it.

The Late Saxon invasion and the creation of a frontier zone

From the end of the 7th century to the beginning of the 9th, Wessex expanded rapidly – conquering Somerset, Devon and finally Cornwall. Somerset and Devon soon took to the language and culture; not so Cornwall. Why not is an enigma. By measuring human remains from cemeteries, Heinrich Härke[27] has concluded that the great majority of Wessex people in the Early Medieval period had the typical physique of the Romano-British. (His research suggested that those of Romano-British stock and the north German newcomers could be told apart by their height, even allowing for other factors such as diet and the environment.) Then, too, river names are highly durable, and Celtic names of rivers increase from east to west. There are other evidences of continuity such as the survival in Devon of church dedications to saints with Celtic names like St Budoc and St Petrock. Given the sheer speed of the conquest, all this continuity is hardly surprising.

An aim of the Saxon conquest was the removal of the Dumnonian elites, who had still been reinforcing their north Somerset strongholds in the late 5th and early 6th centuries. The last date when one of the terraces at Tintagel was occupied coincides with the fall of the north Somerset strongholds at the end of the 7th century.[28] That terrace had suffered from erosion, so the coincidence might have been just that: but the battles in Somerset might have stripped Tintagel of the resources and soldiers needed to sustain it as a base for a Dumnonian king. The *Annales Cambriae* (or Welsh Annals) record that Dungarth the King of Cernyw (Welsh for Cornwall) drowned in 875: thereafter there is no literary record of any Cornish king. King

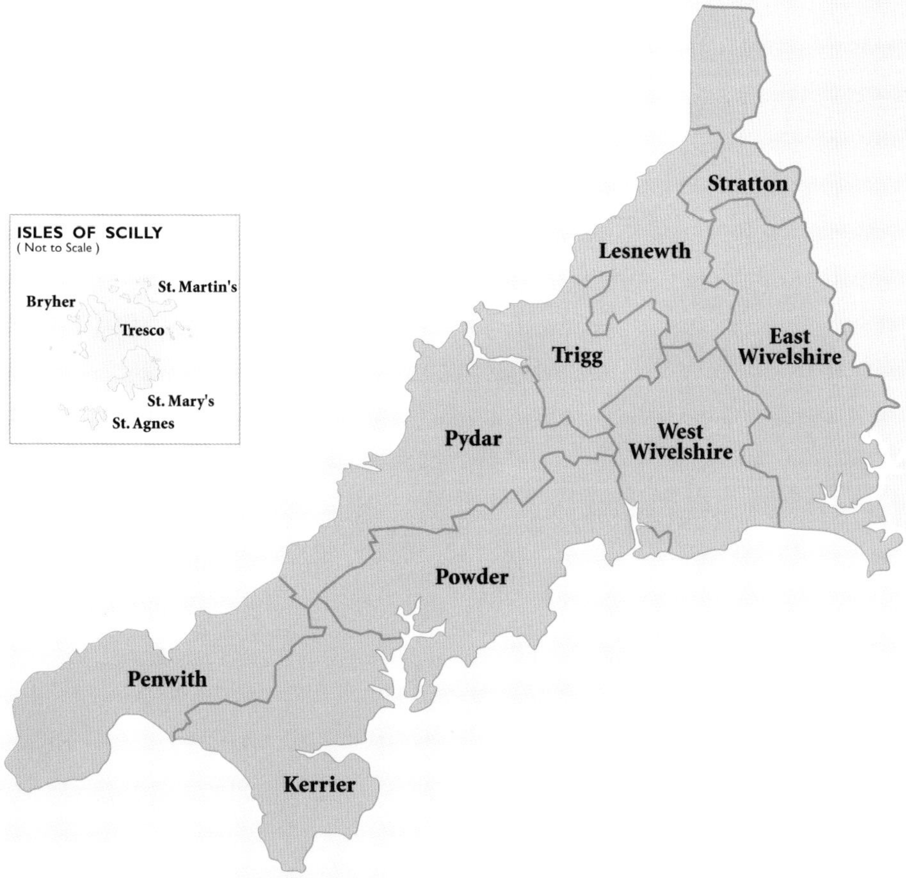

ISLES OF SCILLY
(Not to Scale)

Bryher
St. Martin's
Tresco
St. Mary's
St. Agnes

Stratton
Lesnewth
Trigg
East Wivelshire
Pydar
West Wivelshire
Powder
Penwith
Kerrier

The hundreds of Cornwall are unusually large compared with others in England. A hundred is a subdivision of a county supposed to supply a hundred men for military duty if so required. These Late Medieval hundreds make better comparison with Roman rural districts and could suggest that Roman administration survived to some degree in Cornwall during the period. The hundreds of Trigg, Lesnewth and Stratton were once one, as were West and East Wivelshire – making for an original simple, sixfold division of the peninsula.

123

Hywel, mentioned in the Anglo-Saxon Chronicle for the year 926 has usually been identified as king of Cornwall, but a likelier candidate is the powerful Hywel Dda, King of Gwynedd, as the reference brackets this figure with Constantine King of Scots.[29] The severely reduced Dumnonian state would hardly have merited such a record. William of Malmesbury, writing in the late 15th century, records an incident from a source no longer available. It involved King Aethelstan of Wessex (924–940) expelling the Britons from Exeter – which may represent a policy of wider ethnic cleansing. However, given Härke's evidence above that the ordinary populations remained largely unchanged, this is more likely to have been part of a power struggle to rid the town of its Dumnonian nobility.

Turning Exeter into one of several burhs,[30] demolishing the British secular leadership and wiping out the lann system would have made it easy to eradicate the culture of Dumnonia and absorb it into Wessex. After the Anglo-Saxon conquest a new burh was added in Cornwall, too, to supplement the three in Devon, Exeter, Barnstaple, Lydford and Totnes. Barnstaple and Totnes had replaced the earlier burhs at Pilton and Halwell respectively in the early 10th century. The new burh was set up forward from Lydford, just across the Tamar at St Stephens-by-Launceston. Today's street pattern still preserves in outline the burh's two entrances, central street and burghage or strip plots. The burh was situated immediately to the west of the lann enclosure of St Stephens,[31] and was the site of an Anglo-Saxon mint from 976. However, the siting of this burh was still cautious, and gives the impression that Cornwall was regarded as frontier land.

Although the plan was probably to bring Cornwall culturally in line with the rest of Wessex, it could be that the area served as a convenient sink into which the dispossessed or disaffected British elites could be exiled – to make it easier to consolidate the rest of Dumnonia. As we have already seen, the lann system survived in Cornwall, albeit in an eroded condition, and only the immediate borderlands showed the linguistic creep of Anglo-Saxon. Indeed the county subdivisions in Cornwall – the hundreds – differ in area from the typical English hundred, and match the area of the *pagi* which subdivided a Roman *civitas*.[32] Some of the Cornish hundreds had names that sound like typical *pagi* names – like Pydar, which comes from 'Petuarius'. It must not be forgotten, though, that this process of assimilation lasted less than two hundred years. The Norman conquest halted it, and Norman rule changed what the Anglo-Saxons probably intended to be the course of history by deliberate and active support of Cornish culture – in other words, 'Divide and Rule'!.

The Anglo-Saxon conquest meant changes in church organisation. Some monastic sites became Benedictine monasteries, but most gradually became parish churches under the Latin parochial system. Two groups of rectilinear sites represent this new type of true churchyard,[33] and a rectilinear church surrounded by its rectilinear plot becomes the pattern, rather than the old enclosure. The first group, in East Cornwall, includes Stratton, Whitstone and Callington; the second, in West Cornwall, includes Ludgvan, Sennen and St Enoder. The former sites were in areas with many Anglo-Saxon place-names, were often associated with Anglo-Saxon religious houses, and were usually dedicated to universal saints without Celtic names. The latter all had Celtic patron saints (Ludgvan, Sennen and Enoder) but had 'eglos' rather than 'lann' place-names – signifying churches, not monastic enclosures – and by 1066 many of them were owned by St Petroc's church in Bodmin. An exception to the move to rectilinear churchyards is St Buryan, where Aethelstan provided the churchyard with an outer enclosure or sanctuary like those already in Padstow and St Mawgan.[34] St Buryan's location in a tin-producing area might have increased its wealth. The contemporary Trewhiddle hoard, hidden in tin streaming deposits near St Austell, shows that alluvial tin was still being won.[35]

In religious sculpture, elaborately carved stone memorials like the Doniert Stone near St Cleer (commemorating the last recorded king, Dungarth) gave way to elaborately carved crosses. After about AD 900 a new tradition of wayside crosses was developed; many are now found in the churchyards to which they were later moved. Wayside crosses continued to be put up in the Late Medieval period (AD 1000–1500), though they became plainer. The Penzance Market Cross, dating to the late 10th/early 11th century, has an inscription that has been translated as:[36] 'They lie here in the open. Whosoever in peace comes here, let him pray [for their souls]' – a formula similar to those then used in Ireland and Wales. Because the Latin is of Old

Place-names in Brittany are as yet the best evidence for the migration of Celtic-speaking British people from Cornwall and Devon to Brittany. The map on the left shows the distribution of place-names with the element 'plou' (meaning 'parish'), which Breton shares with Cornish. The map on the right shows place-names with endings 'ay' and 'ac'. The 'ac' endings represent archaic spellings and the 'ay' endings an up-to-date spelling, suggesting that it was only in these areas that the French language continued to be used locally.

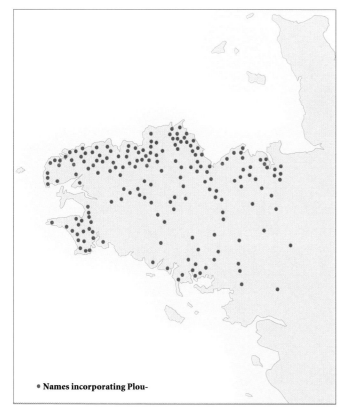

• **Names incorporating Plou-**

• **Names ending in -é or -ay**
• **Names ending in -ac**

English type, however, it could conceal a secret message, which decodes to reveal the author of the inscription as someone with the Anglo-Saxon name of 'Wiweht'.[37] Against that Elizabeth Okasha has pointed out that little of the text is clearly legible, so any such reading must be treated with caution.

Ordinary settlements began to change, too, and longhouses of Late Saxon type have been found at Mawgan Porth[38] and Treworld.[39] Mawgan Porth is particularly informative, making as it does a close-packed group of longhouses with drystone walls. Inside were living quarters at the upper end with stone slabs marking out beds (to be filled with straw or reeds no doubt), and a byre for livestock, complete with drainage gulley, at the other end. Thus the animals would keep warm in winter and themselves warm the humans at the other end of the house. Outhouses could have been used to store food and equipment. Just outside the settlement was a cemetery of long cist graves, but though houses had changed, the design of the cemetery was still deeply rooted in the Late Iron Age and Roman past. These were Christian burials however, like those in the monastic enclosure on Tean in the Isles of Scilly;[40] so the graves ran east to west, and there were no grave goods. Christian reverence for the soul meant that even newly born babies had a proper burial, in a section of the cemetery set apart for infants.

Locally produced pottery represented a continuous tradition from local copies of Roman wares. It is known as 'grass-marked' pottery because of the impressions of grass on and around the base of vessels. This is a fragment found at Tintagel.

Ethnicity in cultural continuity and change

Upon a fragmented tribal society the Romans had imposed statehood and a sense of common identity as citizens of the province of Britannia. The emergence of a native British/Anglo-Saxon divide made native Britons even more conscious of their Britishness: so much so that, when people migrated from southern Britain to Gaul in the Late Roman and Early Medieval period, they called themselves Britons. Here we consider two problems of identity: that of the migrants to Gaul, particularly to Armorica (later 'Brittany' or 'Little Britain'); and the creation of a political unit called 'Cornwall'.[41]

Britons were first recruited as mercenaries by the Roman authorities in Gaul (particularly for Armorica) in the 4th century, and given land *in lieu* of pay – the typical Late Roman arrangement.[42] The threat was then from Germanic invaders like the Franks, but in the 6th century the indomitable Franks themselves enlisted Britons – this time to throw out another Germanic group, the Visigoths. The western parts of Brittany came to speak Breton, the closest language to Cornish, and the eastern parts continued to speak what later became a dialect of French. The western part was also divided into Dumnonia and Kerne (Cornwall), reflecting south-western origins.

The late Breton archaeologist Pierre Giot argued that the settlements of these first Bretons were basically rounds,[43] like the ridge-pole house of Livroac'h in Poullan-sur-Mer, or the enclosure on the Ile de Guennoc, which began as an earthen bank, later replaced by drystone walling. Some migrants adapted what they found and turned megalithic tombs into homes; that happened on the Ile de Brunec around AD 700 and on the Ile de Guennoc around 800. At Plussulien an earlier *souterrain* – a cave like a *fogou* – was reused at about 450, though the date may indicate a continuing interest in pagan ritual. However, as Michael Batt of the Service Régional de l'Archéologie de Bretagne suggests, there are serious problems with these dates, which may more correctly be Late Medieval.[44] The distribution of Breton language place-names is securer evidence.[45] The weak material evidence for British settlement may be due to the assimilation of the incomers into the more metropolitan culture of Brittany.

There were marked differences between East and West Armorica in how they buried the dead, though much of the evidence is from the end of the Early Medieval period.[46] In the Gallo-Roman and Frankish East the dead were generally placed in sarcophagi carved from stone, including granite. The norm in the British-influenced west of Brittany was to bury straight into the ground, either in earth-cut graves or in long cists. For instance, at Saint-Urnel a cemetery of the latter type contained inhumations (including some 8th-century ones) without burial goods, and with many infant burials. On site was a rectangular oratory, originally timber, later rebuilt in stone. The altar of the later stone building directly overlays an inhumation, perhaps of someone special in the community. Memorials to the elites also followed British practice. A reused menhir at Louannec was inscribed 'Bodognous, son of Desiderus', and a stone at Lanrivoaré was dedicated to 'Gallmau' – both in a script typical of the western part of the British Isles.

However, the Britons did not enter an empty land in Armorica, so Breton culture was the child of two traditions – the British and the native Armorican. One aspect of it is striking: the dearth of pottery. Cornwall was the only part of the British Isles that never stopped making pottery from the Late Iron Age to the Late Medieval period. Everywhere else in the British Isles pottery was abandoned at some stage in this period in favour of wood, metal and basketry. Starting with imitations of Roman models, the Cornish sequence continued with the grass-marked wares developed from Roman period forms.[47] The marks came from chopped grass where the pottery had been left to dry on the ground before it was fired – the grass (or very occasionally an old piece of cloth) stopping the pots sticking to the ground. Between the 9th and 11th centuries there were pottery cauldrons (bar-lug pots) for suspending over a fire.[48] Round a bar on either side of these ceramic cauldrons were tied either a rope or thongs, which were shielded from the flames by a lug on the outside of the cauldrons. None of this pottery has ever been found in Brittany. Most of Brittany did without pottery altogether at some stage, and when used it was local or Frankish ware. However, Brittany and Cornwall certainly both imported E-Wares and – on the evidence of just one amphora sherd[49] – Brittany received at least some of the earlier Mediterranean imports.

The relationship between Brittany and Cornwall was firmly established in the Early Medieval period and was one that would continue both to reinforce and to challenge the identity of Cornwall thereafter. The regional similarities on both sides of the Channel are due to the cultural and kinship bonds that the migrations of this period produced. The journey between the two coasts crosses the Channel at its widest; so, for Cornwall, contact with its neighbours in Britain was infinitely easier than it was with its kith and kin in Brittany. The idea that Brittany was a major influence on Cornwall before the Late Roman and Early Medieval periods ignores not only the facts of geography but also the findings of archaeology, which clearly show that in those earlier periods Cornwall was much more closely linked to adjacent parts of Britain, above all to its immediate neighbours in the east. Only now, at the end of the Early Medieval period, does the opposite trend set in and Cornwall become Cornwall and not Dumnonia, with its close neighbours no longer native Britons, but Anglo-Saxons.

Clues as to how the name came into use can be found by comparing the literature with archaeological evidence. The earliest reference to 'Cornwall' is in *Carmen Rhythmicum* by Bishop Aldhelm of Sherborne,[50] in Wessex, written by about AD 705. In it he describes a journey: 'When I had set out for nasty "Domnonia" and was proceeding through Cornwall ("Cornubia") ...'. The date provides some clues to the nature of 'Cornubia'. Given that, by the end of the 7th century, even Exeter was part of Wessex, there can be little doubt that the Dumnonia referred to by Aldhelm in this book and in a letter written to King Geraint of Dumnonia cannot have consisted of more than parts of western Devon and Cornwall. Tintagel was the only major stronghold in Dumnonia, and if Tintagel was then Geraint's capital it would more likely have been in Dumnonia, otherwise Aldhelm would hardly have referred to him as its King.

The continuing Anglo-Saxon conquest during the 9th century would have raised a new question: if the lion's share of Dumnonia had been annexed, what would the remainder be called? The Anglo-Saxon word for Dumnonia – 'Defn', later 'Devon' – was used for the newly conquered territory. The Tamar was a convenient natural boundary, and it also allowed Devon to retain the important tin-rich area of Dartmoor. It may then have been necessary to extend the old Roman name of 'Cornubia' from West Cornwall – where Roman influences had been strongest, and the name had been coined to conjure up a picture of the western headlands ('the horns') – and make it cover the whole unabsorbed country up to the River Tamar. A strength of such an explanation is that it needs no special pleading for Cornwall as a previously separate region. After this period it is easy to show that Cornwall had a distinct and separate culture; before it, the theory has to stretch the facts and somehow to ignore both marked differences within Cornwall and marked similarities across the Tamar.

During the Early Medieval period, Cornwall was at first part of the Kingdom of Dumnonia, oriented to the Mediterranean culturally and spiritually. Monastic settlements represented the conversion of the local population to Christianity. This 'Romanised' culture also linked Cornwall to other parts of the western British Isles and Brittany, while separating it from the Anglo-Saxon east. During the latter part of the period this changed, and Anglo-Saxon cultural and political influences began. The Norman conquest tempered these influences, however, and Cornwall was not fully integrated into the Anglo-Saxon world.

CHAPTER SEVEN

LATE MEDIEVAL FLORUIT: THE EARLDOM, THE CHURCH AND THE STATE

Late Medieval Period (AD 1000–1500)

APART FROM THE BURH AT St Stephen-by-Launceston, the first towns in Cornwall appear in the Late Medieval, and with them the changes that town life brings – social, political and economic. The impetus for the process came especially from the Earls of Cornwall and the incoming religious orders – particularly the Augustinian (or Austin) canons, and friars. As the towns grew so the wilderness shrank as new populations colonised the moors. A feudal kingdom was not a nation state but personal property, granted by God to individuals, who might parcel it into fiefs held by ties of duty, and sometimes ties of blood. Such fiefs did not respect ethnic boundaries, though their tenants could use ethnic division to their own advantage. Myths and legends could furnish 'historical' justification for action taken, property and title claimed. Cornwall was a great prize in this respect, as Arthurian legend gave it a special cachet throughout western Europe.

The Earldom: castles, deer parks and King Arthur

The Anglo-Saxon kingdom had treated Cornwall as a frontier land.[1] When the Normans invaded and took it over, William the Conqueror gave it first as a fief to Alain Duke of Brittany, then to his own half-brother Robert, Count of Mortain.[2] Thereafter the new Earldom went to the reigning king's younger sons or cousins. Some frontier lands might encourage ambitious rivals to exploit their volatility and create new power bases, but not Cornwall; there was no trouble to stir up, and the only way to expand was into the sea. It was an outpost with glamour thanks to its Arthurian connections, and had enough mineral wealth to keep the cadet members of the royal family comfortable. What is more, the Earldom included other properties in the Kingdom – in and around London, in Berkshire, in Dorset and, from the 13th century, on Dartmoor.

That the Earldom of Cornwall went well beyond ethnic Cornwall mattered not to the medieval mind. A fief was personal property bestowed with divine blessing. The story in Genesis of how Jacob tricked his father Isaac into blessing him instead of his elder brother Esau was taken very seriously: no matter how fraudulently come by, the title was sacrosanct. All the more interesting, then, was the belief in Arthur. If Arthur had been King of Britain and Tintagel his capital, then any Earl of Cornwall had (as well as divine right) the inheritance of a most potent name. The Anglo-Norman poet Béroul[3] (Christian name unknown), perhaps in the Earl's pay and perhaps drawing from local legend, placed King Arthur in Cornwall, not Glastonbury or anywhere else. This goes beyond the more official version of Geoffrey of Monmouth, who says only that Arthur was born in Tintagel.

There is archaeological evidence for thinking that Béroul had drawn on earlier local legend. Certainly the Earl and his retinue seem to have set up court in imitation of a royal capital. A recent study of my own shows a fit between three sets of evidence: the distribution of imported luxury pottery from the Early Medieval period around prestige sites; sites associated with Arthur in legend, including the works of Béroul; and the distribution of castles built before 1300. The first set of evidence is the finding that Early Medieval imported pottery is mostly within one day's march of

The distribution of castles in Cornwall up to 1300 shows a concentration in the north. In fact, that concentration is largely within a circle 26 kilometres (16 miles) in radius, representing a day's march, around Tintagel. It is as if the Earl of Cornwall was playing King Arthur with his gentry in the roles of knights of the Round Table. The space in the south-west quarter of the circle has legendary associations with King Arthur's hunting grounds.

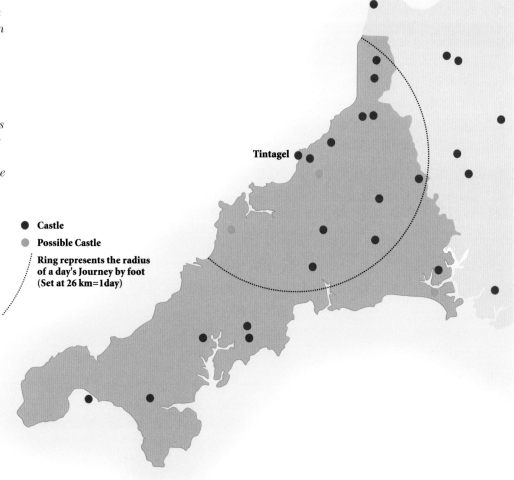

● **Castle**

● **Possible Castle**

⁄ **Ring represents the radius of a day's Journey by foot (Set at 26 km=1day)**

Tintagel

The Late Medieval castle at Tintagel was built as a 'restoration' of King Arthur's legendary castle. Consequently, the walls follow or 'restore' the natural line of the bedrock as if it were the ruins of an older castle (top and right; see also page 131). Likewise, natural terraces were built on as if they were former levels of battlements (above).

a prestige centre,[4] with little if any beyond two days' march. Applying that idea to the sites associated with Arthur and to the castles before 1300, all three distributions match except in one respect. While the imported pottery concentrates round Penwith and Tintagel, and so do the sites associated with Arthur, the castles only match the Tintagel concentration. Interestingly, the castles are built as if in deference to Arthurian sites: they do not intrude on the legendary king's legendary territory, which included Bodmin Moor and Goss Moor.[5] In some of the legends these are enormous deer parks where King Arthur went hunting, and the Castle-an-Dinas that overlooks Goss Moor was said to be his hunting lodge.

The Late Medieval view of the past was that it was like a family tree with new branches representing new generations. The tree is obviously old because of its height, and time can be measured by counting back each generation of previous growth, but the tree is still a tree and one branch like another. Birth, death and rebirth repeat their cycle but there is no sense that time changes anything. Just as Late Medieval painting makes no difference between past and present, so the Earls of Cornwall and the knights in their retinue would have seen Arthur's world as being like their own. They could re-interpret monuments that did not even belong to the Early Medieval period if they looked enough like those of their own age. The Iron Age hillfort of Castle-an-Dinas looks pretty much like the ruins of a Late Medieval ringwork castle, with the same concentric banks and ditches, and lacking only the timber turrets that would be needed for active service. Not all medieval castles were of the motte-and-bailey kind that feature in school textbooks.

So when Richard Earl of Cornwall (1225–72) decided to 'restore' the Early Medieval stronghold of Tintagel, he probably saw no incongruity between the old ruin and his new plan. The ancient stronghold had long been abandoned, the drystone dwellings on the eastern slope of the peninsula were largely under soil wash, and only the odd sherd of Mediterranean pottery eroded out of the hillside would have greeted the new incumbents. Yet the rock formations around the inward and landward side, viewed through half-shut eyes, look like Late Medieval castle walls, and a rock stack at the southern end like a ruined tower. In the event the Late Medieval walls did follow and even extend the line of the rock formations. The curtain wall of the inner ward, for instance, emerges from a ridge of rock and maintains that line, while the wall behind Richard's hall curves strangely round, following the curvature of the underlying rock instead of meeting it straight on. Richard left alone Tintagel's area of castle-like rock formations, which looked like a castle of his own day, and limited himself to what he must have seen as rebuilding at the edges. Richard's son, Edmund, used Restormel as his main residence in Cornwall, and here too is a reminder of Arthur. Edmund built a suite of rooms round the centre of this circular castle, perhaps in imitation of the Round Table.[6]

Although castles were associated with warfare,[7] many of them – like Penhallam[8] (near Jacobstow), a glorified hunting lodge circled by a moat, and the small and flimsy motte and bailey of Week St Mary[9] – could never have stood up to serious attack. The castle of Kilkhampton,[10] on the other hand is a most impressive motte with double bailey, and was built for long-term occupation;[11] aside from the double bailey there are several stone buildings (at least with stone bases). Yet another type was the unofficial castle or adulterine castle, built without royal permission, and only the castle at Truro fits the criteria. Now under the Crown Court, it was hastily built, had a single ditch on the outside and probably contained such timber structures as a turret and palisade. In fact a review of the castles shows that most of them, although built near main roads, were actually built for pleasure – and ostentation. The castle of Upton,[12] for example, on the edge of Bodmin moor, commands views over a peaceful, secluded valley but does not dominate the wider countryside in any military sense.

Earl Richard forcibly purchased all the large and impressive castles, as well as the site of Tintagel. His ambition was to become Holy Roman Emperor and thus, in title if not fact, Emperor of Germany and parts of France and Italy, so he needed suitably impressive accommodation and no obvious rivals within his territories. Richard's plans succeeded for a time; he even bribed some of the German rulers to vote for him and was crowned Emperor in Aachen Cathedral.[13] He added something new to

DEER PARKS
● Medieval
● Post Medieval

Deer parks were not only things of pleasure, but also of prestige. The Late Medieval distribution is concentrated in the northern and eastern parts of Cornwall, and shifts to the southern and western parts (except West Penwith) in the Post-Medieval. The focus of tin exploitation moved gradually westwards over these periods. Where the wealth moved, so did the need for displays of what anthropologists call 'conspicuous consumption'.

Restormel Castle looks like it is built on a motte, but the ground has simply been cut away to give that effect. Although Earl Richard was probably responsible for the gateway to the castle, the circular stone keep with its apartments arranged around a circular courtyard was his son Edmund's design – perhaps inspired by King Arthur's Round Table. The tower extending out in the moat contained the castle's chapel, modified in the 1640s during the English Civil War as a gun deck.

each of his castles. Restormel and Trematon had imposing new gateways and at Lydford, in Dartmoor (also part of the Earldom), earth was heaped up against the stone keep to give the impression that it was built on a motte. Deer parks were another badge of privilege, as deer hunting was reserved for the wealthy; indeed the Normans introduced a new species for the purpose – the Fallow Deer – to join the native Red and Roe Deer. Deer hunting was important in the building and siting of castles.[14] At Launceston[15] the tower within the shell keep has a window in its main upper chamber with an excellent view to the west over the deer park. As for Restormel, it is in the wrong place for a strategic castle. It is overlooked from the crown of the hill above it, and the water it gets from a leat would be at the mercy of any besieger; but the view of the deer park in the valley below is perfect, as it was designed primarily for the pleasure of its owners.

Formal gardens were an important part of courtly leisure too. The 13th-century saint and polymath Albertus Magnus described gardens as being surrounded by a hedge or wall, with ornamental plants and symbolic beds around a turfed lawn. At Tintagel[16] a garden 20 x 14 m (66 x 46 ft) was laid out on the higher ground of the inner ward. Its position is slightly sheltered and it had the extra protection of a wall, though the winds at Tintagel are testing. Small by modern standards it was still special: ornamental gardens of any sort were rare, and no other such garden has been found anywhere in Cornwall. This garden also has literary significance, because a garden at Tintagel was the scene of the tryst between Tristan and Iseult. None of this would have been lost on Richard, who probably had it worked up as an entertainment – perhaps (given the story) for his local mistress, Joan, and not his wife; or perhaps, as he was the living embodiment of legends like these, to impress important guests. The buildings secluded at the back of the Inner Ward next to the garden fit the pattern of accommodation for elite women of the period. They were usually in the least accessible parts of castles but – to mark and enhance their status[17] – they had the best views, over formal gardens and the wider landscape.

The Earls of Cornwall not only used Arthurian legends to promote their own glory, but also to promote Cornwall's ethnic difference. One way in which to do so may have been to set up a rival court. That Cornish heraldic symbols were placed on a par with the English ones is a powerful part of the evidence. Wales was not yet part of the Kingdom. King John was King of England and Earl of Cornwall – two realms. Another way was by administrative action: a town charter granted by Earl Reginald in the 12th century offers equal rights to both Cornish and English.[18] The portrayal of Cornwall through heraldic symbols and maps played on ethnic difference and reinforced an administrative difference. When King John signed Magna Carta, giving his barons a stake in the running of the state, there were two coats of arms at its head, the English and the Cornish. The Cornish flag of a white cross on a black

background (shared with the tinners of Dartmoor) probably dates to the Late Medieval period, too, because both areas were part of the Earldom and the later Duchy. The symbol of the Chough (which was later to be associated with King Arthur) was incorporated into the arms of the local gentry at this time. Families like the Carminows had Cornish mottoes, so the language must have enjoyed some status.[19] Maps like Matthew Paris' map (*c*. 1250) and the *Mappa Mundi* in Hereford Cathedral (*c*. 1300) show Cornwall as a separate entity within the Kingdom alongside England and Wales.[20] The *Mappa Mundi* implies that Cornwall, including Dartmoor, perhaps other bits of the south-west and the smaller area inhabited by Cornish people, occupies most of the fief.

The policy of the Normans was one of divide and rule – ruthlessly, and to show the Anglo-Saxons very clearly who was in charge. The Anglo-Saxon cathedrals at

Dartmoor was a major part of the Earldom of Cornwall. Lydford Castle on Dartmoor is an excellent example of the propaganda of the ambitious and self-promoting Earl Richard. He did not actually build the stone keep, but added a mound of earth around the base, covering up the original ground floor, in order to make it look as if it was constructed on a motte.

139

Winchester and Westminster were demolished, and in their place rose Norman cathedrals. In Cornwall, Robert of Mortain, as the new Earl, stripped St Stephen-by-Launceston of its market rights[21] and built an imposing new castle and market town on the opposite hill at Launceston, even transferring the name Lanstefan to the new location. This was a brutal humiliation of the Anglo-Saxon settlement, leaving no room for doubt that the Norman French lords were the new and absolute masters. As we shall see, the Normans behaved as resolutely French conquerors: they had no wish to deal kindly with the English language or Anglo-Saxon culture until they lost their French possessions in the 15th century.

The Earldom remained special. King John, who was himself the Earl, set up the Stannary courts of Cornwall and Dartmoor to foster and regulate the tin industry.[22] At the end of the 13th century Earl Edmund (1272–99) established a new capital at Lostwithiel to administer it. Lostwithiel has a neat grid system of streets with a central block, which confirms that it was a planned town. In the centre of the town was a complex of buildings called the Shire Hall, later known as the 'Duchy Palace'.[23] It was substantial, as it had to be able to cope with the work of both the Earldom and the Stannary Court. Although it is not obvious to the untrained eye, much of that complex is still visible, and its size is an index of the wealth being generated and therefore the financial power of the Earldom. The most obvious part of the complex is the Convocation Hall where the Stannary Parliaments and Courts were held. It is now a Freemasons' Hall and looks rather like a church. It has thick buttresses and a coat of arms at the north end. Unfortunately the windows and porch are not original as smaller, simpler windows appear on an engraving of 1734. Its basement has a barrel vault and is thought to have been the kitchen. The Great Hall is immediately to its south and, though now divided into smaller properties, was once 33.6 m (110 ft) long and 7.3 m (24 ft) wide – at the time, the biggest hall in the south-west. It also cost a lot because its stone was not local: the walls were made of Pentewan stone from near St Austell and the roofing was Delabole slate from just south of Tintagel.

Changes under the Duchy

In the Hundred Years War the English Crown attempted to lay claim to France. The war put at risk the Duchy of Aquitaine, traditionally the fief of the heir to the English throne, so another – and a secure one – was needed to replace it. Wales already belonged to the heir in the form of a Principality, but having only just been conquered (1284) it was hardly secure. So when the Earldom of Cornwall fell in, the fief was given to Edward, the Black Prince, as the Duchy of Cornwall, and has stayed with the heir to the throne ever since. It thus became identified with the main royal lines of England and later the United Kingdom, although it kept some of the independent structures of the Earldom.

The period of the Duchy (from 1337) was generally one of neglect. It was a convenient source of money, but ceased to be the centre of even the Duke's power base. As undoubted heir to an unthreatened throne, the Duke had no need to develop anything in Cornwall. During the Black Prince's tenure the castles were refurbished after a period of neglect. At Launceston, for instance, the castle keep was used as a prison, which is one reason for its survival, while the Great Hall in the bailey became a ruin. The other castles went into decline, with no further additions and little sign of refurbishment. Neglect and decay are as symbolic as activity, and measure Cornwall's loss of political standing.

While the Duchy let the royal castles crumble, the local gentry started to build in the castle style. Furnished with royal licences to crenellate[24] – in other words, to fortify buildings – they put up castles or castellated manors, not all of which survive. Sheviock (near Torpoint) and Truthwall (near Ludgvan) are two that are lost.[25] A small castle investigated by Michael Tangye on the eastern summit of Carn Brea was probably built as an impressive hunting lodge by the Bassets of Tehidy, and though there have been modifications since it is still to be seen.[26] West of the middle summit of Carn Brea is a long bank and ditch, which formed the boundary of the deer park, and the extent of the deer park seems to be dictated by what can be seen of the hill from the Bassets' estate at Tehidy itself; so the hunt was intended to be visible to spectators at Tehidy. Traces of possible moats can be found at Lanherne and Lee (Morwenstow) and documents from the 18th and 19th centuries of other sites show that Ruan Lanihorne[27] (Roseland), Carminow[28] (near Helston) and St Columb Major[29] possessed moats and walled defences. For a castle of humble status Ruan Lanihorne[30] verges on the magnificent: from a 19th-century description before it was demolished, it had seven towers and possibly an outer court. It overlooked a tidal creek feeding into the Fal estuary, and yet was secluded from it by a high ridge. Just like Upton Castle, on Bodmin Moor, it had access to communication and trade routes and yet provided the privacy befitting someone of high rank.

The Monasteries and the Church

By the Late Medieval period, monasteries had won a measure of independence from local lords and were subject – in theory anyway – to the Pope alone; and as well as monks and hermits there were new categories of religious order – canonries, friaries and knightly orders.[31] Ordained as priests and therefore able to hold services, Augustinian canons were at Launceston,[32] St Germans[33] and Bodmin[34]. At Glasney College, Penryn and Tywardreath priory near St Austell there were Benedictine monks[35] who owned land and, though bound to a life of prayer and contemplation, also dispensed charity. A hermit occupied Roche Chapel. Friars – the Franciscans at Bodmin and Dominicans at Truro[36] – lived in strict poverty and owned nothing, neither the clothes they wore nor even the food for their next meal: everything had to be provided by benefactors.[37] Their mission was to the towns, where the spiritual needs of a worldly and rootless community were unmet, where the poor had no one to turn to and moral danger was everywhere. Finally, there were the Knights Templar, whose order protected pilgrims on their way to the Holy Land. In Cornwall they had a small foundation at Temple on Bodmin Moor to give aid and hospitality to pilgrims travelling from the north coast to the south, *en route* for the Continent – either to the shrine of St James at Compostella in northern Spain, or to Rome or to the Holy Land itself. For all the lack of impressive ruins, Cornwall was host to every variety of Late Medieval monasticism.

All these were daughter houses of monasteries outside Cornwall, although Bodmin priory was an offshoot of an earlier community at Padstow and kept the relics of their founder saint, St Petroc. Some outside monasteries owned acres of Cornish land, yet had no daughter foundation on Cornish soil – like Montacute in Somerset, which owned large areas of Bodmin Moor.[38] Others set up daughter foundations to administer their property: Tavistock owned the priory of St Nicholas, patron saint of travellers, on the Isles of Scilly.[39] A few communities like Crantock, St Buryan and Perranzabuloe remained as collegiate churches.[40] These were centres of learning and had rights akin to those of cathedrals, except that their canons had no role in running the diocese. Towards the end of this period rich benefactors were to found chantries where monks or nuns would pray for their souls or the souls of relatives – to shorten their suffering in purgatory and speed their way to heaven. So far only one such chantry may have been found in Cornwall: at St Benet's (Lanivet, near Bodmin), where a 15th-century chapel and house may represent a chantry and its accompanying almshouse.

The best-preserved remains of the priories are at St Germans and St Michael's Mount, because later urban development did not remove their buildings and lands, which became instead the basis for Post-Medieval estates of landed gentry. The western part of St German's church still stands, but excavations at the eastern end suggest it formed the canons' choir and possibly a Lady chapel.[41] The floor had plain and decorated tiles, the latter red with an inlaid white slip, patterned with chevrons and fleurs-de-lis and covered with a greeny-yellow glaze. Analysis shows they were locally made because they contain local clay. It is the priory churches themselves that mostly survive, and there are fewer traces of their surrounding buildings. On St Michael's Mount, however, the Benedictines built a lighthouse lit by a brazier that has been incorporated in the first defensive wall on the path up to the summit.[42] There are no remains above ground of the friary at Bodmin except for a fish-pond in a park below the present church, though recent excavations have revealed an aisled church dating from the late 12th/early 13th century, with a 15th-century tower.[43] At

*Cornwall's monastic
institutions suffered greatly
at the hands of Henry VIII
during the Reformation.
Above ground remains are
few and in an unimpressive
state. The church of the
Austin priory of St Germans
is a fortunate exception. The
archway is an outstanding
example of the radiating
chevron patterns typical of
Norman architecture. The
arches appear to rest on small
columns carved in relief, and
the effect is like a blazing sun,
symbolising the Resurrection.*

the Benedictine priory of Glasney College (Penryn) the church had imported Caen
stone for its ornamental features and a floor of coloured tiles. A watching brief
(where an observer checks for anything coming to light from development work) has
revealed the location of the gatehouse in the defensive, seaward wall of the priory. A
16th-century illustration shows it then even had gunports,[44] gunpowder having been
part of British warfare since the 15th century.

Monasteries affected not just urban life but the countryside too – including the
moorlands, where poor soils naturally made landowners more generous in their gifts
of land to the church. The example of St Neot parish, Bodmin Moor, shows that land
ownership went in slices from the high moor to rich lowland soils and river valleys
at the bottom.[45] During this period monasteries began to put together the parcels of
moorland they had been given. To the original owners, the odd patch of moorland
had been good for little more than summer grazing at best, but monasteries could

exploit the economies of scale. By putting sheep out all year round on big enough holdings they could produce wool surpluses for the market. Contemporary documents show that much of the surplus went to supply the local and English markets, but some also went in export to Flanders, for weaving into cloth.[46] Even some cloth was produced,[47] and place-names like Tuckingmill in Camborne[48] show that 'tucking' or fulling (preparing cloth for dyeing) took place in Cornwall.

Signs of Christian devotion were everywhere and conspicuous. Besides the land itself, owned in such abundance by monasteries and churches, there were also small drystone-walled chapels like Madron and Fenton Ia, holy wells and wayside crosses. Some elements of church buildings of this period show new influences from Brittany, like the decorative spire of Lostwithiel church and the well-house of Dupath.[49] Burial continued to be in stone slab-lined cists as in the previous period, and followed the same Christian practice of east-west alignment.[50]

Urbanism and state formation in Cornwall and western Europe

The growth of towns, particularly from the 13th century, forced a major break with the past.[51] Although once part of an urban-based state under the Romans, and then of the looser, more rural Dumnonia, Cornwall never lost its character as a kinship-based rural society. In the context of Europe and the Mediterranean, the British Isles supplied raw material, whereas the Low Countries, the Rhineland and the

Cornwall is unique in Britain in having theatres during the Late Medieval period. The form of the theatre is clearly derived from rounds and lann enclosures, as can be seen here at St Just-in-Penwith. However, the idea itself appears to have come from Britanny. Fortunately, there is a medieval manuscript with an illustration of the layout of the small stages, placed at points along the outer bank of the enclosure with a small one in the centre. The scenes alternated between the different stages, so that the audience was placed literally in the midst of the action.

Mediterranean (including Islamic Spain, North Africa and Arabia) manufactured high-quality goods. In the British Isles, ambition offered the rich and powerful only two options: to conquer or to produce more raw materials of more kinds to pay for more fine goods from abroad. For Cornwall there was no land to seize, so secular society and the church vied with each other to promote such expansion.

The creation of towns and ports allowed more materials to be efficiently processed and shipped out. The process was not entirely spontaneous, as secular and religious authorities invested in particular locations. Wool, fish, tin and even silver could be brought to these new towns to be weighed, taxed and packaged in ever larger quantity – in return for smaller cargoes of fine cloth, fine tableware and probably spices.[52] Meanwhile the towns increasingly drew in people from the countryside, cut them off from their rural roots and took them away from just providing for themselves and trading the surplus. These new townspeople now needed supplies of flour and meat, clothes, shoes and pottery, so the towns developed service industries to support the main local industries and their workforce. But subsistence did not vanish entirely. In these early towns the burghers had house and garden plots with a dwelling and enough land to grow vegetables and fruit, even to keep a few animals. The outline of such plots can still be seen in towns like Helston and Week St Mary.

By way of entertainment for these uprooted populations there were theatres in the towns (perhaps one or two in rural areas as well) known as *Plênys-an-Gwarry* or 'Playing Places'. The material was allegorical and religious – 'miracle plays' in fact – and took place in embanked enclosures shaped like small Roman amphitheatres, though their origins probably owe more to the continued use of rounds as places of public assembly. There is a very well-preserved example in the middle of St Just (West Penwith). The monks of Penryn's Glasney College were among the foremost playwrights in the *Plênys-an-Gwarry* tradition and wrote many plays in Cornish – notably *Origo Mundi* (the origin of the world) and *Beunans Meriasek* (the life of St Meriasek). Although attempts have been made to cite the Cornish tradition as part of the origins of English theatre,[53] the plays were in fact exclusively in the Cornish language, and were closely linked to Breton and French theatre traditions.[54] There is even some documentary evidence of similar open-air theatres in Brittany.[55]

It seems that, Liskeard and Lostwithiel apart, towns and ports began as markets round religious centres, and that these developed further in the period of Anglo-Saxon rule so that there were five markets by the time of the Norman Conquest, and perhaps three boroughs – markets with the status of towns. They mainly sprang up from the 12th to the 14th centuries, and most of them were coastal or inland ports like Truro, Lostwithiel and Fowey. Although sherds of bar-lug pottery of the 9th to 11th centuries have been found in Pydar Street, Truro[56] in a pit behind some Post-Medieval houses, the sherds were obviously not in an original context. Because they were associated with Late Medieval pottery dating to 1250–1500, they are most likely to have been heirlooms. A similar situation occurred at Penryn where sherds of grass-marked pottery were found under the priory church, particularly near the west end. Eventually the towns and markets were so well distributed that only the Lizard and the higher parts of Bodmin Moor were more than six or seven miles from a market centre. This was no small achievement, given Cornwall's extremely rural character at the beginning of the period.

These towns[57] contain a number of characteristic elements:[58] a broad market street, often with two or three side roads; burghage plots at right angles to the streets; a church; a monastic establishment; a *Plênys-an-Gwarry*; workshops – potteries, smiths, tanneries; a guildhall; a coinagehall in the stannary towns; defensive walls in some cases; and town houses, though only a few rather late 15th-century examples survive. Of these, church buildings were the most abundant: Bodmin had a priory, a friary, five chapels, two hospitals and two leper houses,[59] whilst many of its forty guilds were religious or charitable. St Neot, on the edge of Bodmin Moor, had active and wealthy religious guilds, which provided high-quality stained glass for its church in the 16th century, most of it still surviving.[60] Late Medieval glass is rare, because it usually contains potash and therefore weathers badly; this late example shows what once existed. In the church at St Just-in-Penwith guilds contributed to a magnificent display of wall paintings that include a representation of Christ of the Trades and another of St George, both of which can still be seen.

As for industries, no coinagehall – where tin was assayed for purity – has been physically identified except at Lostwithiel, though some craft workshops have been. Smithies have been found in Launceston castle, kilns at St Germans; and quantities of waster sherds at Lostwithiel point to the existence of potteries there too. There is other such evidence from villages and smaller settlements, like leather working at Gwithian and ceramic production at Landulph, but the evidence from larger towns is still elusive.

All these activities and wealth needed defences. Those at Launceston, for example, were fairly impressive: the castle motte and keep, the bailey and the town had high stone walls and gatehouses. One of the town gates still stands. St Ives had a blockhouse and bastioned ramparts, but the remains are not obvious to the casual visitor. At Fowey there were blockhouses, a sea-facing wall and a fortified manor.[61]

The reorganisation of the countryside

In this long economic advance, half the impetus came from the burgeoning towns; the other half, just as crucial, came from the reorganised countryside. Hitherto people had farmed and won minerals mostly to subsist; any surplus, such as it was, paid for exotic goods for the elites. Now the aim was to take from the land all it could yield. So the first step for the Late Medieval landlords was to bring as much land as

they could into production. They used the moorlands not just in summer but all year round, exploited rough dune pasture as well and sometimes kept a newly introduced animal – originally from north-west Africa, reared in special farms called warrens, it was the rabbit. The ensuing agricultural boom owed something to a long warm spell known as the 'Little Climatic Optimum'.[62]

There was more streaming and mining than before, especially on Dartmoor where large areas of artificial earth mounds (called pillow mounds) testify to the amount of fresh rabbit meat available to the settlements of tinners.[63] Dartmoor was at first the main centre in the Earldom and Duchy of mineral extraction (especially of tin); the Tamar Valley and East Cornwall gradually became more important. In the far west, rising sea levels turned Scilly into the undeniably plural Isles of Scilly: the lowlands of the large island of Ennor were submerged, creating islands like St Mary's, Tresco, Bryher and St Martin's. People were forced to settle the higher ground permanently.

The new village settlements are particularly well preserved on moorlands, where later developments have not, as in low-lying areas, removed their traces. These villages consist of longhouses – rectangular drystone-wall buildings with a plot of land

Late Medieval churches were bright, colourful places, but the zeal of later ages to remove traces of 'popery' has left little to see. St Just-in-Penwith has one of the best remaining church murals, dating to the 15th century. It shows St George fighting the dragon to defend a princess, who was to be sacrificed to save the great walled city in the background. A Near Eastern saint, George became popular during the Crusades.

147

LATE MEDIEVAL FLORUIT

The Late Medieval period saw people return to live permanently on Cornwall's moors for the first time since they were abandoned during the Late Bronze Age. A village of medieval longhouses is visible in this photograph of Fernacre (Brown Willy) on Bodmin Moor. The village is on the slope of a hill overlooking a stream, surrounded by a field system made up of long narrow strip fields.

round them. These would have been thatched, and unlike the houses of the elites would have had no windows. The light would have come through doorways or from the fire in the hearth. Their occupants would have spent much of their time working outdoors anyway. Although the settlements were clusters of six or seven houses on average, each house and plot was separate from the next. For the first time since the courtyard houses of the Roman period, there were rooms inside to define private space. These separate properties reflected the fact that the responsible unit in rural society had become the family. Each family now answered for itself, its property and its tax – usually paid to the landowner in the form both of produce and days of labour on his fields. None of this meant instant dissolution of the old ties of kinship, but over time those relationships would have felt the strain of property disputes between families now jealous of what was their own. The settlements on Bodmin Moor and Black Moor (now the China Clay area near St Austell) were a long way from others. Their occupation would have meant people weakening their ties with everyone left behind, further loosening the bond of rural communities. In the uplands of West Penwith the new village of Old Lanyon,[64] near Madron, looks like a settlement shift from nearby Chun Castle. As West Penwith is narrow, the uplands are no great distance from lowland areas and the coast, and upland settlements were viable even during the period from later prehistory to the Late Medieval.

Longhouse settlements were based mostly on subsistence agriculture. Peasants held land as tenants of their lords, which could be monasteries. With any surplus they made after tax they could buy goods like pottery from the nearby towns. The longhouse settlement on the slopes of Garrow Tor, for instance, contains Lostwithiel Ware Pottery.[65] Houses in the settlements comprised[66] a livier or general living area for people; a shippon or byre for livestock with a central drain to remove animal waste; a cross passage between the two, separated from the shippon by a low screen; and sometimes a private room at the back, possibly for storing dairy products, but more likely a sleeping area for at least some of the householders. In the centre of the livier was a hearth lined with stones. The wealthy in their manors and castles might sometimes have chimneys, but never the rural poor. Set apart from the longhouses were outhouses to store tools and produce. Further out from the settlement with its buildings and small enclosed gardens were strip fields. Good examples of these are to be found on Bodmin Moor, at Garrow Tor for example, and also along the ridge just south of Goss Moor. Small, corbelled structures called 'beehive huts' found near Late Medieval settlements on Bodmin Moor – like those on Brown Willy and Louden Hill – were probably contemporary.[67] Their smallness and their being in sheltered spots on highly exposed hillsides suggest that they were shelters for people out herding livestock.

The longhouse settlements on the moors were eventually abandoned. Although popularly known as 'deserted medieval villages', many, such as Garrow Tor and Old Lanyon, survived well into the Post-Medieval period. A less friendly climate, soil exhausted from over-exploitation and even the Black Death have taken the blame for their demise. The most likely reason, however, especially given their late survival, is that the villagers were moving into the growing towns to better themselves. For the monasteries and secular landlords, too, it was now more efficient to manage the upland pastures with fewer people. It could be that some of the peasantry went to work on lowland farms that were situated closer to their markets; this would have meant that they were able to deliver fresher produce more quickly and cheaply (see Chapter Eight).

Crafts, industries and trade

The new urban economy was stoking a demand beyond the power of cottage industries to supply. Late Medieval industry needed free capital, so craft work had to come out of the home, and thanks to the individualisation of property and responsibility the period saw the beginnings of paid labour. Domestic servants and craftsworkers were paid a wage, and could thus save money and move up the ladder. Some of the upwardly mobile went on to be traders in towns, and in the countryside some accumulated plots of land to create their own farms or estates – as at St Neot.

On a grander scale, the very powerful could amass money to plough into infrastructure, as Edmund, Earl of Cornwall did in founding Lostwithiel and its port.[68]

Although most of the large scars running across the moorlands of Cornwall and Dartmoor are due to later mining, some are the legacy of this period, and Sandy Gerrard has investigated a number of them – such as the tin works at North Penkestle, Bodmin Moor. At the top of the leats is a scattering of prospecting pits and a dam. The weathered rock exposed lodes, which were dug out, and a stream using water released from behind the dam. Alongside the leats banks of waste material were arranged in a herring-bone pattern. Elsewhere, at the Calstock and Bere Alston silver mines, people were using a technique called cupellation (the extraction of silver from its ore), then new to Cornwall and the south-west, and a study shows how complex the whole process was.[69] It relied on tallow and iron brought from Launceston, Bodmin, Tavistock or Lostwithiel; it consumed sea coal, imported via Fowey, Saltash and Sutton as well as 'moor coal' or peat from Dartmoor; it used cows' hides from places like Buckland and Buckfast, hemp from Yeovil and Bridport; and it shipped in an array of other items like oats, bellows, locks, rope, anvils, refinery ash and nails from Tavistock, Sutton and Exeter. The ore itself had to be mined, not merely streamed like tin, so there had to be adits to keep the workings dry and drain the water off by gravity to vents cut into the hillside. Out of the ground came an ore which repeated heating reduced to 'fertile lead', a silver-lead mixture ready for the cupellation itself. In this final process the fertile lead went into a hearth lined with an absorbent material called ashes of tan – which was refuse oak bark from Exeter and Buckland. The high temperatures oxidised the lead, which was then absorbed into the hearth, leaving the silver on top. Apart from the adits and the hearths, the remains at the sites also included a crazing mill for crushing the ore.

Finally, ports like St Ives, Newquay and Fowey began to turn pilchard fishing into an industry.[70] A huer's lookout at Newquay is a good example (though heavy restoration has altered it) of what was a vital component in the fishing strategy. The huer watched for the shoals, signalled back to the port when he sighted them and directed the boats, which then went to work with large seine nets. As for the harbours of this period, there is a good example in Old Town, St Mary's (the Isles of Scilly): a thick pier of large unmortared and undressed rocks separates the harbour from the rest of the bay.[71] The fish were salted and shipped off to large cities in the Mediterranean, as food for the long fast of Lent. Although most of the salt was imported from Brittany and the Vendée some – at least at the beginning of the period, according to 'Domesday Book' – was apparently produced in Stratton, though archaeological traces have yet to be identified.

As we have already seen, distinctive kinds of pottery were made in towns and bear their names – like St Germans Ware and Lostwithiel Ware – and it may be that

This charming jug, imported from western France, was a luxury item during the Late Medieval period. It is Saintonge Ware, prized for the light creamy colour of the clay, an ideal background for simple, colourful designs. The belly of the bird mirrors the curvature of the jug, while its beak is suggestively within a hare's breath of the spout.

Sandy Lane pottery had an urban source in West Cornwall.[72] However, there was a whole network of potteries in rural locations that connected with these towns, so that St Germans Ware was made in potteries along the Tamar Valley, not just in St Germans itself. At the same time pottery from Devon and further afield was coming into Cornwall. Saintonge Ware and Beauvais Ware pottery from France and Merida Ware from Islamic Spain were imported in modest quantities.[73] For that and other sorts of overseas trade the invention of the 'cog' was an important step forward. This was a ship with a fixed rear rudder, and a tiller to turn it, instead of a side rudder just like an over-sized oar on one side. In keeping with the temper of the times it was larger than previous ships, and therefore more productive.[74]

The key developments of this period were, of course, the growth of towns and the creation of a distinct administrative identity around the Arthurian legend. The authority of tribe and kinship was being replaced by that of the state. Industries like mining and fishing began to be significant factors in the local economy. The countryside changed, too, with moorlands colonised by small villages exploiting the wool and mineral resources there, though lowland farming – with the advantage of being nearer to towns – gradually took over. Christianity coloured everything – people's minds, their lives and the whole social order.

Crockery was limited, because people still cooked and ate communally. This Beauvais Ware jug, produced in northern France, was a luxury item and would have been passed around the table as a drinking vessel.

CHAPTER EIGHT
CAPITALISM AND CLASS CONFLICT
The Post-Medieval Period (1500–1750)

IN THE POST-MEDIEVAL WORLD, Cornwall's new towns with their busy industries and thriving trade would open it to regular, sustained contact with other communities and other countries. It was a world where nations were born out of trade (and not out of allegiance to a divinely appointed lord), and where shared culture and language were the key to commercial success.[1] So, with ample capital and the will to rule, the large nations of the Atlantic seaboard would colonise the Americas and Asia, taking their languages with them – English, Spanish, Portuguese, French and Dutch. In the British Isles the gradual assimilation of the Norman French had led to the triumph of English culture, and to English being the language of commerce and power. As a nation instead of a feudal lordship, England strove towards uniformity of culture. In Cornwall the elites resisted all this Englishness at first, but then took to it and joined an upper class identified with fashionable cities like Bath and London and with life at court. The rest of Cornwall developed a new identity that helped it to negotiate rapid technological and economic change and to absorb the new and diverse cultural influences the period produced.

The age of capitalism, colonialism and nation-building

Early capitalism could create the infrastructure to move goods – shipping, ports, towns – but the lack of a shared culture and shared ideas that could aid communication was a real handicap. As more and more people of all classes became able to build up surpluses, sometimes with new technology, they found it more practical to speak the national language rather than the local dialect. But the problem was not just linguistic;[2] differences in material culture can also hinder trade, for goods only change hands when both parties understand them. Post-Medieval Cornwall preferred at first to cling to its own ways and language, while trade within Europe and beyond it gathered pace and volume. The new colonies and their exploitation by European traders brought new influences, some of which were to be more significant in the Industrial period.

Religion helped to shape Cornwall's sense of identity. In the Reformation and Counter-Reformation rulers had absolute power to choose their subjects' religion –

152

but this in an age that increasingly demanded personal responsibility. In Cornwall Catholicism was originally strongly associated with the defence of Cornish culture, while Protestantism equated with English culture. By the Industrial period Cornwall stood at the other extreme by embracing a wholehearted evangelical Protestantism associated with a new Cornish identity based on its fledgling industrial communities.

Shipping and fishing

The industries that grew up at the end of the Late Medieval period had begun to transform the economy. Once it had been mainly subsistence farming[3] yielding small surpluses, supported by a little manufacture; now that farming counted for less, surpluses increasingly counted for everything. Those who controlled these industries were starting to think like capitalists before there was any such word. They invested in new enterprises for personal gain, and the idea that as heads of a wider kinship group they had social obligations faded from their minds. They used the towns, ports, even rural communities as sources of profit and cash,[4] while the ordinary members of those communities still felt the old ties of kinship and duty. They saw the future as changing and dynamic, while ordinary people saw their lives in fixed terms of morality and religion, of life and death. The growth of industry therefore seemed to those working at the rock face, on the shop floor and at sea a spiritual challenge for which their reward would be in heaven. The gentry and rich merchants saw technology, science and business acumen as the means to rewards in the here and now, and left moral and spiritual matters in a domain of their own. Profits had nothing to do with holding any moral position, they were simply a function of skill and reason.

Under the heading of the spiritual come a lot of traditions in Cornish fishing. There is a correct way of eating fish, from the head to the tail. There are taboo words: for example, *cleeta*, from the Cornish word for *belfry*, is used for *church* – taboo because of a belief that anything to do with the clergy brought bad luck to fishing.[5] In contrast, offerings of fish were made to the 'bucca', who was a hobgoblin or imp. Newlyn men would set up a post, which they called the bucca, and to which they made offerings; at Mousehole the offerings were simply left on the beach.[6] There are legends about mermaids.[7] One of the most famous, the Mermaid of Zennor, was even carved on a bench end in Zennor Church. Mermaids derive from classical Greek and Roman mythology and continued to be part of the lore of the Mediterranean. The trade in salted fish, particularly pilchards, to Spain and Italy was the likely vehicle for these legends to come to Cornwall. Since the fall of the Moorish state of Granada, the sea routes into the Mediterranean were in the hands of European and Christian countries – Spain and Portugal – which meant that these markets were now open to European traders, including the Cornish.[8] The more

Folk beliefs supplemented Christian belief in Cornwall. The trade in fish to the Mediterranean brought the idea of mermaids – one is carved here on a bench end from Zennor Church.

shipping there was, the more shipwrecks – and witches and the odd evil creature like the Mermaid of the Lizard were widely blamed. The elites saw it differently, and Sir John Killigrew had a lighthouse set up on the Lizard[9] where the present day lighthouse stands; unfortunately this eminently reasonable solution failed because the merchants refused to pay their dues.

It was the fishing industry that reinforced, reinvigorated and perhaps to some extent reinvented the relationship at the level of ordinary people between Cornwall and Brittany. In the Late Medieval period there were families of Bretons in Cornwall to keep the connection alive,[10] and it was all very natural while the Duchy of Brittany also formed part of the domains of the Norman and Plantagenet dynasties. That easy state of affairs ended, however, with the defeat of Brittany by France; and the marriage of the heiress Duchess Anne to the French King brought about Brittany's union with France. The rupture, formally at least, was sharp and prolonged.[11] Indeed England and France were often at war or menacing each other until the *Entente Cordiale* in 1904. The reality on the ground (or at sea) was rather subtler. No doubt Cornish people in Anglo-French wars were pitted against Bretons, but the fishing industry continued to bind them in a spirit of co-operation. Salt was necessary to preserve fish for export to the Mediterranean and western France,[12] and most of the salt was imported from Brittany and the Vendée – areas of France exempt from salt tax.[13] When a salt tax was imposed in England and Wales from the late 17th century, smuggling became not only attractive but, so extortionate was the tax, vital to the survival of fishing.

It is not clear how effective tax collection was in the ports, nor even how much money it raised. Lack of any force to patrol the long Cornish coastline meant it was almost impossible to police smuggling in the Post-Medieval period.[14] Formal smugglers' caches are more likely to date from the late 18th/early 19th centuries when more serious counter measures were taken by the revenue. The remains of small fishing operations are evidence of ample facilities in small coves, where salt and anything else could have been hidden. An example of just such a Post-Medieval fishing cellar is at Porth Godrevy,[15] Gwithian, and has formed part of a study by the Cornish researcher Michael Tangye (whose name, interestingly, is Breton[16]). A little ledged hollow in the low cliffs to the side of the road just beyond the second National Trust car park contains traces of drystone walling. These represent a fish cellar and two fishermen's boat sheds, while a round socket once contained the capstan for winching the boats up onto the shore. The lower levels of the fish cellar's drystone walls are still visible, and square hollows in the masonry bear witness to equipment that once was there. The hollows make a line of sockets that each took one end of a pressing pole; the other end bore down on a hogshead or barrel of pilchards, under the heavy weight of oval granite boulders with iron hooks attaching them to the pole.

The resulting pressure would have compacted the fish in the hogshead, and squeezed the oil and brine (the 'train') from between the staves and into a 'dreg-' or 'drug-pit' – which unfortunately is no longer there at Porth Godrevy. The floor of the cellar at that site was partly a slate platform of the underlying bedrock, which sloped towards the centre where it met the cobbled part of the floor. Slates now lying over the cobbles are from what had been the cellar roof, which presumably protected the processed materials from inblown sea, sand and rain. Traces of fishing cellars are not always obvious, but pressing stones like those found at Porth Godrevy and Gurnard's Head, Zennor can be good indicators that there were cellars nearby.[17] They are often

Pentewan stone, a type of soft granite, or elvan, was sought after in the Post-Medieval for decorative elements of important buildings. The entrance to the Henrician (Henry VIII) keep of Pendennis Castle is a case in point. With good money lavished on its coat of arms and gargoyles carved out of Pentewan stone, it was not built purely for defensive reasons, but also as a symbol of royal authority and national unity.

to be seen in gardens in St Ives and Newlyn, and their weight means that they cannot travel far without strenuous help. Pressing stones not only bear witness to the processing of fish but also to the wider connections of these small operations. The oval boulders used are found in raised beaches – beaches left high and dry by former interglacials – in the cliff faces of West Penwith, notably at Nanjulian, St Just.[18] These had to be brought into towns or ports and taken to a blacksmith who would drill a hole in them to take an iron hook embedded in lead. The process illustrates just one of the links between fishing and the whole trading infrastructure.

That infrastructure was, of course, created by the local gentry. While most of the small harbours in Cornwall were built or altered in the Industrial period, a few have their origins in the Post-Medieval, like the Custom House Quay built by the Killigrew family in their new borough town of Falmouth, using the same sort of building technique employed for the Elizabethan outworks of Pendennis Castle. The masonry is local slate set in alternate courses, horizontally and vertically. Although it is only for small pleasure craft today, the harbour would have been pretty impressive at a time when ships were generally about the size of a large modern yacht. There was an earlier harbour guarded by Little Dennis blockhouse and a protective wall that joined them, below Pendennis Castle; the entrance to it was made by widening a fissure in the slaty shales of the headland to allow a supply vessel to get in at high tide.[19] At Penryn, just westwards from Falmouth up the creek, wharves were simply waterside walls and needed no breakwater or enclosing harbour. While new harbours at places like Falmouth, St Ives and Fowey were impressive and heralded changes in the way that shipping would be handled, most of the coastal settlements had no more than a capstan at the top of the beach. Small boats would have had to bring contraband like salt, tobacco and brandy onto the shore.

As for the ships themselves, a revolution in maritime transport saw the end of the old broadsail rigging in ships with a mixture of sail types. Broadsails were large rectangular sails suited to the strong, steady winds of the Atlantic and North Sea, but unhandy in light or changeable winds. Lateen sails were added to ships because their triangular shape, developed in the Mediterranean, works well where the wind is fickle. They can quickly be trimmed to catch the wind, and they make it easier to keep the ship on course. A great variety of ships was developed over this period, with different numbers of masts, kinds of sail and sizes of sail. There were also more ships altogether, their increasing numbers reflected in the greater incidence of shipwreck along the Cornish coasts.[20] Not all this shipping had to do with Cornwall's industries: the Packet Ships from Falmouth[21] carried the Royal Mail to the Americas and Africa as well as passengers, and many ships were simply in passage to and from ports anywhere in Northern Europe – though they might put into Cornish ports for repair, maintenance and stores.

Because navigational infrastructure was poor and instruments to measure longitude were inaccurate till the late 18th century, ships were not always aware that they were near Cornwall's rocky coastline. The most dramatic case was the wreck of the *Association*.[22] This was the British naval flagship that struck the Western Rocks between the Bishop Rock and St Agnes in May 1707, along with three other ships of the fleet – the *Eagle*, the *Romney* and the *Firebrand*. These shipwrecks have yielded coins, navigational equipment, ships' fittings, pewter tableware, ceramics, a copper kettle, buckles, and shot and iron cannons. In other words, the finds range from arms to everyday items, reminding archaeologists that these ships were floating settlements as well weapons of war. Some of these items can be seen in the Isles of Scilly Museum in St Mary's, and others in the museum at Charlestown. Other wrecks indicate the range of commercial and naval vessels passing by – or indeed failing to pass by. A mid-17th-century merchantman wrecked off Mullion, on the Lizard,[23] has revealed evidence of the trade between Bristol and the continent. Although it was badly worn by the movement of shingle, a steep-sided gully has prevented the dispersal of the material, and a layer of concretion has actually fixed some finds to the seabed. At least 23 iron cannons demonstrate that the ship was armed, and other finds make up a very mixed cargo. It included lead ingots, circular copper 'cakes', handmade brass pins (the most common item, probably from Bristol), brass buttons, musket and pistol barrels, a pewter plate, a medallion, a saint's statue of brass, iron nails and clay pipe bowls marked E.B. – standing for Edward Battle, a Freeman and merchant of Bristol. Such wrecks show that trade did not involve bulk shipments but mixed cargoes for more complex transactions. Similar evidence comes from the wreck of the Portuguese ship *St Anthony*, sunk in 1527 off Gunwalloe; but here local people helped themselves. In Gunwalloe Church six painted wooden panels of saints are of 16th-century Iberian origin, and are likely to have come from the wreck.[24]

Mining and quarrying

The maritime revolution of the Post-Medieval period coincided with the invention of the printing press and the use of paper[25] instead of the previous medium for the written word – vellum made of calf skin. The result was a greater dissemination of ideas as well as goods. In the late 16th century German miners were brought over to England to improve mining technology and production, and some came to Cornwall; but was technology all they brought? It may be that the tradition of the Knockers in Cornwall also has something to do with these German immigrants. A 16th-century German mining engineer, George Bauer (or 'Agricola') wrote a treatise on mining, *De Re Metallica*, which included a chapter on the spirits and fairy folk living under the earth and in mines.[26] The behaviour and ways of dealing with German Kobalts and Cornish Knockers described by Agricola[27] are very much like the folk tales of the knockers recorded at the beginning of the 19th century before they could be forgotten. A miner who came across mining tools or worked tin that were hard to explain knew that knockers were about and made offerings to propitiate them. Historians and antiquarians in this very period were only gradually realising that past and present were materially different, and most people looking at ancient tools in an old working would not instantly assume they were archaeological; plainly they were contemporary and belonged to the knockers, perhaps just disturbed at their work. To thank them they would leave offerings like candles, food or a share of the tin they had found.

Cornwall was full of workings, including those of older periods already mentioned – like the medieval workings at North Penkestle on Bodmin Moor. The orthodoxy is that people reopened earlier workings and followed the lodes down, and any artefacts they found in doing so must have been left there by accident. However, it is hard to pass off finds made in 1835 of a block of tin and a number of coins at

Roche, or a large 16th-century ceramic pitcher full of tin from streaming works found in the 1820s, probably at the Boscarne works, simply as forgetfulness on the part of earlier miners.[28] A particularly interesting find is that of a crowned tin figure seated on a throne, dug up in 1853 on Bodwen Moor, Lanlivery near an old smelting house.[29] On it are Hebrew characters that make no sense. The legends of the knockers recorded by Richard Carew in 1602, and more fully worked up in folklore gleaned in the 19th century, identify the knockers as Jews who had killed Christ and had been banished by the Roman Emperors to toil in the Cornish mines in eternal penance.[30] (Even Constantine the Great [306–337] is mentioned, so no pedantic date was going to kill a good story.) That the Hebrew characters make nonsense might mean that people who knew nothing of Hebrew copied them blindly, and that the figure was some sort of offering to the Jewish knockers. This object is on view at the Royal Cornwall Museum. Incidentally, miners took great care not to offend the knockers on account of their race or beliefs, and it was unlucky even to make the sign of the cross in a mine.

As for the mines themselves, most tin during this period came from surface and shallow workings. Even the cliff workings were shallow, like those near St Just (West Penwith);[31] they are identifiable as rows of small artificial caves, about two to four metres deep. Lode-back mining involved digging pits close to one another along the line of lodes, and it has left conspicuous traces on moorland – near the Hurlers stone circles, for example, in Minions, Bodmin Moor.[32] Some of these formed shallow shafts up to five metres deep, which may have interconnected below the surface. Openworks such as in the Witheybrook, also near Minions, formed an essentially continuous opencast cutting along the lode. The ore was usually treated close by – as in the 16th-century mill complex at Retallack,[33] near Constantine (Kerrier). Near an area of workings, it contains at least six crazing-mills, as well as stamps. Any massive ore would first be crushed into coarse lumps in the stamps, where iron-shod hammers shattered it on large mortar stones. Those lumps and the finer ore would then go to the crazing-mills to be ground between two millstones. Water-wheels powered both those operations. The remains of a blowing house with a mould stone in the centre marks the end of the process. Here there were bellows, again powered by water wheels, to force-feed the furnaces with oxygen; and at last the molten metal would pour into the mould stone, to cool into an ingot ready for transportation.

Finally, there was quarrying. In this period the signs of quarrying on the granitic moorlands are rows of chiselled slots.[34] The remains of incomplete or spoilt work, like millstones and blocks, can be found among clitter or boulder scatters and on tors. No doubt much of the stone was for local use, but some was actually exported – to western France, for instance, where chemical analyses of the stones have traced them to Cornish sources.[35] One fine-grained granite or elvan, Pentewan stone from near St Austell, was particularly prized. It was used for decorative stonework in august buildings like the keep of Henry VIII's castle at Pendennis,[36] and Antony House near Torpoint.[37]

The agricultural landscape and rural settlement

The gradual reduction or abandonment of moorland villages that had begun in the Late Medieval period continued right into the 17th century.[38] Farmsteads and isolated houses replaced them, but not always where the villages had once been. For, as we have seen, it was not just that people moved from moorland to lowland and from country to town, but that the countryside was operating differently. Sometimes rural communities diversified: on the coasts they went in for seasonal fishing (and making bags from the grasses growing on sand dunes, according to the early 17th-century author Richard Carew of Antony[39]); inland there was mining and quarrying. Fewer people did the main work on farms. Tenant farmers now paid rent in cash, not in kind, and there was no longer a system of labour *in lieu* of tax. Money was the new basis of rural relationships, and there was much variation in wealth.

Among the wealthier farmhouses of this period is Stonaford,[40] North Hill, just north of Bodmin Moor. Here a sequence of building and rebuilding on the same spot began with a Late Medieval longhouse and ended with a 19th-century farmhouse. The late 16th and early 17th centuries saw the dwelling transformed from a semi-communal space into something more private and divided. The walls were heightened to take a first floor with a slate roof, instead of a thatched roof. The ground floor was divided into two rooms or possibly three, of which two had fireplaces and chimneys built into the walls. A two-storey porch was added to the northwestern door, to make it the formal front entrance, and the other door was blocked to stop people just dropping in. The extra space and the fireplaces and chimneys would have represented a major improvement in the occupants' standard of living. The formal front porch would have deterred casual visitors, the partitioning into rooms would have prevented them from getting any further into the house and a lean-to dairy at the back kept work and living quarters apart. Less wealthy versions of such buildings, with one main room above and one below, were more common – like that of Leaze,[41] in St Breward.

Some poorer people remained in longhouses until the 17th century, as at Old Lanyon[42] (West Penwith), while others lived in one- or two-roomed cottages. Peculiar to Cornwall are houses with buttressed chimneys, many of them made with drystone walling. The chimney used no bricks or finely cut stone and mortar, but was just an integral part of a very thick, semicircular drystone buttress built up against a corner of the house. The mass of the buttress supported the height of the chimney structure, and also contained the stresses caused by the heat of the fire. Such but-

tresses look like semicircular mounds of stone on the corner of the low, square or rectangular, drystone walls that remain of the Post-Medieval cottages, such as the one on the east face of Roughtor.[43]

Outhouses became increasingly a part of these farming settlements – dairies, pigsties, barns and cowsheds among them.[44] On Bodmin Moor they built beehive huts[45] like those of the Late Medieval period, except that these – as at Leaze and Garrow – were actually in and around the farmsteads. Holes drilled at the sides of some entrances show that there had once been doors. Similar huts for a variety of uses occur elsewhere in Britain and Europe. In Cornwall they lack shelves, so they cannot have been dairies. Current theories are that they were shelter for animals – chickens, for example – or places to store the lime spread as a dressing to counter acidity, or to store sand, used in the house to keep floors clean.

Beyond the settlements there were other developments, perhaps influenced by the cooling temperatures sometimes known as 'The Little Ice Age'.[46] Fuel came from peat, known as turf, which was cut from moorland peat bogs and stacked to dry

This old cottage, photographed in the 19th century, illustrates the changes that occurred over the Post-Medieval period in the houses of ordinary people. Instead of the Late Medieval longhouse with its two-entrance cross-passage, here there is one entrance with a formal porch in front. Even the poor began to claim privacy, as the porch is a barrier to free entry. Thatching rather than slates was the norm for roofs, fireplaces shifted to the wall and chimneys were added.

161

Peat, or 'turf', was used as a fuel on Cornish moorlands up until the early to mid-20th century. Turfsteeds such as this on Bodmin Moor were constructed to dry out the peat. A square or rectangular platform was surrounded by a ditch and an outer bank. The peat was placed in a stack over the platform, and the excess water drained into the ditch.

on roughly rectangular platforms surrounded by ditches. These turfsteeds are found on other Cornish moorlands, too: there are a number, for example, at Trelan[47] on the Lizard. Finally, farmers began to consolidate their medieval strip fields by purchase and exchange into larger and more productive fields. A good example can be seen at Treskilling in Luxulyan, where one large, open field with strips is bordered by smaller fields that are obviously combinations of former long strips.[48]

The rise of the gentry: metropolitan life in Cornwall

Although the gentry in Cornwall are seen historically as having mixed views on the English state – as witness the 1497 and 1549 rebellions – the archaeological evidence shows them as increasingly drawn into its orbit. Private armies had been banned but some private fortification remained. Fear of invasion by French or Spanish armies meant that the Crown needed a coherent system of defence, and new fortifications built by the Crown in Cornwall were run by members of the local gentry given the authority to do so. The latter, in their private capacities, built themselves stately homes and laid out ornamental gardens in the prevailing taste of their times.

Coherent defence was the strongest integrating force. Henry VIII created the first national system of coastal defences, which ran all the way from the Thames Estuary to the Isles of Scilly.[49] That system began by assimilating castles and strong points that were already there – at Fowey, St Michael's Mount and in the Old Town of St Mary's in Scilly; and it was steadily reinforced, then and in later reigns. The

Great Map of the West drawn up around 1540 sets out the original concept and shows, for example, that a pair of castles at St Mawes and Trefusis Point were to have guarded the mouth of the Fal; the choice was Trefusis, not Pendennis, in order to protect the approach to Penryn. Yet if an enemy could capture Pendennis, he would have an excellent beachhead, easy to supply from the sea, and beyond the reach of any cannonball from St Mawes. So, on second thoughts, they built at Pendennis where the estuary is also narrower, and even then the design of the castle changed even as they were building it. Excavations[50] have shown that the sequence began with a cylindrical keep with three gun decks, but the lowest of these quickly became redundant when a chemise was added. A chemise is a gun deck with a bank of rubble and earth faced with a crenellated stone wall, and the effect was to bring the lower cannon forward. In the 1550s a governor's residence with a gatehouse and bridge was added. Finally, in 1598–99 bastioned earthworks were added around a much larger area and the original castle became militarily redundant, and perhaps simply turned into an extension of the governor's residence.

In Scilly, King Charles' Castle (Tresco) and Harry's Walls (St Mary's) were an addition to the existing Late Medieval Ennor Castle on St Mary's, now surviving only as traces of low stone walling.[51] Harry's Walls was to have been a battery in the new Italian design, but local topography meant that it could not be fully completed. King Charles' Castle (originally and more properly known as Tresco Castle) overlooks the harbour of New Grimsby and was built between 1548 and 1552. It had a semi-octagonal frontal battery, with rectangular rooms behind, including a kitchen. The Isles of Scilly were on key trade routes, and some of the material found in the castle probably comes from shipwreck. Colourful Spanish majolica wall tiles were used for the floor, alongside tiles that may well have come from St Nicholas' Priory, the dissolved monastery on the island. 17th-century earthworks beside the Castle date either to the Civil War or to continued Royalist resistance during the period of Cromwell's Commonwealth. After the Parliamentarians took Scilly the castle was plundered for a new one – Cromwell's Castle – closer to the shore.

As well as combining in national schemes of defence, the gentry were taking up with people of their own station across the region and the country as a whole. This meant that the owners of Cornish stately homes and their gardens now reflected the taste of their social equals nationally, and ties of class took precedence over the claims of neighbourhood. Stowe House, near Kilkhampton in North Cornwall, vividly exposes the trend.[52] Early in the 18th century the main male line of its owners – the Grenvilles, Earls of Bath – died out. The house was abandoned, then demolished 30 years later, before it could be touched by the improvements that overtook other aristocratic houses of the late 17th century. Little more than its great footprint is left – to the east of the later farmhouse, Stowe Barton. The plan is typical of the

extreme formality of its early Post-Medieval times, and consists of a rectangular block 192 x 103 m (630 x 338 ft), divided into eight compartments ranged in two lines of four laid out east to west. The northern four compartments had an entrance court in the east leading up to stairs that flared out to give access to the house, with two gardens behind. The southern four compartments were walled gardens giving warmth and shelter from the strong westerly winds to disciplined rows of plants. A long drive from the valley below drew the eye up to a house that declared itself aloof from the habitations of ordinary people. Wherever they appeared in England, walls, drives and imposing buildings let it be known that here were the homes of substantial people who were happy to distance themselves from any poor relations nearby and from the local community, and unashamed to disown the obligations that once applied to them.

The other side of this distancing from actual neighbours was the closeness of shared sensibility with others of the same class far away. Visiting one another, the gentry would all have felt comfortable in settings that would have been alien and somewhat forbidding to poorer local people. Stowe House was built to a design derived from Sir Roger Pratt's Clarendon House of 1665 in London, and also bears a resemblance to Belton House in Lincolnshire. Even the bricklayers and stone carvers who built Stowe House were brought in from London. There had been a

pedimented doorway opening onto the principal or privy garden – reminiscent of the contemporary Kirby Hall, Northamptonshire, where a similar doorway from the privy garden led to the main suite of rooms in the house. The bricks for the house and for the walled gardens are the earliest surviving brickwork in Cornwall, though there is more impressive 17th-century brickwork to be seen at Ince Castle, Saltash.[53] Most of the remains of Stowe now consist of earthworks, though decent stretches of brick wall are to be found in the northern compartments. The gardens were laid out with shrubs and pathways in characteristic formal patterns. From the late 18th century, the parkland or 'English Garden' replaced these formalised gardens with an idealised 'natural' landscape.

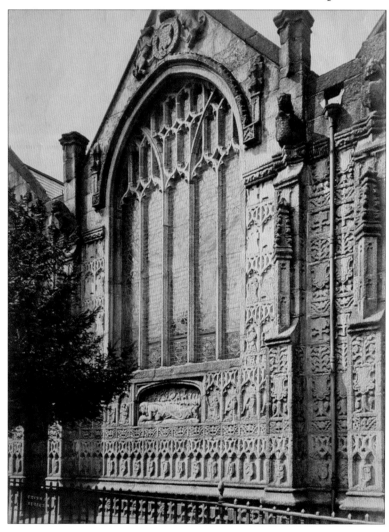

There are some churches with elaborate carved stonework that still survives from the Reformation – the most spectacular being at St Mary Magdalene in Launceston. There is hardly any exterior space left undecorated.

Conflict and division in churches and religious imagery

The Reformation in England was complicated, with changes in religious policy from one reign to the next, and with differences in the degree of its influence from one region to another. In Cornwall a certain amount of resistance does seem to be evidenced in the archaeology. For example, at Probus Church in mid-Cornwall, niches in the tower are now empty where statues would once have been – which may suggest conformity. In the 19th century, however, repairs and improvement revealed two skulls walled up in a secret niche.[54] That the church has two saints, St Probus and St Grace, suggests that these may be pre-Reformation saints' relics. In the late 19th and early 20th centuries many High Anglican churches in Cornwall had their rood screens restored or brought out for all to see, not always in their original place. Some are reproductions but some – as at St Buryan and St Ewe – were restored from the original screens, or parts of them, that had been hidden away.[55] Wayside crosses,[56] a major feature of Late Medieval Cornwall, remained untouched, even those with representations of the crucifixion like that of St Just (in the south-western corner of the churchyard), as were holy wells such as those at Luxulyan and Perranwell.[57]

Apart from being the arena of religious conflict, churches were places where communities met and left a social record. Memorials were no longer restricted to the gentry but, from the late 16th century, also commemorated the wealthy and the growing merchant classes. They could be brasses or stone plaques, sometimes of imported stone like marble, sometimes engraved in Latin rather than English. The gentry, of course, created ever more magnificent monuments, like that of John Robartes (a mayor of Truro) and his wife – richly decorated and complete with their statues under a canopy – in St Mary's Church, Truro, and now in the northern transept of the Cathedral.[58] Patronage gave the gentry a splendid means of advertising their wealth and piety. In the early 16th century, Sir Henry Trecarrell rebuilt much of St Mary Magdalene, Launceston in finely carved granite. In decorative relief on the exterior walls are St George and the Dragon, St Martin of Tours, a Royal coat of arms and a recumbent Mary Magdalene at the east end of the church under the window.[59] This is the richest decoration on any Cornish church. For those not quite so wealthy pews were introduced, and pew rents charged; the least wealthy often had to stand.

The Post-Medieval period in Cornwall was therefore one of increasing wealth but also increasing social division. Wealth, class, ethnicity, religion and even outlook on life divided sections of Cornish society. On the other hand, industries that later became emblematic of Cornwall had become well established by the end of the period. The combination of lateen and broadsails produced a maritime revolution that led to more reliable and frequent traffic by sea, and so to greater movement of goods in and out of Cornwall. Trade links created contacts with the Mediterranean and Germany, and these could account for traditions and folk beliefs that have left their mark on the archaeological record.

CHAPTER NINE

CORNWALL AND THE DIASPORA: A WORLD INDUSTRIAL CULTURE

The Industrial Period (1750–1880)

THE INDUSTRIAL REVOLUTION brought Cornwall dramatic economic growth, larger settlements and a mobile population. It also widened the growing social gulf of Post-Medieval times. In fact the wealth it generated was so unequally divided that the gentry and the masses almost inhabited different universes. The gentry identified with England, with places like Bath and London and with English high culture; whereas ordinary people began to identify themselves not only with their community in Cornwall but also with the wider Cornish community round the world. Thanks to its early lead in hard-rock mining, Cornwall could export skilled labour and technology to the United States, Australia, Mexico, New Zealand, Chile, Bolivia, Canada and South Africa.[1] Although rich benefactors paid for some of the education behind the new skills, evangelical Christianity was probably the single greatest influence on Cornish minds. Old legends did not perish, because they were hastily being put on record, but folk memory treated them as idle and valueless stories, with sad results for some of the ancient monuments that embodied them.

For all these changes and the accompanying social deprivation, confidence and hope were the spirit of the times. Belief in religion, the community, the family and new ideology are all in the archaeological record. One increasingly powerful idea was the sense of Celtic identity. Being of ancient British stock only connected the Cornish to Wales, Scotland and Brittany, but to be Celtic implied a long Classical heritage. As Celts they were supposed to be related to Iron Age people like the Gauls who sacked Rome and the Galatians who invaded Ancient Greece.[2] It was in this period that private individuals, parish churches and, later, museums began to collect material relating to a 'Celtic' past. As for the contemporary Cornish, their material culture was highly distinctive, in spite of industrial mass-production.

A crucial factor in Cornwall's powerful role in the birth of a global economy was that it was part of the largest empire on earth. Great Britain was the first country to industrialise and, within it, Cornwall was one of the first regions to do so. The British

Empire had spread over different climatic zones, could get at different sorts of mineral wealth, had a foothold (at the very least) on every continent and possessed strategic islands in every ocean. By supporting revolutions in Latin America against Spanish rule in the 1820s, Britain won lasting and advantageous trade agreements.[3] After colonies and ex-colonies, Latin America was the next most important destination of Cornish migrants.[4]

Change and innovation in Cornwall's industries

Cornwall had been an industrial centre even before the Industrial Revolution partly because it had minerals and fish but – just as important – also because of its access to the sea. The main industries of the Industrial period were mining, fishing, china clay, quarrying and (to feed all the people employed) farming. Crucial to the success of every one of them, however, was transport. It was changing fast and radically in the four key areas of shipping, turnpike roads,[5] canals and railways – and of these shipping was the most important for Cornwall.

Many new ports were built and others improved. In fact most of Cornwall's small quays were built in this period, like the square quay at Woodgate Pill on the Fowey, which is made of horizontally lain stones mortared together, and which juts out into a tidal creek.[6] Navigation in Cornwall's treacherous seas was a serious obstacle to the growth of seaborne trade. Among dozens of wrecks was that of the Hanover in 1763: a postal packet ship bound for Falmouth from Lisbon, it was swept miles off course by a violent storm and eventually struck the cliffs of St Agnes.[7] The wreck was preserved by a sandy gully below the cliffs, and yielded gold coins and more than fifty iron cannon of different sizes (which seem to have been a job lot of unofficial cargo, picked up by the captain by way of very private enterprise). There was a market for cannon because wars with Spain and France meant that even merchantmen needed

Port facilities were improved significantly during the period. At St Ives, the pier was tackled twice. The first stage was Smeaton's Pier extending out to the stone lighthouse; the second saw a slight change in direction, ending in a slender metal lighthouse. Many of the buildings around the harbour were constructed as dwellings for workers or for maritime purposes, such as sail lofts. They are now mainly holiday cottages and cafes.

*Fear of French invasion saw
the Tamar estuary bristling
with fortifications. One of the
most spectacular is Tregantle
Castle, which guarded a
potential overland route to
the Lynher and thence to the
Tamar and an attack on
Plymouth itself.*

to be armed. To make the approaches to land less dangerous, more lighthouses and
day marks were built. The Wolf Rock lighthouse between Land's End and the Isles
of Scilly was successfully completed in 1869.[8] Its landing platform and tower were
made of granite blocks, and the first 12 metres (39 feet) are solid except for a space
for the water tank. An ingenious inward opening door made of gunmetal solves the
problem of suction created by the retreating surge during storms.

Port facilities improved. Lighthouses were built on breakwaters: one of the most
impressive, on Smeaton's Pier in St Ives, is made of granite blocks in the shape of a
pawn from a game of chess.[9] Signal stations used semaphore to warn ports and the
authorities generally of approaching ships – identifying them as commercial, naval
or hostile. The Admiralty ran the earliest of these, like those on Dodman Point,[10]
near St Austell and at St Martin's Head on the Isles of Scilly. The former consisted
of accommodation, an enclosure for a flagpole secured by metal links to the four corners and a small tower for a telescope lookout; the latter[11] had larger accommodation, an old ship's mast as a flagpole, a latrine, a storeroom, even an animal pen.
Later, commercial operations took over from the military. For example, G.C. Fox
and Company built a two-storey signal station with castellations and a signal platform
on the roof at Bass Point on the Lizard (which was subsequently bought by Lloyd's
of London[12]). Shipping had to be protected, and the forts at Falmouth and Plymouth
were upgraded while new fortifications were built at St Ives on the Island.[13] A whole
series of forts went up on either side of the Tamar,[14] notably on the peninsula
between the English Channel and the Lynher, with its huge stone and earthwork
forts, and there was even a railway line connecting some of them to a port on the
Lynher side. Tregantle, as the first of the so-called Palmerston forts,[15] built because
of fears that Emperor Napoleon III of France would threaten Britain, had a fortune

spent on it.[16] It had special bastions known as caponiers, with several levels of gun and rifle ports and a stone keep complete with drawbridge, which made for a strange mixture of modern thinking and medieval fantasy.

Meanwhile inland transport improved – paid for by industry or tolls.[17] Roads like the Old St Ives Road or 'Watershed Way' and the Old Land's End Road had just followed high ground to avoid wet valley bottoms,[18]but the new roads were metalled with sand and gravel. The 'new ' St Ives to St Just road runs along the edge of the coastal platform below the high granite ridges. Dug into the hillside along its length are small quarries for its construction and maintenance. The first signposts appeared: small, carved stone obelisks gave the distances to the nearest towns, and were testimony to growing literacy. One at Crows-an-Wra even has a hand helpfully pointing the way.

Another important development at the end of the 18th century, especially at the Devon end of the north coast, was canals.[19] There had been little hope for industry without them on the north coast where rivers with silted sandbanks ran down to a shore of high cliffs or shallow sandy bays. The greatest of the canal systems was built from 1819 to 1826,[20] stretching miles inland from Bude to the specially created Tamar Lake at Alfardisworthy. It served Marhamchurch, Hobbacott, Red Post and Venn on its main branch, and minor branches took in Blagdonmoor, Bridgerule and

Industrialisation made a significant impact on farming. A large area of poor marginal land called the Culm Measures, in the north of Cornwall and part of Devon, was transformed by the importation of shell sand from coastal dunes that neutralised acid soils. This photograph is of the Bude Canal, which allowed barges to take heavy loads of sand to inland farms.

Druxton Wharf. It provided a large area of north Cornwall and Devon with calcareous shell sand from the shore to 'sweeten' or lower the acidity of moorland soils, and thus help to increase the acreage and output of once marginal land. To help boats go upstream, buckets of water dropping into wells pulled ropes attached to the boats. In other parts of the canals, wheels driven by water power pulled the ropes.

Railways started essentially to serve mining interests. The earliest were designed for horse-drawn carriages, as a Director's Carriage in the Royal Cornwall Museum at Truro shows. The most impressive of the railway monuments of this early phase is the Treffry Viaduct, near Luxulyan, built in 1842.[21] It is about 230 m long and almost 33 m high (700 x 100 ft), and contains an aqueduct sealed under granite blocks, with ruts for the rails that ran above them. The carriages were pulled by horses, and served Treffry's clay pits, whilst the water drove water-wheels to provide power on the inclines further along the railway. The first steam loco-motive was produced by Richard Tre-

The great engineer Isambard Kingdom Brunel extended the Great Western Railway into Cornwall, connecting up many smaller industrial lines. The original pillars of the viaduct on St Georges Street, Truro, are still standing beside the ones presently in use. They are smaller, though, and this 19th-century photograph shows why. The original viaduct had a wooden superstructure.

vithick in Camborne in 1801.[22] A reconstruction built for its bicentenary by the Trevithick Society shows what thermal efficiency he achieved by putting the furnace within the boiler itself[23] – thus launching the revolution in steam locomotion. Interestingly, the chimney was at the back, not at the front of the locomotive as it is today. The smaller industrial lines connected with the Great Western Railway from 1859 when Brunel built the Royal Albert Bridge over the Tamar,[24] which is still very much in use. Not so Brunel's viaducts in Cornwall, however. In many places, like St George's Street in Truro,[25] the supporting columns of Brunel's viaducts can be seen alongside the later ones that now support track, but they are not so high – the reason being that originally they had superstructures made of wood.

The mines that the railways served variously produced tin and, particularly, copper. Although it had been cheaper in Wales, especially at Parys Mountain on Anglesey, copper mining still paid because of strong demand – arising particularly from coinage, gunmetal and brass in all its uses.[26] The deepest mine in Cornwall, Dolcoath in Camborne, was primarily a copper mine though tin was mined at the greatest depth.[27] Mining's ancillary work usually had its site in river valleys. In the western Cot Valley,[28] near St Just, there are stamps, dressing floors, buddles for separating ores from lighter sediment and streaming works; they were close to water because it is essential to the work of concentrating ore. China Clay was another industry that exploited valleys. After some experimental work on Tregonning Hill,[29]

Many small fishing operations flourished at this time. The long building behind the beach at Penberth Cove here is the fish cellar where pilchards would have been processed for export. To the right of the boats is a capstan, used to winch boats ashore in this windswept part of West Penwith.

the industry started in earnest at St Stephen-in-Brannel in the late 18th century. China Clay needed water too – to power water-wheels and to fill the settling tanks that separate the finer from the coarser grains of the decomposed granite.[30]

Mining made good profits, but it taxed the lives of ordinary people – not least the children who had to cut narrow 'adits', or drainage channels, through rock with little or no light to help them. These can be seen in the shaft open to the public at Geevor mine. The 'Bal-Maidens',[31] or mining women, had a tough life too. They worked above ground, breaking up lumps of ore in all weathers, while the stamps that crushed the broken ore made a noise that deafened them. Imagine their relationship with their menfolk, whose eyes were weakened from working long hours in the dark.

Farming, of course, was crucial to the support of a growing industrial population that no longer produced much of its own food. The enclosure of moorlands into crofts with regular rectangular and square fields around them virtually obliterated some areas of once open landscape, and any earlier archaeology that went with it.[32] The moorland of Carnmenellis bordered by Helston, Redruth and Penryn all but vanished, except for a few small patches.

The fishing industry was carried out on a massive scale from a multitude of small ports, but the technology was still surprisingly primitive. A typical example is Penberth[33] – a small windswept cove just east of the Logan Rock in West Penwith. Here an animal-powered capstan winched the boats up the shore, and fish cellars were used for curing and packing the fish. The huer's hut on the cliffs is little more than a windbreak formed of large granite boulders. It is thought that an upturned boat was put over it to give extra shelter from the rain. Little wonder that free-trading – or smuggling in official parlance – was a popular way of making ends meet.

Meanwhile smuggling facilities became increasingly sophisticated. Kegs of brandy and rum could be tied together and anchored to the seabed by granite boulders with grooves round the middle to take the other end of the rope.[34] One such boulder is on display in the Museum in Hugh Town on St Mary's, Isles of Scilly. Smugglers' caches ashore were ever more elaborate – like the so-called *fogous* at Porthcothan, south of Padstow, Ethy Woods and Norway House on the Fowey.[35] These are either cellars or artificial caves carved out – as marks on the walls show – with metal picks. In west Cornwall the 'hulls' or underground storage chambers no doubt reflected a real need of space for storing farm surpluses, but came in useful if anything needed hiding too. A good example of a hull is at Home Farm, Bolenowe Lane, Troon (near Camborne).[36] The entrance is at the base of a hedge belonging to a deserted cottage. Two granite uprights support a lintel leading to a crawling passage (which has partly collapsed): it extends about 5.5 m (18 ft) to a bend, then on for some 3.7 m (12 ft). These subterfuges were a response to the ever tougher measures taken by the customs. An instance is a large brick chimney called the 'King's Pipe' on Custom House Quay in Falmouth.[37]

Smaller service industries fared even worse than mining and fishing. Pottery found on sites of this period is increasingly imported rather than locally produced. A number of local potteries produced coarse wares – like those from Penzance, Mawgan-in-Meneague, Truro, St Columb Major and the area around Bude, Stratton and Holsworthy (Devon).[38] By the end of the 18th century the local product was less able to compete with factory-produced white china.

The emergence of an industrial culture and its dispersal

The county was affected by mass-production, but it still kept many of its own ways of doing things. As Cornwall itself was one of the first places to industrialise, there was no ready-made body of rules about how industrial communities were supposed

Smuggling was a major industry in Cornwall, but controls were becoming more stringent by the early 19th century. The 'King's Pipe' on Custom House Quay, Falmouth was a large brick chimney prominently positioned by the customhouse. Contraband tobacco could be publicly burnt to ensure a clear message and to prevent it being corruptly put back on the market.

to run, so the close-knit extended family and the chapel continued to permeate Cornish society. The mores of the time left a lasting impression on industry, country life and the home not only in Cornwall but also in Cornish communities abroad. This 'Cornish transnationalism'[39] can be seen through its industrial and domestic culture.

Industrial processes were self-replicating because workers and their families identified so strongly with their industries that new styles and technologies quickly became tradition. The distinctive design of 'Cornish Engine Houses' (for Trevithick and later engines[40]) is so powerful an image that few are aware of the earlier designs for Newcomen and Watt engines. In fact only three survive: at Wheal Pool, near Helston; Wheal Henry, near St Day; and Carnon Stream, near Devoran.[41] To cope with the stresses produced by the then wooden beams, the walls were internally stepped; and anything bulky and heavy – like the boiler – went in through a large rear door. Even these early designs were peculiarly Cornish. The later Cornish engine houses typically have a strong bob-wall at one end to support the metal rocking beam, reinforced by an arch underneath. Whilst the building was of local stone, the upper courses of the chimney were laid with bricks imported from Somerset.

Industrialisation brought mass-produced appliances such as the Cornish Range, which replaced the open fire and the cloam oven for cooking and heating. Fuelled by coal, the range had an oven and hot plates.

Ordinary houses could become a marker for Cornish culture too, even though they used mass-produced materials. Investigations of a cottage at Carn Euny, Sancreed (1750 to 1800[42] and then in its mid-19th-century phase) showed that it had regional features as well as industrial products like mortar and lime plaster. On the right of the hearth and separated from it by stone walling was a furze cupboard, where furze or gorse was stored in the late 18th-century phase – the furze being fuel for the fire. All the cooking was done over an open slab on the fire. (In other cottages, cupboards that had once held furze, whatever their later use, had been identified by the scratch marks it left behind.[43]) A later recess lined with coal soot[44] from the mid-19th century, when the fireplace probably acquired an oven, is likely to be a 'fringle'. A fringle was a smaller channel and flue set into the main hearth, with its sides made up of stones, mortar and even some earth. It was to save fuel when a larger fire was not needed.

Such features were carried by the ethnic Cornish overseas. The round-buttressed chimney of Post-Medieval Cornwall had survived into the Industrial period, but now incorporating lime plaster and mortar. In the military settlement of Victoria in Port Essington (Coburg Peninsula, Northern Territory), five such chimneys have come to light.[45] In 1838 the British attempted to settle north Australia in order to control the lucrative trade in *trepang* or *bêche-de-mer*, a shellfish caught in those waters and exported to markets in China. The first simple bark huts for the troops were followed by five slightly larger buildings for those bringing their families. These too were made of 'bush materials', and each of the cottages had a round-buttressed chimney: a fallen tree has demolished one, but the other four are intact. The chimneys were built of local stone, with the external faces shaped and the internal surface finished off with lime plaster. The arches over the fireplace were brick, which helps to date these structures to the building phase after 1839. Inconsistencies in construction revealed by gaps in the masonry, particularly in the timberwork, show what a lot of improvisation went into early colonial settlements like these. Another site at Glenelg in South Australia dating to 1836–38 may, on the evidence of a contemporary picture, be a related site as some of the marines were transferred from Glenelg to Victoria in 1838.

In many cases communities went *en masse*. In the Burra area of South Australia the town of Redruth was founded and laid out in a typically Cornish manner. There were small cottages arranged in front of the footpath and methodist churches.[46] The local mine was set out with three Cornish engine houses with circular chimneys.[47] The isolated nature of working-class frontier settlements tended to reinforce the role of community and put a premium on frugality.[48] So people recycled rather than throw anything away, built houses to a standard design and shared what they had. The example of Kawau Island, Northland (New Zealand)[49]

Amazingly, miners' cottages in Australia, such as these in Redruth in the Burra area (above), were built to the same dimensions as those back in Cornwall, despite all the available space! Colonial Cornish industrial settlements were spartan and facilities basic, though this was made up for by a close-knit community spirit. This was a far cry from the lawless 'Wild West'. The mining settlement in Miners' Bay, Kawau Island, New Zealand (left) consisted of weatherboard houses, simple and unadorned.

177

FRUGAL LIVES

It is not just the dwellings and workplaces of the Cornish that were frugal and simple. These images from Kawau Island, New Zealand show that clothing was not fancy or decorative either. Miners were supposed to provide their own work clothes, and work tools too! Alcohol was frowned upon, so tea and tobacco were among the few treats that were consumed. Pipes were cheap and mass-produced, made of clay, such as the one illustrated here.

revealed that in the settlement at Miners Bay from 1844 to 1854 there was little sign of luxury except for some blue teaware probably connected with the church. Most of the goods were standard stuff, bought on the local market, and it is their strikingly religious connotation that marks the settlement as Cornish.

Cornish influences were not one way, however. The communities abroad sent back money that made a real difference to their kith and kin, and when their members returned they brought ideas from the new lands with them. There are a variety of exotic place-names that date from this time: Californian Moor at Four Lanes, Australia Terrace at Drump Lane and Chili Road at Illogan Highway.[50] People brought back mementoes of their overseas experiences. For instance, a copper badge was found at Tresavean Mine inscribed 'Junction Shaft, C.A. Mine, Bisbee, Arizona'. It was issued by the Calumet and Atlanta Mining Company (C.A.).[51]

Religion and belief in Cornish culture

Religion had become a source of class conflict by this period, with the interiors of churches dominated by plaques commemorating the rich and influential; and the right to sit in a pew had to be bought. Some of the gentry even built private chapels where they could pray without rubbing shoulders with the lower orders. William Rashleigh, for instance, built a chapel of ease in 1815 at Tregaminion, on his Menabilly estate near Fowey, with a memorial to his wife Rachel.[52] Above the porch is his family's coat of arms just in case there should be any doubt as to its private nature. A more impressive private chapel is at Trelowarren (near Helston), which forms a wing of the main building.[53] Inside, the walls and ceilings are covered with exquisite stucco – ornate plaster decoration supported by hidden frames. Such private splendours hardly encouraged the working classes to trust in the religious leadership of the gentry and the priests who seemed to be in their pockets.

Outside the churches there was revolution in the graveyards. For the first time headstones began to commemorate ordinary people,[54] for cheaper stone slabs from the quarries meant that more people could afford them. (Earlier examples do exist but they are rare.) Typefaces became familiar as printed books became more common, and stone masons could work from cheap copy-books in a variety of lap-idary styles. Cheap quarry-cut stone increasingly brought standardisation, and ever more people could afford memorials. Even so, the graveyard was hardly a classless society. Mausoleums in churchyards like those at Treslothan and Veryan, panelled slate chest tombs in St-Mawgan-in-Pydar and the impressive Hawkins monument in Probus churchyard all testify to the difference that wealth could make to sepulchral splendour.[55] The Hawkins monument[56] is dedicated to Sir Christopher Hawkins, who died in 1829, and consists of four large 17th-century cavaliers with breast armour, swords and sashes: they kneel as they bear the upper corners of the tomb on their shoulders. The main part of the tomb is decorated with baroque pilasters, car-touches and cherubs.

In spite of the social division, this period did witness a growth in religious fervour – in particular in the growth of Nonconformism as a popular alternative to Angli-canism.[57] Although Nonconformism existed before the arrival of John and Charles Wesley in the 1740s, the Quakers[58] and Presbyterians who made up the Old Dissent were not populist. Not only was the new Methodism of the people, but the working class also saw it as being of their own Cornish people. There is a tale of a Sunday school lesson in the 1850s, related by A.K. Hamilton Jenkin, where the teacher explains that Cornwall is not a 'furren country' but 'kidged to a furren country by the top hand'.[59] In other words, Methodism was seen as a kind of Cornish 'national' reli-gion. From Cornwall to Devon there is a marked drop in numbers of Nonconformist chapels – which in Cornwall easily outnumber Anglican churches. Often the chapels served smaller or new communities that had no church. For example, the area strad-dling Pendeen between Carnyorth and Bojewyan has seven chapels to one church, and three of those chapels predate Pendeen church.[60]

The earliest places of Methodist worship were private houses or open-air loca-tions such as Gwennap Pit, or even the courtyard houses at Chysauster.[61] Whereas Anglican churches embodied a history of the faith, the chapels were seen as enact-ing a living covenant between their congregations and God. Nevertheless, they fol-lowed the Anglican trend of the time – towards the Classical and away from the Gothic. They were variously rectangular, round or octagonal; they had galleries; and their architecture emphasised the Word of God. At first they had prominent pulpits with the seating ranged round them: from 1850 the rostrum replaced the pulpit, as it made for easier access and afforded space for more preachers. There was much more seating than in Anglican churches, the pews were all of the same design and there were free pews for the poor. The earliest example of these gallery box pews is in the Wesleyan Chapel at Carharrack, built in 1815.[62] At first the singing in chapel was unaccompanied, and the introduction of organs was resisted until 1822. The Queen Street Chapel in Penzance installed an organ as early as 1827 and thereafter

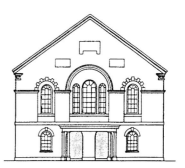

Ostentation was usually reserved for the exterior façades of Nonconformist chapels, such as this one in St Just-in-Penwith.

The style of chapel interiors could vary enormously within a 'circuit', or church district, because of differences in the social status of the respective congregations. The Chapel Street church here was in a fashionable and wealthy part of Penzance and boasts a double-decker mahogany pulpit, panelled box pews and stained-glass windows.

organs became a feature of chapels. Education was seen as important to the Nonconformist mission, so Sunday schools and day schools were added or built nearby. In 1865 at Charlestown, large windows suitable for lighting up a warehouse were built into the first floor of the building behind the chapel for the schoolroom.[63]

Chapel religion radiated from the pulpit and the classroom. Anglican and Catholic churches also laid new stress on religious education, with less effect on local culture; but all denominations united in decrying 'superstition' and immorality. The Wesleys made clear their opposition to Cornwall's folklore, particularly the beliefs about fairy folk, and disapproved of folk dances and the sport of hurling. All this side of folk culture went into sharp decline and people came to see their identity as linked to the human community rather than to their native land. The land itself was simply a commodity, to be altered at will without social or religious cost. The landscapes, now romanticised, were scarred by railways, canals, sprawling settlements, waste dumps, mine tailings and rivers silted up and poisoned with effluent.[64] A good example is Kilmar Tor on the eastern side of Bodmin Moor – a site of extensive quarrying.[65] Terraces of stone rubble levelled to simplify yet more quarrying cover up the natural outline of the granite. Running from the valley below, between Kilmar Tor and Bearah Tor, are the remains of a railway. Ramps leading down from the tor end at a platform of just the right height – that of the trucks that carry the stone away.

If no one thought twice about scarring the landscape, there was nothing sacred about ancient monuments either. Bronze Age barrows like the Rillaton Barrow were plundered for treasure, as the art historian and antiquarian William Penaluna recorded in 1838. Cornish people had once believed they were the haunt of Spriggans (pronounced 'Spridjans'),[66] who brought bad luck – even death – to anyone who violated their barrows or cairns and rifled their treasure. That treasure was now there for the taking – to join some collection as evidence of the ancient Celts, or just to be sold. Once, if only once, the vandalism went too far. William Borlase, in his *Antiquities* of 1769, writes about rock formations that were held in awe, and in a discussion of 'rock-idols' he mentions the Logan Stone[67] at Treryn Dinas in West Penwith. (All such stones – Men-Amber in Cornish – rocked naturally on their point of balance, and some were credited with powers of speech and prophecy.) When a certain Lieutenant Goldsmith[68] and the crew of his revenue cutter decided to see if they could topple it completely in 1815, using the latest engineering technology, they were all too successful. Such was the outcry, however, that he had to put it back, but it has never rocked since.

On the positive side, village rivalries began to break down, and they were replaced by a spirit of mutual support that was essential for coping with widespread poverty and with the effects of emigration by so many of the young and strong. One example of social cohesion in action was the temperance movement. Alcohol, mass-produced and cheap, was now a real threat to industrial communities, and members of the temperance societies pledged themselves never to touch it. In the St Ives and Penzance areas in particular there was a plethora of Teetotal Chapels. On the Island in St Ives there is an actual Teetotal Street, and there are chapels in Fore Street and Chapel Street in St Ives and one in Ludgvan.[69] There is a certain irony to be detected in this stern social control considering that, as the Celts they thought they were, it should have been in character to be wild, emotional and uninhibited. Be that as it may, the mechanism that kept people together in this time of change and uncertainty was evangelical Christianity.

Evangelical Christianity – Nonconformist and Low Church Anglican – spread with Cornish people to other parts of the world, and took moral strictness with it. Archaeological finds from Miners Bay on Kawau Island, New Zealand can be interpreted in religious and moral terms.[70] The glassware contains few bottles for alcohol, and only one that might have held perfume. Local newspapers of the time record a thriving Temperance Society on the island and print the names of those who broke the pledge – suggesting powerful social control. Perfume bottles are common in colonial mining settlements, and are often associated with the recorded presence of prostitutes. In Miners Bay the family-minded and godly community wanted none of that unseemliness.

Teetotalism was a significant feature of many Cornish communities, and could be adopted by whole chapel congregations. Even this street on the Island in St Ives was named 'Teetotal Street'.

The Cornish engine house is probably the most recognisable and iconic monument of Cornish culture – no matter where it may be found. This is the engine house and chimney (1865) from Wheal Hughes, a copper mine in Moonta, South Australia, which contained a Cornish pumping engine produced by Harveys of Hayle, Cornwall.

Social life and identity of the wealthy

In social life, class division and separate identity were writ large. The upper classes identified with a trans-regional elite and focused on places where the genteel gathered like London, Bath and Weymouth. The lower classes identified with the region, Cornwall, but increasingly focussed on their worldwide community. For many the metropolitan centre was New York or San Francisco rather than London. These two separate but parallel universes co-existed almost like two separate ethnic groups. In Scotland the term 'Anglo-Scottish' is often used to describe some of the Scottish gentry, and there ought by analogy – at least for this period – to be such a label as 'Anglo-Cornish'. An extreme instance of this identification with England is the folly on Kit Hill, near Callington.[71] Here Sir John Call of Whiteford, Stoke Climsland, erected what he thought of as an old Saxon castle to commemorate the victory of the Saxons over the Cornish in AD 838 at nearby Hingston Town. It seems to have been meant as a motte and bailey castle (Sir John's knowledge of the past was obviously sketchy), with the idea that the keep on the motte should be visible from his estate at Whiteford.

The emergence of Bath as a royal spa town and a fashionable centre for balls and other elite entertainments gave Cornwall something to aspire to, and Truro especially took Bath as its architectural model. The Assembly Rooms were built in the late 1780s, and the façade still survives on the north side of High Cross (the square in front of the Cathedral).[72] Built of honey-coloured Bath stone and designed in the classical style, it has two roundels with heads in profile – one of Shakespeare, the other of Garrick, the most famous actor of the time. Above and in the centre is a third roundel with a relief image of Thalia, Muse of Comedy. The Assembly Rooms were used for a variety of cultural entertainments and were important to the functioning of Society with a capital 'S'. Unmarried young women, for example, could meet eligible young men in a safe and socially controlled way with their chaperones.[73] That they could marry only from their own class meant that they had to make dangerous forays into a world of unknown suitors from beyond their familiar neighbourhood.

Bath was the pattern for the rest of the town too.[74] Thomas Daniell built the Mansion House in Prince Street with a frontage of Bath stone[75] from a quarry belonging to his wife's uncle, Ralph Allen, who was mayor of Bath. Lemon Street, built by Sir William Lemon in the early 19th century, is still largely untouched, apart from the intrusion of a cinema. Classical frontages of Bath stone line both sides of the street, and St John's church at the top of the eastern side – Italianate and complete with cupola – was added shortly afterwards in 1827–28. When the River Kenwyn was diverted to run underground, the present centre round Victoria Street and River Street became available for new building, and a miniature Bath crescent – Walsingham Place – went up on the eastern side of the square. Splendid frontages with columned porches lead up to this narrow and exclusive little location. Other streets got their names from the fashion of their times: the naming of King Street, Prince Street and Duke Street even suggests a delicate, but still grand, order of precedence.

On the private estates there were other diversions. The influence of the newly popular spa town of Weymouth can be traced to the 1780s, when the Duke of Gloucester and King George III began to patronise it.[76] When Dr Richard Russell

For Cornwall's elite, Truro was their own miniature Bath. Not only were building styles imitated, but the honey-coloured Bath stone was even imported for new buildings. This splendid Classical façade is that of Truro's Assembly Rooms.

183

published *A Dissertation on the Use of Sea Water in the Diseases of the Glands* in 1750, the great new health fashion was the sea. People bathed in it, drank it and took salt water baths for every ailment. It gave the rich and leisured new ways of socialising and spending ostentatiously, for those who owned access to the sea could build private baths. In Cornwall there are a number of them at Portreath, Stackhouse Cove near Marazion and Polridmouth near Fowey.[77] The most impressive set-up is at Portreath, where Lord de Dunstanville (of the Bassett family of Tehidy) had his mason carve out six baths in the cliff face in 1782. They are in the smaller cove on the western side, and are still very visible today. The best example is a bath on the cove side of the small seaward promontory at Portreath. It is about 1.5 m (5 ft)[78] above beach level, and is sunk into the rock. The bath itself, with rock walls on the

The wealthy Cornish gentry families created their own private spa facilities in imitation of the popular resort of Weymouth. Lady Basset's bath from Portreath is a good example of a salt-water bath, fed by the tides. The overflow drain is visible in the bottom left of the picture, and traces of iron from a rail at the back of the bath are on the right.

back and western sides, measures about 2 m by 1 m (7 ft x 3ft 6in). Sinkings with small traces of iron are found at either end of a small ledge at the back of the bath, and there are traces of a handrail on the top step of three cut into the rock. To maintain water level in this tidally fed bath, a wedge-shaped drain was carved at the top on the south side and a hole was drilled at 0.33 m (1 ft) down. In order to reach the baths today you have to climb iron rungs, unrelated to the baths, that lead to a higher ledge.

The gentry spent lavishly on their stately homes and gardens.[79] The formal patterned layouts of early 18th-century gardens gave way to idealised parklands inspired by the poetry, painting and general mind-set of the Romantic Movement. Well-known architects took a hand. The famous landscape architect Humphry Repton produced designs for the gardens at Antony House near Torpoint,[80] and some of his advice was clearly acted on. The parterres of geometrical planting round the house disappeared and the new view was of *bosquets* – bold clumps of woodland. A central vista stretched down to the river, and the walled garden was moved. Two lodges were built, one at the main gate, the other by Antony passage. At Caerhays, John Trevanion managed to bankrupt himself by trying to outdo everyone else.[81] He employed John Nash to build not the usual Classical house, but a mock castle with an imposing castellated gatehouse at the shoreward end. Meanwhile, the hunt was on for exotic plants. The St Aubyns of Clowance introduced plane trees to Britain,[82] and one of the most famous plant collectors was Augustus Smith, from 1834 the lessee of Tresco in the Isles of Scilly.[83] Thanks to the climate of the islands, tender plants brought from the Mediterranean thrive in the formal gardens he created around the ruins of the old Benedictine Priory of St Nicholas. In effect the Abbey Gardens have turned what had been a real priory into a 19th-century garden folly.

The Industrial period was one of two worlds: those of a highly religious working class with a distinctive culture spread globally and of an increasingly wealthy and worldly upper class that saw itself as English. Generally, however, the technology and culture of Cornwall traversed the constraints of national boundaries. At home, though, the monuments of the Cornish prehistoric past were seen as relics of superstition, and many were destroyed. The technical achievements were great, but the landscapes were industrialised and polluted.

The gentry poured money into follies and landscape gardens. John Bettesworth Trevanion's Caerhayes Castle proved his ruin, due to the high fees of its architect, John Nash. The gardens follow the trend of parkland, inspired by romantic poetry and painting extolling nature.

CHAPTER TEN

DISCOVERING 'VANISHING' AND 'ENCHANTED' CORNWALL IN THE RECENT PAST

The Consumer Age (1880–)

AS 19TH-CENTURY INDUSTRIES gradually declined, tourism gradually grew – its growth made possible by the transport links that the Industrial period produced. The attractions were romantic images of Cornwall's historic past, especially King Arthur, the ancient Celts and various fairy folk – and the mild climate. Literature, painting and, later, electronic media all created a package that drew visitors from all over the world, and ugly industries that had scarred the landscape mellowed into picturesque ruin.

It was a more democratic age, and hitherto suppressed national and ethnic feeling started to find expression in more overt forms, within state boundaries and across them. One influence on Cornwall's sense of identity was the reflection back upon itself of the image projected by its own tourism and heritage industries. It even absorbed the outside world's ideas of it – for this was also a more globalised age. The result was that Cornwall and the Cornish have almost became brands.

Globalisation: popular culture and consumerism

The new networks of world trade and communication meant that ideas that would shape popular culture spread further and faster than ever.[1] The electronic media, especially, were the great disseminators, and Cornwall was one of the world's first and busiest switchboards. The cable station at Porthcurno relayed telegraph and telephone messages from 1870 between Britain and the Mediterranean, then the Americas and eventually as far as New Zealand.[2] Marconi set up a wireless station – a wooden hut and a mast – at Bass Point on the Lizard,[3] and was able to send signals to the Isle of Wight, before going on to send messages to America from Poldhu.[4] Finally, after the Second World War, a battery of dishes at Goonhilly Downs Earth Station[5] has sprung up to send and receive telephone, internet and TV signals via

FRANK
SHERWIN

PENZANCE

IN THE CORNISH RIVIERA

CHEAP MONTHLY
RETURN TICKETS
ISSUED DAILY

FREE GUIDE FROM
TOWN CLERK, Dept.P.,
PENZANCE (Postage 3d)

satellites linking Britain to the whole Western Hemisphere, the Eastern Hemisphere being covered by its sister station not far from Malvern in Gloucestershire. All three of these sites are open to visitors. The dark side of globalisation was global war, and it has left its marks everywhere – for example, in coves like those at Mount Edgcumbe and Trebah[6] (on the Helford River), where concrete matting and other concrete structures are the remnants of temporary harbours for the embarkation of soldiers during the D-Day operations of 1944. The existing fort of Pendennis was re-fortified in the early 20th century, before being retired in the 1950s as an ancient monument. Vulnerable from the air, it would have been useless in any nuclear war. Instead, behind barbed wire fences, a new generation of military bases like RAF St Mawgan and RNAS Culdrose rely on intelligence and early warning.

In a world awash with messages, product producers and political parties use slogans and images to grab their share of mind: in this turbulent market Cornwall is no mean brand. Literature ranging from Tennyson's *Idylls of the Kings* (1859 and 1888)[7] to Daphne du Maurier's *Vanishing Cornwall* (1967) and *Enchanted Cornwall* (1989);[8] Gilbert and Sullivan's operetta *The Pirates of Penzance* (1880);[9] and works of art throughout the period by such as Stanhope Forbes[10] and Barbara Hepworth:[11] all these are components of the idea of Cornwall, printed, played and reproduced all over the world. All this attractive image-material, and a lot more supplied by people who were actually Cornish, is matched by a kind of editorial control within the county. In 1888 Cornwall County Council was formed as a part of local government reforms.[12] Like other counties it had to furnish itself with a coat of arms (which represents fishing and mining, but curiously ignores farming), set up an administrative centre (Truro) and foster a public image of what the county represented. The reality, however, included new types of industry and changes to the old ones, occasioned by new sources of energy.

The Second Industrial Revolution and its impact on Cornwall

The Second Industrial Revolution brought the new power sources of the internal combustion engine, electricity and compressed air;[13] and from the mines came arsenic, tungsten, bromine and nitrates – minerals for niche markets, albeit large ones. This specialist output was a lifeline in a period of gradual industrial decline.

Electricity was the most important energy source of the new age. Tourism felt the benefit first when in 1898 the Poldhu Hotel, near Mullion, put in an oil engine and dynamo to generate power for the hotel.[14] In 1902 the Urban Electric Supply Co. Ltd set up the Camborne & Redruth Tramway to take passengers;[15] that was followed by a mineral tramway to East Pool Mine, part of which can still be visited by courtesy of the Trevithick Trust. The economic uncertainty of the 1920s and 1930s meant that many other such projects never came to fruition, and the Camborne & Redruth

Tramway closed in 1927. It was electricity that also made possible compressed-air drills, which the Holmans firm manufactured in Camborne for hard-rock mining all over the world. Finally, in Cornwall as everywhere else, electricity gave rise to the electronic revolution in mass communication.

The internal combustion engine was a great stimulus to the growth of small coastal villages. As early as 1934 John Betjeman in his *Shell Guide to Cornwall*[16] could point to small resorts far from the nearest railway station that had grown purely because tourists could get there by car. Popular guides like Baring-Gould's *Book of the West* (1899)[17] had encouraged visitors long before that. Early tourism included excursions of horse-drawn carriages from Penzance to the Logan Rock combined with a stay in the Logan Rock Inn,[18] and yet another destination was a Victorian tea shed at Porth Godrevy, evidenced by charcoal and broken teacups.[19] By the 1920s people went on outings in charabancs, till the name faded away in the 1930s and the 'sharry' became a motor coach.[20]

Older industries saw hard times and either found new applications – which helped to buoy up a shaky labour market – or gave way to entirely new industries. From the 1890s to the 1930s the old arsenic industry turned to specialist markets in pest control.[21] For the Colorado beetle that destroyed potato crops, and the Boll weevil infesting America's cotton plantations, calcium arsenate was the answer.[22] Geevor Mine has a good example of a calciner used to roast the ores, and it is on view to the public. The balmaidens (women mine workers) had to scrape the arsenic off the sides of the chimney – at severe risk to their health. Using materials like sulphuric acid (another by-product of mining) and nitric acid made from saltpetre imported from Chile,[23] an industry producing nitro-glycerine-based explosives was set up at Upton Towans, near Hayle, in 1890.[24] 'Towan' is Cornish for 'sand dunes' – ideal for minimising any damage that might arise from accidental explosions. There are remains both of a tramway running between mounds on which wooden cartridging huts once stood, and of concrete magazines (looking a little like bunkers) with barricading and mounds around them. If there was an explosion, the barricading sand would protect other buildings. The prominent chimney stack on the site is from the nitric acid factory. The works were set up by Cornish mining interests to supply armaments manufacturers in competition with none other than Alfred Nobel, ironically the founder of the Nobel Peace Prize.

Among entirely new industries, a tungsten mine was set up at Castle-an-Dinas in mid-Cornwall[25] on the northern side of an Iron Age hillfort overlooking Goss Moor. Gorse and brambles cover the area of the shafts; concrete footings for the overhead conveyor system and a track for vehicles run diagonally through the hillfort to derelict concrete buildings. These were for the initial processing and storage of the ore, and in the mid-20th century this one mine supplied about half the world's tungsten.

CORNWALL IN THE RECENT PAST

New specialist industries emerged during this period, such as the arsenic industry. Arsenic is a by-product of mining for metal ores. This calciner is next to Levant Mine in West Penwith, and was used to roast and extract the arsenic. The process created toxic fumes that went through a series of passages and settled on the brick walls. The arsenic workers had to scrape it off, without access to any safety equipment or protective clothing.

190

Demand for bromine created another new specialist industry. This highly toxic element is used for making tetraethyl lead, an anti-knock additive for petrol. From the North Quay near the mouth of the Hayle Estuary bromine was extracted from sea water from 1939 to 1970.[26] Leaks into the estuary gave the plant a bad press, and with stiff competition from Amlwch in Anglesey (which was nearer the manufacturing plants in Cheshire) the works at Hayle had to close.

Even farming and fishing had to diversify and specialise. From the late 19th century daffodils and other spring flowers became a crop:[27] thanks to the trains and refrigeration they arrived in the London markets fresh. Ice kept the fish fresh too (so no need of pressing and salting), and trawling replaced the old seine nets.[28] From the early 20th century large, commercial fishing fleets from outside began to threaten the livelihood of Cornish fishing villages – so they increasingly turned to pleasure trips, cafés and tourism generally. The community in Porthgwarra, West Penwith, created a specialist lobster fishery.[29] They built 'hullies' for holding lobsters, crabs and crayfish, by walling up the sides of cavities between the rocks on the shore. Grooves in the rocks show where joists were pushed in to be the base of a wooden grid to stop the lobsters escaping through the channel at the bottom; more grooves round the rim of the hullies held the lid. The catch went to Newlyn, then onwards to Billingsgate Market in London.

Tourism archaeology and its wider impact

Early spring flowers, especially daffodils, have long been one reason that people think Cornwall basks in central heating delivered by the Gulf Stream. Another is the Great Western Railway. It did a great deal to project the image of Cornwall as a subtropical paradise in its poster campaigns in the 1920s and 1930s.[30] The 'Cornish Riviera' picture[31] was not entirely fantasy, though, because private estates and local councils had planted all manner of exotics from the Southern Hemisphere – Chile, Argentina, South Africa, Australia and New Zealand. Wisely they kept away from anything subtropical, and chose languid-looking but hardy plants, notably the New Zealand flax and the 'dracaena palms' from New Zealand. In fact these are not palms at all but arborescent lilies, briskly known in their native lands as 'cabbage trees'.[32] They became so popular that a long street in Falmouth called Dracaena Avenue has them planted on both sides. They are also a common garden plant and have come to be identified as typical of Cornwall. The Eden Project is just the latest expression of enthusiasm for the exotic. Cornwall has the highest biodiversity in the British Isles – much of it in the form of imported species.[33]

Old ports like Newquay and Falmouth softened their industrial characters to become resorts.[34] At the end of the 19th century Newquay was a fishing port with fish cellars (the remains of which can still be seen with their characteristic holes for

Even farming in Cornwall adapted as quicker rail transport and then refrigeration made the transportation of fresh flowers possible.

pressing poles), a huer's hut and quays complete with a railway, part of which is now a pedestrian route in the town above the cliffs. All this changed in 1897 with the building of the Headland Hotel by the Cornish architect Silvanus Trevail.[35] This elegant hotel, with its ornamental Art Nouveau brickwork, was designed to be the finest hotel in south-west Britain. Its social and geographical positioning were a perfect match, because it stood on a prominent headland dominating Newquay. (Not everyone was pleased: there were riots by those who saw it as an elite confiscation of common land.) In due course the cachet of royal patronage – there were several visits by King Edward VII and Queen Alexandra – stamped it as a grand hotel indeed, and that reputation was confirmed in the early 1930s when the Black and Silver Ballroom opened. Fashionable London orchestras and the BBC Palm Court broadcasts attracted an upmarket clientele, who also enjoyed the private golf links outside.

At the beginning of the 20th century, affluent holiday-makers in Newquay had only five large hotels competing for their custom; or they might buy a large house as a holiday home, and move in for August with all their servants. An even more exclusive pleasure-seeker was Pendarves-Vivian, who owned the Glendorgal estate at Porth (next to Newquay) between 1876 and 1882.[36] He had a private harbour built into the side of Trevelgue Head, just west of the ramparts of the cliff castle and facing Glendorgal over Porth cove – just as mooring for his steam yacht. There are still

New monuments and structures, like Truro cathedral, built between 1879 and 1910, stress Cornwall's unity and separateness. It was the first Anglican cathedral built on a new site since 1220, and the first Cornish diocese separate from Devon since the late 10th century. The motivation was not nationalist, though; improving the prestige of local Anglicanism was vital in stemming the alarming tide of conversion to Nonconformism (the Methodists in particular were almost seen as a Cornish 'national' church).

193

traces of the harbour: a granite block, some metalwork, rock-cut steps and several metal rings.[37]

From the 1920s a new middle-class tourist had discovered Newquay. Hotels like the Tolcarne charged reasonable prices, offered good facilities and various sorts of entertainment. Tolcarne built two large garages at the back equipped with petrol pumps and inspection pits, and it had the first ballroom in the town itself – complete with a maple floor. The hotel had a lease on the beach below, and rented out beach huts which, by the 1950s, had permanent concrete terraces to give them a secure foundation. Beach huts were part of a growing craze for surfing, which in those days was not confined to any particular age group. In the 1930s, however, surfing began to be taken seriously as Surf-O-Planes replaced the simple plywood 'belly boards'.

Designed by Cornish architect Silvanus Trevail to be Cornwall's premier hotel in 1897, a magnificent Art Nouveau exterior announced the opulence and trend-setting nature of its anticipated clientele. Its situation on a headland, like other grand hotels of the time in Cornwall, provided it with excellent vistas over the sea and coast.

It was not just hotels that promoted tourism. The towns themselves provided amenities for the public and began to do so quite early on. In 1906, for instance, Newquay laid out Trenance Gardens in the Tolcarne Valley beneath the railway viaduct, with a stream flowing through into a small pond. Later the town added hard tennis courts, a bowling green, a boating lake and even a dance hall – which was later converted into flats.[38] In Penzance the terminus of the Great Western Railway attracted tourists into what they saw as the mysterious far west of Cornwall. A host of public amenities welcomed the visitor: the Morrab Gardens, the Promenade and Britain's biggest outdoor seawater swimming pool, the Jubilee Pool,[39] were built. The Pool was a magnificent piece of Art Deco architecture that could have been taken out of a Hollywood movie set of the 1930s. Smooth concrete terraces open out onto a curvaceous pool erected on a rocky peninsula jutting into the sea just west of the harbour.

From popular mythology and ideology – another new identity

Idealised notions of past and present identity are important in establishing norms of behaviour and shared assumptions. A culture needs to reproduce symbols that every one of its members can understand and relate to – be they artefacts, building styles or images. Even the stock phrases of conversation are full of allusion to well-known stories, events or people. Some folk myth connects to a real past, and some was never anywhere but in the mind, but all of it is common coin within the culture.

A good example of the real past working on present minds is that people are not merely aware of that past but cherish it. They recognise that ancient monuments are not to be destroyed just because they are pagan, or too remote in time, or just in the way. The Old Cornwall Society, formed in the 1920s, began to place plaques by ancient monuments, as did the Ministry of Works and its successors. The recent campaign against 'English' Heritage's use of controversial and unpopular signs stressing Englishness, including the defacing of its signs and plaques, indicates the strong identification of the Cornish with their past. All this is a far cry from the mind-set of the previous period.

Overseas, Cornish communities have been concerned with their heritage. The mining settlement of Cadia in New South Wales, for instance, has had itself listed on the NSW Register because of the early Cornish engine houses there.[40] There is also real pride in the achievements of the Cornish in Pachuca and Real del Monte in Mexico. In Pachuca a number of monuments testify to its Cornish heritage.[41] A 40-metre (131-foot) tower is dedicated to the Mexican Revolution and built by a Cornish mine captain, William Rule, hard by a Methodist chapel; elsewhere the Casa del Conde Rule,[42] built by Francisco Rule, now serves as the municipal government building. The local mines were fitted with nine Cornish steam engines, which were hauled overland all the way from the coast by the miners, high up to the edge of the Sierra Madre.[43]

From the less than real past come all the legends – notably of King Arthur, and of pirates. Just how potent the Arthurian legends are is plain from what they have done for tourism around Tintagel. On cliffs to the east of the 'Vale of Avalon' and opposite Tintagel Castle, the Camelot Castle Hotel built by Silvanus Trevail in 1899[44] has crenellations round the roof, and corners like towers. The whole building rests on a

The most impressive seaside structure has to be the Jubilee Pool at Penzance. This Art Deco lido is built on the rocks off the headland of Penzance itself at the eastern end of the Promenade. The smooth curves and pleasing design are still a delight, despite the passing of time and fashion – and it is still in use.

raised, flat mound that mimics a Late Medieval motte. The village itself has many cafés and shops with Arthurian names. This is all harmless fun, of course, but it is worth bearing in mind the power of the fabulous in propaganda. Recent research into Cornish politics of the early 20th century has revealed a secret plan by the Nazis in Germany to create an experimental SS state in Cornwall.[45] This state would have deliberately played on the Celtic origins of Cornwall and its legendary King Arthur to justify its separation from the rest of Britain. It would have become part of the domain of Heinrich Himmler, the SS chief. Himmler was an Arthurian fanatic and even built himself a round table in the basement of his headquarters in Austria – the Wewelsburg.[46] It was complete with a throne for himself, as King Arthur, and seats for his chief officers, who were to be his knights.

The idea of piracy in Cornwall is even less rooted in fact. It begins with Gilbert and Sullivan's operetta, *The Pirates of Penzance*, first performed in 1879, and is followed by Robert Louis Stevenson's *Treasure Island*, published in 1882.[47] *Treasure Island* is full of characters with names like Squire Trelawney, Jim Hawkins and Redruth, the squire's gamekeeper. Although acts of brigandage on land and sea were common throughout Britain before the introduction of a proper police force in the 19th century, piracy was not a long-term dedicated profession here as it was in the Caribbean. Indeed Cornwall was more a victim of piracy, with people from coastal villages and ports sometimes being carried away by Barbary pirates from North Africa during the Post-Medieval and early Industrial periods.[48] Theme parks and tourist souvenirs exploit the fantasy of pirates, however, and myths of piracy have become a feature of modern Cornwall. The Admiral Benbow Inn in Penzance is just such an example, capitalising on the story of *Treasure Island*.[49]

Out on the headland facing the original Tintagel Castle is the Camelot Castle Hotel, complete with turrets, a fitting piece of architecture for the land of King Arthur.

Popular fantasy sometimes finds physical expression in modern-day Cornwall – as at this pub in Penzance, named after the inn in Robert Louis Stevenson's Treasure Island.

The rise of Cornish nationalism and the Celtic tigers

Cornish nationalism is not to be defined simply as a political force: a sense of identity has only to be strong enough for people to see themselves as ethnically separate,[50] without their having to call for independence. It must be remembered that in the Industrial period, the consensus in the county's upper echelons was that there was no such thing as a separate ethnic group called 'the Cornish' – as governments have denied to this day. The current and growing confidence that people have in their Cornish identity and culture rests in part on the concept of Celtic culture, linking Cornwall to archaeological finds and to other more powerful cultures. Ireland is the

exemplar. Its independence, its cultural strength, its communities overseas and its recent economic success all prove that being Celtic is no handicap.

It may be that the plainest signs of change lie in political nationalism. By the late 19th century the suppression of ethnic and nationalist sentiments had led to a dearth of material signs of the separate powers of the Late Medieval Earldom and Duchy. The Duchy Palace of Lostwithiel was all but lost. After a period of lying in ruins it became just an ordinary block of Victorian houses on Quay Street:[51] only the chapel, transformed into a Masonic lodge, looked at all unusual. The great castles of that era also lay in ruins. Then, in the 1920s, the tide of sentiment turned, and people began not only to respect but even to revive many old monuments, and put them back into use. From 1928 The Gorseth Movement took to holding its ceremonies at places like the Boscawen-Ûn stone circle.[52] More recently there have been annual gatherings at St Piran's Oratory on St Piran's day, and there is a campaign to reopen the oratory itself. From the 1960s a crop of plaques and statues has sprung up to celebrate the past. Mebyon Kernow – the main party of Cornish nationalism[53]– set up a plaque in the 1960s to Thomas Flamank and Joseph an Gof, the leaders of the 1497 rebellion (against the heavy and unjust taxes levied to pay for Henry VII's war against the Scottish – fellow Celts): it is by the gate of the churchyard at St Keverne on the Lizard. Life-size statues of them went up in 1997 on the road from St Keverne to Helston.[54] More recently a large granite slab recording the Prayer Book Rebellion of 1549 (against, among other things, the imposition of the English language into church services previously held in Latin with sermons in Cornish) has been placed on the grass verge below the bowling green at the entrance to the old town of Penryn.

Not all Cornwall's quays and ports have been converted into seaside resorts. The port of Charlestown was built as an outlet for the china clay industry. It is now a major attraction on the heritage trail, with a maritime museum and the port complete with sailing ships. This enables its character to be retained in some measure.

197

One feature of many monuments and signs is the increasingly common use of the Cornish language.

Since the beginning of this period, artists have been attracted to Cornwall's scenic landscape and seascape. The 'Tate of the West' in St Ives is just the latest manifestation of this interest.

The new nationalism came in all sizes, not always monumentally large: jewellery, clothing and other artefacts were its emblems too. Old Cornish designs were revived, and some influences came in from a wider exchange of themes among Celtic countries. Broadly, the common sources were archaeological material from the Iron Age of north-west and north-central Europe (perceived as being Celtic), from the Early Medieval British Isles and from the folk idiom of modern Celtic cultures. As we saw in Chapter One, the term Celtic is meaningful only as it applies to those who have defined themselves as Celts since the early 18th century, when the word first emerged in its modern sense. Today's Celtic cultures see themselves as interrelated, frequently borrowing elements from each other's material culture, and so foster feelings of kinship and friendship. Material elements like the triskell – the three curved lines meeting at a point – have become symbols common to them all. The creation of the Cornish National Tartan and other Cornish tartans is a good example of this continuing Celtic cohesion.

Even subtler are the symbols that have moulded Cornwall into a more unitary, distinctive and cohesive whole then it had ever been. The Cornish colours of black, white and gold cover literally anything, from rugby supporters to supermarket products, as icons of Cornishness. Cornish standardisation reaches right into the planning process, so that there are rules governing hedge building.[55] A particular style of stone hedge, the 'Cornish Hedge' that developed over the Post-Medieval and Industrial periods, has become the officially permitted hedge (not counting the Devon Turf Hedge, which is allowed in parts of North Cornwall). Unfortunately, the wealth of different styles of hedges from different periods and different parts of Cornwall[56] – all authentic – is usually overlooked in favour of the 'national' style. The Cornish pasty, on the other hand, is a recent success story in its acknowledgement of Cornwall's diversity.[57] For much of the 20th century there was only one sort – the steak pasty – even though in earlier times there had been fish pasties and jam pasties. In California and Mexico, Cornish pasties are today made with Mexican spices, while in the late 19th century large pasties were divided into savoury and sweet halves. Now many bakeries have pasties of every kind, reflecting Cornwall's more confident and cosmopolitan nature.

From the small elements of the Cornish culture to the larger ones like the Eden Project, the Consumer Age has been characterised by popular images and their reproduction in the actual material world. Co-opting real and imagined histories, Cornwall is projected as a unitary and sleek brand. Its diverse nature should not, however, be forgotten. Industries have been more specialised as the traditional ones became less secure, and sometimes the industrial past has been marginalised or romanticised. What is less marginal, however, is the growing confidence of the region and of its people in their own sense of identity and will to succeed. It is to be hoped

A curious feature of Cornish identity today is the way images of a Celtic past and an industrial past jar, or at least sit awkwardly together. As some traditional industries collapse, places like Geevor Mine in West Penwith are turned into heritage centres or museums. The problem of how to marry the two identities is then thrown into starker focus.

that this new sense of confidence will recognise and celebrate Cornish culture as diverse, adaptive, and vibrant – as all living cultures should be.

Cornwall's past has been diverse and changing. A few common factors recur in different periods, though. For example, since the end of the Ice Age, when sea levels rose, Cornwall has occupied a pivotal position in routes of transport and communication between the Irish Sea, Atlantic Ocean and English Channel. Cornwall's geology has made it rich in mineral wealth, though relatively poor in agriculture. This has meant that its links to other far-off communities have been almost inevitable. The idea of 'remoteness' sometimes attributed to Cornwall derives from its political marginality. Its poor agricultural resources have generally placed it in a weaker position *vis-à-vis* its neighbours throughout its past.

A number of stereotypes of Cornwall obscure its past. I have challenged these or put them into a more reasonable perspective. And I have attempted to create an impression of the lives of people from all periods. Instead of a dry rendition of archaeological data, I have looked at the hows and whys of human behaviour. This is evident in the later periods, during which the folklore and popular culture of Cornwall are seen to have achieved physical form. People recreate their own views of themselves and their past continuously, even altering or manipulating earlier monuments to their own ends. Each age has its own ideas and its own messages. This diversity is not to be glossed over but, rather, celebrated.

This section is divided into the modern administrative districts of Cornwall. For each district, I have attempted to provide at least one site to represent each period, although this was not possible when there was no meaningful or accessible site available. I have included site directions, grid references, accessibility information and a brief description with each site record.

Grid references are from the National Grid. The letter codes (SV, SW, SX and SS) refer to squares on the National Grid. The letter code is indicated either in the key of an OS (Ordnance Survey) map or sometimes on the map itself. The six-figure numbers should be read as follows. Take the first two numbers and read them off west to east along the grid. The 3rd number is the subdivision of the square eastward beyond the first two numbers. This marks the exact position of the first coordinate. The next three numbers (4th–6th) are read in the same way, here to pinpoint the south to north coordinate, and with the 6th number as the subdivision of the square northward beyond the first two numbers (4th–5th). The meeting of the two coordinates (west–east and south–north) marks the location of the site.

Access information is given under the following categories.

To find

Easy = directly next to the road or street

Moderate = a little complicated to find, but still close or right by a road or street

Harder = follow the directions carefully

To walk (counting the distance from the nearest road or street)

Little = extremely little

Moderate = a small distance is involved

Long = suitable for those who are not in a hurry and who are reasonably fit

Danger One should always consider precautions against potential mishaps in the countryside. However, the sites identified here are those where the dangers are increased during spells of very poor weather – such as cliff edges and high moorlands well away from traffic.

THE ISLES OF SCILLY

The main islands of St Mary's, Tresco, Bryher, St Martin's and St Agnes have regular ferry services. Boats (at a higher price) provide sightseeing tours that take in smaller islands. The main islands do have some transport facilities, but you will access much more of the islands' archaeology if you are prepared to walk. If requiring road transport, book or check up beforehand. Archaeology guided walks are available – enquire through the islands' tourist information service.

Early–Middle Neolithic

Innisidgen entrance graves, St Mary's

GRID REFERENCE SV 921127 & SV 922126

TO FIND Moderate   TO WALK Moderate

Take the A3111 east from Hugh Town, then the A3110 northwards. Instead of following the A3110 eastwards, take the road straight ahead past the prominent Telegraph Tower. Take the northward path of McFarland's Downs to the coastal footpath. Turn eastwards along the coastal footpath past Bar Point. At Innisidgen, there is a fork in the path. The left path leads to the lower entrance grave near the shore, and the right path leads to the upper entrance grave near a rocky crag.

Late Neolithic–Early Bronze Age

Barrow and statue *menhir*, Chapel Down, St Martin's

GRID REFERENCE SV 944157

TO FIND Moderate   TO WALK Long

Danger Avoid in poor weather conditions

From the quay at Higher Town take the coastal footpath to the east. At a fork in the path, take the north fork up on to the moorland. The barrow (and very small statue *menhir*) is on the eastern headland overlooking the island of Nornour to the south.

Early Iron Age

Shipman Head cliff castle, Bryher

GRID REFERENCE SV 876160

TO FIND Moderate   TO WALK Long

Danger Avoid in poor weather conditions

From the Town quay, take the road northward, and then the footpath to the northern headland. A rampart cuts off the headland from the rest of the island.

Roman Period

Halangy (pronounced 'Linjy') Down Romano-British courtyard house settlement, St Mary's

GRID REFERENCE SV 910124

TO FIND Moderate   TO WALK Moderate

Take the A3111 east from Hugh Town, then the A3110 northwards. Instead of following the A3110 eastwards, take the road straight ahead past the prominent Telegraph Tower. Take the northward path of McFarland's Downs to the coastal footpath. Turn westwards along the coastal footpath, following the signs to the settlement.

Early Medieval

St Helen's Oratory, St Helen's

GRID REFERENCE SV 901169

TO FIND Moderate   TO WALK Little

Danger Avoid in poor weather conditions

The oratory consists of low drystone walling, and is found to the east of the Industrial Period Pest House. There is an enclosure wall, oratory, cemetery and monks cells. The island can be seen as part of a guided boat trip, but not by means of a regular ferry.

Late Medieval

Ennor Castle and Old Town Quay, St Mary's

GRID REFERENCE SV 913104 & SV 914101

TO FIND Easy   TO WALK Little

The castle mound or motte is not directly accessible, but is clearly seen from outside the churchyard in Old Town looking north-east towards the town. It is a mound covered with trees rising above the level of the houses.

The quay is on the eastern side of Old Town Bay, and consists of a wide breakwater of uncemented rocks.

Post-Medieval
Star Castle, the Garrison, St Mary's
GRID REFERENCE SV 899107
TO FIND Easy   TO WALK Little
Enter Hugh Town from the quay, and turn right up Garrison Hill. Go through the Garrison Gate House, and straight ahead is Star Castle. The Castle is also a hotel and restaurant.

This late 16th century castle has a dry moat and bastions. It was designed for cannon warfare, and defended the entrance to the harbour of Hugh Town.

Post-Medieval
St Agnes Lighthouse, St Agnes
GRID REFERENCE SV 880082
TO FIND Easy   TO WALK Little
From the quay, go up past Higher Town to Middle Town. The lighthouse is at the top of the hill.

The lighthouse was built in 1680 for a brazier light (the brazier is now in the Abbey Gardens on Tresco). It also possesses gunports. Cannon were fired (without cannonballs!) during fog to warn ships off the rocks.

Industrial Period
Telegraph station, St Martins
GRID REFERENCE SV 942161
TO FIND Moderate   TO WALK Long
Danger Avoid in poor weather conditions
From the quay at Higher Town take the coastal footpath to the east. At a fork in the path, take the north fork up on to the moorland.

Consumer Age
Abbey Gardens
GRID REFERENCE SV 894142
TO FIND Moderate   TO WALK Little
From the quay at Crow Point, go straight ahead through the airport following the signs to the Abbey Gardens. From the quay at New Grimsby, take the road southwards, following the signs.

The gardens were the creation of the Smith and Dorrien-Smith family, and incorporate some earlier archaeological sites, including the ruins of the Late Medieval Priory of St Nicholas. There is also a collection of figureheads from shipwrecks.

PENWITH

Early–Middle Neolithic
Tregiffian chamber tomb
GRID REFERENCE SW430244
TO FIND Easy   TO WALK Little
Located on the B3315 from Penzance to Land's End (via Treen), to the west of Lamorna. It is just west of the Merry Maidens Stone Circle on the grass verge beside the road.

The chamber of the tomb is intact, though one stone at the entrance decorated with cup-marks is a replica. The original is in the Royal Cornwall Museum in Truro.

Late Neolithic–Early Bronze Age
Round barrow, Godrevy
GRID REFERENCE SW 580430
TO FIND Moderate   TO WALK Little
Take the B3301 between Hayle and Portreath. Just north of Gwithian is a small road bridge. The bridge is narrow and does not permit more than one vehicle to pass at a time. Immediately north of the bridge is a turning to the west leading to the National Trust car park. Go past the National Trust car park to a second National Trust car park. Walk along the footpath northwards until you reach a large, prominent mound (the round barrow) on the low cliff.

Late Neolithic
The Merry Maidens stone circle
GRID REFERENCE SW 433245
TO FIND Easy   TO WALK Little
Located in a field to the south of the B3315 from Penzance to Land's End (via Treen), to the west of Lamorna. This is one of the best stone circles to visit. There are also two stone uprights, The Pipers, in a field across the road to the west.

Iron Age
Bodrifty Iron Age settlement
GRID REFERENCE SW 445354
TO FIND Harder   TO WALK Little
At roundabout west of Penzance Heliport, take the road into Penzance. Take the first turning to the right under the road bridge in the direction of Gulval, the B3311. Next take the road northwards signposted 'New Mill'. Alternatively, New Mill can be reached via the road to the south, just past Boswednack on the B3306 St Ives to St Just road. At New Mill, take the narrow road to Bodrifty Farm to the North West. The settlement is on the moor to the north of the farm.

The settlement consists of an unenclosed settlement of hut circles, connected to relicts of an associated field system. Note the incorporation of *in situ* large granite boulders into the settlement, which suggests some respect or even veneration of natural phenomena.

Roman Period
Carn Euny courtyard house settlement
GRID REFERENCE SW 402289
TO FIND Moderate   TO WALK Moderate
Take the A30 from Penzance to Land's End. At the crossroads in Drift, take the signposted route to the north. Just before Sancreed, take the signposted route west to Brane Farm. There is a small car park past the farm. A footpath leads to the settlement

This is a particularly fine example of a courtyard house settlement. The *fogou* or underground passage is easily accessible and of large dimensions with a round corbelled roof chamber. An 18th–19th-century cottage on site contains a mixture of industrially produced products such as lime plaster and mortar, along with local features such as the furze cupboard to the right of the fireplace.

Early Medieval

Chun (pronounced 'Choon') Castle, Men-an-Tol and Maen Scryfa (pronounced 'Main Screefa')

GRID REFERENCE SW 405339, SW 42349 & SW 455318

TO FIND Moderate–Harder TO WALK Moderate

Take the north road from the Heamoor roundabout on the A30 at Penzance in the direction of Morvah. Alternatively, take road south at Morvah to Penzance from the B3306 St Ives to St Just road. A lane to the west of the road in a valley between Morvah and Lanyon Farm leads to Little Bosullow Farm and Chun Castle. On the other side of the road to this lane is a small lay-by. A footpath from this lay-by signposted for Men-an-Tol leads eastwards to Men-an-Tol stone circle. Further along in a field to the north side of the path is Maen Scryfa inscribed stone.

Chun Castle began as an Iron Age hillfort, but was reoccupied in the Early Medieval period. The walls of the dwellings that appear like spokes of a wheel belong to this period. To the immediate south of the hillfort is a quoit, and to west a courtyard house settlement. Men-an-Tol is a stone circle with a later Early Bronze Age holed stone and cist added. Maen Scryfa bears the inscription: 'RIALOBRANI CVNOVALI FILI'; 'Of Rialobranus, son of Cunovalus'.

Early Medieval

Inscribed stones and lann enclosure bank, Phillack churchyard

GRID REFERENCE SW 565384

TO FIND Easy TO WALK Little

At the Loggan's Moor roundabout on the A30 to the immediate east of Hayle, take the turning into Hayle following the signs to Phillack. In Hayle, the second turning to the right leads to Phillack. In Phillack churchyard is a stone with a 6th–7th-century inscription. The inscription reads: 'CLOTUALI MOBRATTI'; 'Of Clotualus, son of Mobrattus'.

Traces of the original lann enclosure bank were revealed by excavation to the south-east of the church. Directly over the arch of the south porch of the church is a 5th-century inscribed Chi-Rho stone.

Late Medieval

Madron chapel and holy well

GRID REFERENCE SW 447382

TO FIND Moderate TO WALK Little

Take the north road from the Heamoor roundabout on the A30 at Penzance in the direction of Morvah. Alternatively, take road south at Morvah to Penzance from the B3306 St Ives to St Just road. It is reached via a lane just north of Madron, on the east side of the road. A signpost indicates the lane.

The chapel is a rectangular drystone-walled building with an altar at the east end. In one corner is a small reservoir. The holy well is hard to miss, being close by in a marshy area with trees festooned with votive ribbons. The present chapel structure is Late Medieval and not earlier, as is sometimes claimed.

Post-Medieval

St Michael's Mount monastery and stately home

GRID REFERENCE SW 298515

TO FIND Easy TO WALK Moderate–Long

The buildings are on a tidal island immediately south of Marazion. At low tide simply walk across on the causeway. At high tide, there are boat services to take you across for a small fee. The National Trust also charges a fee for visiting the historic buildings and gardens.

The monastery was founded by Benedictines. A small lighthouse provided by them is on the right just before the summit. Later buildings belong to the site's history as a stately home. Ornamental gardens dominate the seaward terraces. Recent work by Pete Herring of the Historic Environment Service has also revealed traces of a Neolithic Hilltop Enclosure.

Post-Medieval

Porth Godrevy fish cellar

GRID REFERENCE SW 582427

TO FIND Moderate–Harder TO WALK Little

Danger Avoid in poor weather conditions

Take the B3301 between Hayle and Portreath. Just north of Gwithian is a small road bridge. The bridge is narrow and does not permit more than one vehicle to pass at a time. Immediately north of the bridge is a turning to the west leading to the National Trust car park. Walk past the National Trust car park and then just after the second National Trust car park, look for a grassy hollow in the low cliff. A steep path leads down into the hollow where the remains of a 17th-century fish cellar, with its low drystone walls, are visible.

Note the small square holes in the wall for the pressing stones. The large hole cut out of the rock on the platform was probably the socket for a capstan for hauling boats and equipment on shore.

Industrial Period

Geevor and Levant mines

GRID REFERENCE SW 375344 & SW 369340

TO FIND Easy TO WALK Little–Moderate (if doing the Geevor tour)

Both are on the north side of the B3306 St Ives to St Just road. The entrance to Geevor is in the village of Pendeen. For Levant Mine, take the road north of the B3306 at Trewellard (Levant Road), just to the west of Pendeen.

The Levant mine is a good example of 19th-century mining technologies, whilst the Geevor site is mainly concerned with 20th-century mining. A short and level stretch of an earlier Post-Medieval mine at Geevor has been opened up as part of a guided tour to explain the conditions underground. Entrance fees are charged.

Consumer Age

Jubilee Pool, Penzance – an Art Deco lido

GRID REFERENCE SW 475299

TO FIND Easy TO WALK Little

Entering Penzance from the east, follow the main direction of traffic down Wharf Road. From the main car park, walk along Wharf Road (continuation Quay Road) until the pool appears on the left, seaward side.

Entrance fees are charged. The pool is open-air, being built on rocks jutting out into the sea. The architecture is worthy of a Fred Astaire and Ginger Rogers movie. It is open to the public for swimming.

KERRIER

Mesolithic–Middle Bronze Age
Poldowrian (pronounced 'Pol-dow [as in 'now'] - rian') Mesolithic to Bronze Age settlements
GRID REFERENCE SW 748168
TO FIND Harder   TO WALK Moderate
Take the B3293 from Helston to St Keverne, taking the second road to the south after Zoar Garage at a crossroads. After passing the hamlet of Ponsongath, take the first road to the south. Next take the left-hand road at a fork in the road and head to Poldowrian Farm. The museum and site are open free of charge by appointment (contact Mrs Hadley 01326 280130/434) every Wednesday in August, 10am to 5pm.

The Late Mesolithic site is located on a ridge overlooking the way down to the sea. There is also a Middle Bronze Age hut circle and a Beaker encampment. Though the museum lacks the chic of a public museum, it contains an excellent collection of everyday artefacts from the site.

Mesolithic
Stithians reservoir
GRID REFERENCE SW 714365
TO FIND Harder   TO WALK Moderate
Follow the signs to Stithians from either the A393 or the A394. In Stithians, head down the main street to the church. From the church, take the road signposted for Four Lanes westwards through Hendra. On the left-hand side just after Hendra, turn left to the south. The route is signposted for the dam of Stithians Reservoir. At the dam, there is a car park. At the northern end of the car park is a footpath which circles the reservoir. Follow the footpath to a peninsula jutting out into the water. This is the location of the Late Mesolithic site, and still has amazing panoramic views, even though the valleys are submerged. Look north-west to the water-sports area. In contrast, just to the left of this is where a Neolithic camp was located in a more ecologically useful placing next to a former marsh.

Early–Middle Neolithic
Carn Brea Neolithic hilltop enclosure and Iron Age hillfort
GRID REFERENCE SW 685406
TO FIND Moderate–Harder   TO WALK Moderate
Do not confuse with Carn Brea village (you will not find it there!). Instead, coming down the A30 dual carriageway north of Camborne and Redruth, take the junction signposted to Pool to the south. Drive to the roundabout beside McDonalds in Pool. Go straight ahead (southwards), and go past the Carn Brea Leisure Centre (on the left-hand side of the road). Follow the road to Carnkie. Take the left turning into Carnkie. Half way down the street is a turning to the left and up the

hillside, signposted to the monument of Carn Brea. Follow the winding and poorly surfaced road up to the top. There is some limited parking on the saddle of the hill. The castle of Carn Brea further up on the eastern tor is a restaurant, which has parking for customers only.

The middle and eastern tors have terraces and enclosure walls from the Neolithic period. A large rampart and ditch enclosing these tors and some hut circles in the saddle of the hill belong to the Iron Age. The castle on the eastern tor has Late Medieval origins. A deer-park enclosure bank and ditch is found to the west of the middle tor. The enormous cross on the middle tor and the quarried tor stones around it are from the 19th century.

Late Neolithic
The Nine Maidens stone circle, near Wendron
GRID REFERENCE SW 683365
TO FIND Harder   TO WALK Little
The stone circle is on the east side of the B3297 (the Redruth–Helston road) between Four Lanes and Wendron in a field on the top of a hill south of the junction with the B3280. It was part of a row of three circles. You need to look over the stone hedge to see it.

Middle–Late Iron Age
Castle Pencaire (pronounced 'Pen-care'), Tregonning Hill
GRID REFERENCE SW 599300
TO FIND Moderate   TO WALK Long
On the A394 from Helston to Penzance, take the turning to Germoe. Drive through Germoe to Balwest. A lane and footpath lead up to the hillfort on the summit of Tregonning Hill. Do not deviate from the footpath as there are many quarry pits and mine shafts over and around the hill. There is a fork in the path. The left path leads over the ditch and rampart into the hillfort. The interior contains the remains of roundhouses. The right path leads down the hill to two Romano-British rounds with ovalhouses.

Roman Period
Trebarveth Romano-British salt works, the Lizard
GRID REFERENCE SW 796193
TO FIND Moderate   TO WALK Long
Danger Avoid in poor weather conditions
Go to Coverack, south of St Keverne on the Lizard. Walk along the Coverack to Lowland Point coastal footpath. Once past the houses, the footpath is narrow and the cliff elevated. Continue past a rocky headland. Beyond the headland there is a wide level area with low cliffs extending all the way out to Lowland Point. Before reaching Lowland Point, there is a low headland called Pedn Myin, strewn with boulders on grass. The salt works site is here on the edge of the cliff. An oval house is already half eroded away. A low bank marks off the other side of the site.

Early Medieval
Inscribed stone, Mawgan, the Lizard
GRID REFERENCE SW 707248
TO FIND Easy   TO WALK Little

Take the A3083 from Helston in the direction of the Lizard. Go past RNAS Culdrose, and at the roundabout go left down the B3293. Follow this road until a roundabout. Take the turning for Mawgan. The stone is on a grass area at the junction of three roads in the centre of Mawgan village.

The weathered inscription reads: 'CNEGVMI FILI GENAIVS' – 'Of Cnegumus, Son of Genaius'.

Late Medieval
Gunwalloe church
GRID REFERENCE SW 660205
TO FIND Easy   TO WALK Little
Take the A3083 from Helston in the direction of the Lizard. Go past the RNAS base of Culdrose, but take the turning right before the roundabout at the end of the base. Follow this road all the way through Gunwalloe village and past the Halzephron pub. Park in the National Trust car park and walk straight ahead, where the church is nestled in the side of the promontory on the left. Look out for the 15th-century screen from the Portuguese shipwreck, the St Anthony. The church itself is of aisled construction with a separate belfry.

Post-Medieval
Clowance estate with ornamental landscape
GRID REFERENCE SW635349
TO FIND Easy   TO WALK Little–Moderate
Take the B3303 from either Camborne or Helston. The entrance to the estate is on west side of the road between Praze-an-Beeble and Nancegollan. The estate is a country club with holiday accommodation. The estate is surrounded by a wall, and contains landscaped gardens, exotic trees and water features. A Victorian country house has replaced earlier buildings.

Industrial Period
Portreath industrial port, railway incline and rock-cut baths
GRID REFERENCE SW 653454
TO FIND Easy–Moderate   TO WALK Moderate
Portreath is a small port to the north-west of Redruth. The B3301 from Hayle as it goes down a steep hill into Portreath is flanked on its south side by a deep and broad cutting. This cutting is where the railway incline came down. On the north side of the port is an elaborate harbour with a long pier and two inner docks. A day mark stands above on the cliff. The late 18th-century rock-cut baths are on the seaward side of a small cove at the western extremity of Portreath beach.

Consumer Age
Goonhilly Earth station
GRID REFERENCE SW 727213
TO FIND Easy   TO WALK Little–Moderate
Take the A3083 from Helston in the direction of the Lizard. Go past RNAS Culdrose, and at the roundabout go left down the B3293. Follow this road; the Earth station will appear on the left-hand side. The Earth station is one of two major satellite and cable communications centres in Britain. There is an interpretation centre and a guided tour through the

site. Additionally, just past the Earth station perimeter fence is a small lay-by. Here there are the ruins of a WWII RAF radar station, and on the flat open moor beyond is a grid of small cairns set up as anti-glider defences. There is also a Neolithic standing stone or *menhir* near the perimeter fence of the Earth station.

CARRICK
Late Neolithic–Early Bronze Age
Carland Cross barrow cemetery
GRID REFERENCE SW 845538
TO FIND Easy   TO WALK Little
Carland Cross is the junction between the A30 and the A3076 north of Truro. In the fields to the south-west of the junction are a number of bowl barrows, and to the north-west of the junction is a large bell barrow (in other words, a bowl-shaped mound on a platform with a ditch around it) partially obscured by vegetation.

Late Bronze Age onwards
Bolster Bank
GRID REFERENCE SW 715497 to SW 716500
TO FIND Moderate   TO WALK Little
From the A30, follow the signs for Porthtowan at the junction at Scorrier. From Porthtowan, take the road to St Agnes. The earthwork begins in a field to the east of the road just before a junction where four roads meet. At this junction, turn right for St Agnes and the other visible end of the earthwork is in a field to the south. The earthwork is probably of Late Bronze Age date given the pattern elsewhere in Britain, though may well have continued in use in later periods.

Middle–Late Iron Age
Round Wood, multiple enclosure fort, near Feock
GRID REFERENCE SW 837404
TO FIND Harder   TO WALK Little
On the A39 between Falmouth and Truro, take the B3289 to the south (signposted for King Harry Ferry) at Playing Place. At Penelewey, turn east. Past Trelew, take the lane going directly eastward, rather than turning round the corner. The road is poorly surfaced, so take care. Down the hill, the multiple banks and ditches of the fort will appear on your right-hand side. The site is placed on the cliff overlooking the Industrial Period quay. The weak nature of the 'defences' makes a secure enclosure with separation of livestock a likely explanation, as does its location within a natural theatre with high hills all around it and easy access to the waterways of the Fal river, known as the Carrick Roads. Multiple enclosure forts are generally found in good agricultural areas.

Roman Period
Carvossa Romano-British rectilinear enclosure
GRID REFERENCE SW 919483
TO FIND Moderate   TO WALK Little
On the A390 between Probus and Grampound east of Trewithen Gardens is a small road to the south. It is opposite a turning northward for Grampound Road. Going south down this road, take a turning down the first lane on the left. On your left is the high bank and

ditch of the rectilinear enclosure. Go down the turning to the right just past the earthwork. In the small field to the right is the interior of the enclosure. It is still possible to make out the largely ploughed out continuation of the bank and ditch. The site is placed down from the high point of the hill, making warfare an unlikely reason for its construction. The view over the Fowey and the good agricultural land make trade and agriculture more likely.

Early Medieval
St Clement inscribed stone
GRID REFERENCE SW 850439
TO FIND Easy   TO WALK Little
At the Trafalgar Roundabout on the A39 just north of the wharves, take the turning to the east up a hill. Follow the signs to St Clement. In St Clement, the inscribed stone is to be found in the churchyard. The inscription reads: 'VITALI FILI TORRICI' – 'Of Vitalus, son of Torricus'.

Early–Late Medieval
St Perran's Church, Penhale Sands
GRID REFERENCE SW 772565
TO FIND Moderate   TO WALK Moderate
Following the B3285 out of Perranporth to the east, turn north at the junction by Gear Sands Holiday Park in the direction of Mount. Just before Gear Farm, there is a footpath on the left-hand side. Take the footpath over the dunes. The ruins of the Late Medieval church are easy to see, built here because of the pilgrimage attracted by the early oratory. To the south-west is where the Early Medieval oratory of St Perran is located buried under the sand. Recently archaeologists from the Historic Environment Service have detected the enclosure bank of the Early Medieval monastic settlement around the oratory.

Post-Medieval onwards
Pendennis Castle
GRID REFERENCE SW 824318
TO FIND Easy   TO WALK Moderate
Follow the main A39 into Falmouth. Go straight over all the roundabouts. At the end of the A39 is a roundabout, next to the Falmouth Hotel. Turn right at the roundabout up the hill, following the road as it swerves to the left. Pass the turning to the swimming pool on the right; take the next turning to the right into the Pendennis Castle car park. There is a footpath around the castle defences, and signs indicate where to find the entrance to the castle. English Heritage charge fees for entry to the interior of the castle. The Keep was an early 16th-century gun deck, and the outer earthworks and bastions are late 16th century. Within the castle and other locations around the headland later military structures continued to be built. In woods on the northern slopes, there are even WWI practice trenches.

Industrial Period
St Anthony Fort, the Roseland Peninsula
GRID REFERENCE SW 847311
TO FIND Moderate   TO WALK Moderate
Join the A3078 either at its junction with the A39 and via Tregony or at Ruan High Lanes (from the King Harry Ferry crossing route). Follow the A3078 until the road signposted for Porthscatho and Gerrans. Pass through Gerrans and continue to the end of the road, ignoring the turn-off to St Anthony and Place Manor. At the end of the road is a National Trust car park with a noticeboard showing a map of the site.

This fort was a 19th-century replacement for St Mawes Castle, placed at the end of the Roseland Peninsula opposite Pendennis to guard the Fal estuary. It is hard to spot from the distance, which was part of the strategy. The ditches and weapons were hidden by the carefully landscaped earthworks.

Industrial Period
Devoran mineral tramways and quays
GRID REFERENCE SW 798389
TO FIND Easy   TO WALK Moderate
Take the turning south-east into Devoran from the A39 at the bottom of the hill. Outside the village hall straight down the street (the route of the old mineral tramway) is an interpretive panel explaining the site. At the end of the street the quays and the remains of their storage facilities can be seen alongside the creek. On the opposite side of the A39, a little west of the Devoran turn-off, is a bicycle route along the route of the old mineral tramway down the Carnon Valley to the mines, which made the area the richest in the world during the mid-19th century.

Consumer Age
Truro Cathedral
GRID REFERENCE SW 826449
TO FIND Easy   TO WALK Little
The cathedral is located in the centre of Truro and can be seen easily from most vantage points. Entry is free, though contributions are encouraged. The cathedral is Neo-Gothic with statues of kings and queens of England adorning its western façade. In its southern side it incorporates part of the original aisled parish church of St Mary's. On its northern side there are traces of an abortive project to build cloisters in what is now a green area with park benches.

RESTORMEL
Early–Middle Neolithic
Helman Tor hilltop enclosure
GRID REFERENCE SX 061617
TO FIND Harder   TO WALK Little
From Bodmin, take the A389 past Lanivet. Turn left under the dual carriageway bridge before Innis Downs roundabout. Immediately past the bridge, turn left again. Drive on to Reperry Cross and take the second turning on the right heading south-east for Trebell Green. Continue over another junction to Trebell Green and beyond. Along this woody and shady road, look for a turning to the left in the direction of a large hill with tors on it. There is only one such in the area. Follow this road, which runs along the foot of the hill and curves around

its southern slope. At the southern end of Helman Tor is a car park. A footpath leads up to the monument.

The tors are connected by low stone walls built of large boulders with smaller stones in between. The flat terrace areas were shown to have traces of habitation. The hill is surrounded on three sides by marshy wet areas with surrounding hills behind them. To the south, there is a low ridge. The site dominates the surrounding area.

Early–Middle Neolithic
Lesquite quoit
GRID REFERENCE SX 070628
TO FIND Harder   TO WALK Little
From Bodmin, take the A389 past Lanivet. Turn left under the dual carriageway bridge before Innis Downs roundabout. Immediately past the bridge, turn left again. Drive on to Reperry Cross and take the second turning on the right heading south-east for Trebell Green. Continue over another junction to Trebell Green. At Trebell Green, turn left for Fenton Pits, and in Fenton Pits turn right. About a kilometre (1.6 miles) down this road, the quoit lies in a field on the left-hand side. The quoit has partially collapsed and is placed below Helman Tor.

Late Neolithic
Castilly henge
GRID REFERENCE SX 030628
TO FIND Moderate   TO WALK Little
The henge is located in a field isolated by the Innis Downs roundabout on the A30 (near Lanivet and Bodmin) and a small lane. The small lane cuts across from the A30 to the A391 to the south-west of the roundabout. The henge is actually visible from the A30 immediately west of Innis Downs roundabout.

This is one of Cornwall's few henges. It has a clear high bank and an inner ditch, and lies mid-way down a slope. Excavations revealed that its bank had been modified and heightened after its original construction. It may possibly have been re-used during the Civil War (mid-17th century).

Middle–Late Iron Age
Castle-an-Dinas hillfort
GRID REFERENCE SW 945624
TO FIND Easy   TO WALK Moderate
On the A30 between Truro and Bodmin is a stretch without dual carriageway. Just west of the narrow railway bridge that goes over the A30 is a turning to the west signposted for St Columb Major. 2 kilometres (1.25 miles) along this road is a lane to the right up the hillside. It is signposted for Castle-an-Dinas. There is a car park at the end next to the buildings of the former tungsten mine (do not enter). Follow the footpath to the hillfort. To the north of the hillfort is an overgrown area that is fenced off. This is where the tungsten mine was, and is too dangerous to explore.

Late Iron Age–Roman Period
The Rumps cliff castle
GRID REFERENCE SW 934811
TO FIND Harder   TO WALK Long

Danger Avoid in poor weather conditions
From Wadebridge, take the B3314 northwards past St Minver. When the B3314 makes a sharp turn eastwards, go straight ahead down the road for New Polzeath and Polzeath. Follow the signs left at the next junction. Ignore two turnings to the left, and instead take the right-hand turn after these turnings up the hill past Pentireglaze Farm. There is a National Trust car park before Pentire Farm; alternatively, you can pay the farmer for parking in the farmyard. From there, take the footpath to the headland where the cliff castle is located. The walk is about a kilometre (1.6 miles).

The cliff castle has multiple banks and ditches cutting off the headland. The oval houses in the interior are hard to make out. However, the two large stacks on the headland and the third out at sea probably have much to do with its siting.

Early Medieval
Mawgan Porth settlement and cemetery
GRID REFERENCE SW 851673
TO FIND Easy   TO WALK Little
From Newquay, take the B3276 northwards until Mawgan Porth. After crossing the bridge, there is a turning into a public car park on the right-hand side of the road. From there, walk to a crazy golf course and caravan site also on the right-hand side of the road. The settlement can be seen on the upper slope of the hill in the same field as the crazy golf course. You can enter the site with the golf course owner's permission.

The houses are divided into a living space and a byre for livestock. Each byre contains a drain. The drystone walled houses are placed close together, probably indicating a close-knit kinship-based society.

Late Medieval
Restormel Castle and the Duchy Palace
GRID REFERENCE SX 104614
TO FIND Easy   TO WALK Little
At the north-west end of Lostwithiel on the A390, turn onto a smaller road headed northward. This road is signposted for the Castle. At the end of the road just before the farm buildings follow the signpost to the left up to the Castle. English Heritage charges fees for entry. In Lostwithiel itself are a museum and the Duchy Palace, the best preserved part of which is found in Quay Street. From the A390, turn down Fore Street to the south. Continue past the church on the left, and turn right into Quay Street. The Freemason's Lodge on the corner is the most obvious surviving part of the palace, which originally took up the whole block.

Post-Medieval
St Catherine's Castle
GRID REFERENCE SX 118509
TO FIND Moderate   TO WALK Moderate
Danger Avoid in poor weather conditions
Go to Fowey and take the street following the coast of the estuary south-westwards. Further down, follow the signs along the footpath to the headland where the 16th-century Castle is situated. The castle is two storeys high

with gun ports in the lower one. In Fowey and Polruan (facing Fowey across the estuary), there are two late 14th-century blockhouses representing the earlier Late Medieval defence system for the Fowey.

Industrial Period
Wheal Martyn china clay works and museum
GRID REFERENCE SX 005554
TO FIND Easy   TO WALK Little
The museum and site are on the west side of the B3274 north of St Austell, between Ruddlemoor and Carthew. This is a good place to understand how the region's china clay industry worked.

Consumer Age
The Eden Project
GRID REFERENCE SX 049548
TO FIND Easy   TO WALK Little–Moderate
Take the A391 from Innis Downs roundabout on the A30 or from just east of St Austell. Follow the signposts at a double roundabout near Penwithick for a turning eastward to the Eden Project. From there the route is well signposted.

A former china clay pit has been transformed into a celebration of Cornwall's almost 300 year-old tradition of being a haven for imported exotic flora that could not be acclimatised elsewhere in the UK. Large domes cover the tropical rainforest and arid zones in the European Union's answer to the USA's Biosphere.

CARADON
Mesolithic–Early Bronze Age
Dozmary Pool campsite
GRID REFERENCE SX 193743
TO FIND Moderate   TO WALK Little
Turn off the A30 for the Jamaica Inn. Opposite the Jamaica Inn, the road for Dozmary Pool is signposted to the south. The Mesolithic, Neolithic and Early Bronze Age campsite is at the western shore of the pool.

Like all such sites, it is the location rather than extant remains that is important. Except for the modern reservoirs, it would have been the only such pool on the moor. As such it would have attracted animals sought by these prehistoric hunters. Its atmospheric location has also made it part of the legend of Jan Tregeagle, who was sentenced for eternity to empty it using a shell with a hole in it. Eventually, a storm emptied it, setting him free.

Early–Middle Neolithic
Trethevy quoit
GRID REFERENCE SX 259688
TO FIND Harder   TO WALK Little
From Liskeard, take the B3254 northward, then the turning north for St Cleer. Just past a crossroads, take the turning to the right for Tremar and Darite. Drive through Tremar on the turning northward to Darite and Trethevy quoit. The quoit is in a field to the left of a crossroads, on a low knoll below Caradon Hill.

The quoit, or dolmen, consists of uprights around a chamber supporting an enormous capstone. This is perhaps the most impressive of this type of monument in Cornwall. It is worth remembering that it would have originally been viewed with Caradon Hill towering over it, and that it thus merely mimicked the hill's now missing tor.

Late Neolithic
Duloe (pronounced 'Dew-low [opposite of high]') stone circle
GRID REFERENCE SX 236583
TO FIND Moderate   TO WALK Little
On the B3254 between Liskeard and Looe, go to the village of Duloe. In a field just north of the church is the small but impressive stone circle. A signpost indicates the path to take. The stone circle consists of large quartz uprights in a small circle. It is partly the result of reconstruction as some of the stones had been incorporated into a nearby hedge.

Late Neolithic–Early Bronze Age
The Hurlers and Rillaton Barrow
GRID REFERENCE SX 257714 & SX 260719
TO FIND Easy   TO WALK Moderate
From Liskeard, take the B3254 northward to Upton Cross. In Upton Cross, take the road westwards to the Minions at the crossroads. Before entering the Minions, a car park with a Cornish engine house will appear on the right-hand side of the road. Park here. The engine house contains a free interpretation centre. Immediately beyond the engine house to the left are three stone circles in a row. Due north is a single large round barrow. This is the Rillaton Barrow, where the golden beaker in the British Museum came from (a replica is in the Royal Cornwall Museum). Amazingly, the beaker's exact twin was found in a barrow in Kent recently.

Neolithic–Middle Bronze Age
Stowe's Pound
GRID REFERENCE SX 258726
TO FIND Easy   TO WALK Long
Danger Avoid in poor weather conditions
Follow the route for the Hurlers (as above), then just follow the footpath northward to the hill. At the top of the hill is the natural tor formation of the Cheesewring. The broad rock wall at the top is the Neolithic hilltop enclosure. The second walled enclosure on the northern slopes is the Middle Bronze Age settlement enclosure with a scattering of hut circles inside and outside it. Below the Cheesewring is the quarry begun in the Industrial period.

Roman Period
Goonzion Romano-British rectilinear enclosure
GRID REFERENCE SX 172677
TO FIND Harder   TO WALK Little
On the A38 between Bodmin and Liskeard, take the turning for St Neots. In St Neot's turn west on the road for Mount and Cardinham. The enclosure is in the second field on the left-hand side past a crossroads. It consists of low, straight-sided earthworks around a level area on the brow of the hill. Like other such enclosures, it was clearly located to maximise agricultural resources.

In this case, it was placed among the rich soils of the lowlands with transhumance opportunities on the adjacent moors looming above it.

Early Medieval

The Doniert Stone

GRID REFERENCE SX 237688

TO FIND Easy   TO WALK Little

From Dobwalls on the A38 (between Bodmin and Liskeard), take the road north for St Cleer. Continue on this road past Redgate, and the Stone will appear in a grassy niche beside the road on the right-hand side.

This decorative inscribed stone is dedicated to Doniert or Dumgarth, the last recorded King of Cornwall, who drowned in AD 875. The inscription reads 'Doniert Rogavit Pro Anima' – 'Doniert requested this [to be erected] for the benefit of his soul'.

Late Medieval

St German's church (priory)

GRID REFERENCE SX 359578

TO FIND Easy   TO WALK Little

Just before Tideford on the A38, take the turning south down the B3249 for St Germans. On the left-hand side of the road in the village is a church with an unusually large and magnificent round decorated archway in the Norman style. This is St German's church.

St German's was once the church of an Augustine priory. The present building is only part of the original construction. The remains of the rest under the ground surface extend into the Port Eliot estate behind.

Post-Medieval

St Neot's church

GRID REFERENCE SX 186679

TO FIND Easy   TO WALK Little

On the A38 between Bodmin and Liskeard, take the turning for St Neots. In St Neot's, turn left, and the church is on the right-hand side of the road.

The church is famous for its rare 16th-century stained-glass windows. The guilds in this wealthy town were sponsored by all the local guilds, which are also represented, along with religious themes.

Post-Medieval onwards

Mount Edgcumbe estate, blockhouse and D-Day landing

GRID REFERENCE SX 452527

TO FIND Easy   TO WALK Moderate

From the A38 at Trerulefoot, turn down the A374 for Torpoint. Turn to the right down the B3247 for Crafthole and Millbrook. Continue past Millbrook to Mount Edgcumbe, which is on the end of a peninsula in the Tamar opposite Plymouth.

Within the estate, there is a 16th-century stately home and a blockhouse on the shore. The small northern bay contains concrete matting from the D-Day operations during the Second World War. The road leading to the bay was constructed at that time.

Industrial Period

Kit Hill folly, mines and quarries

GRID REFERENCE SX 375713

TO FIND Moderate   TO WALK Moderate–Long

From Callington, take the A390 north-eastwards. Take a left turn up the road in the direction of Monkscross and Luckett. On the left-hand side, take the road up the hill. Parking is available. Walk up to the top, where you will find Sir John Call's late 18th-century folly in the form of a motte-and-bailey castle. All around the hill are old mines and quarries that can be visited. Follow the trail that has been marked out for safety reasons.

NORTH CORNWALL

Paleolithic–Mesolithic

Booby's Bay

GRID REFERENCE SW 854759

TO FIND Moderate   TO WALK Moderate

From Padstow, take the B3276 until just past Windmill. Turn right to Harlyn. Drive through Harlyn, and take the right-hand turn for Trevose Head and Constantine Bay. Take the next right for Trevose Head. On the left-hand side there are parking spaces, and a footpath to the coast. Alternatively, drive up the road and park in one of the car parks. The Palaeolithic and Mesolithic sites are located along the slopes and on the low cliff of Booby's Bay. The Late Mesolithic site is just above a small quarry pit at the head of a stream, part way up the slope. This spot has panoramic views along the coast and inland, illustrating the changing relationship of Late Mesolithic people to the natural world.

Early–Middle Neolithic

Woolley Barrow

GRID REFERENCE SS 263166

TO FIND Easy   TO WALK Little

Follow the A39 north of Kilkhampton. The barrow is situated just before the border with Devon on the right-hand side of the road. It is in the corner between the A39 and a minor road. The site is on a slope overlooking the source of the Tamar river. Originally part of a long barrow cemetery, this is the only surviving barrow. It has no chamber inside, and has ditches on either side. Cornish long barrows frequently do not contain any funerary evidence.

Neolithic–Iron Age

Showery Tor and Roughtor (pronounced 'Row [as in 'now'] -ter') prehistoric landscape

GRID REFERENCE SX 149813 & SX 146808

TO FIND Easy   TO WALK Long

Danger Avoid in poor weather conditions

Take the A39 to Camelford. Just before exiting the town on the northern side, turn down the Roughtor Road (signposted). Follow until the end, where there is a National Trust car park. Walk up the hillside to the northernmost tor, Showery Tor, surrounded by a flat cairn. On the way up, you will notice a low broad stone wall – an embanked avenue first aligned on Showery Tor and then changed to face what was the central tor, quarried away in the Industrial Period. Around the main part of the ridge, Roughtor, is a Neolithic hilltop enclosure, later modified to make an Iron Age hillfort.

Middle Bronze Age

Leskernick settlements and field systems

GRID REFERENCE SX 182800

TO FIND Moderate   TO WALK Long

Danger Avoid in poor weather conditions

Take the turning for Jamaica Inn on the A30, but do not follow the turning under the dual carriageway bridge. Instead take the road to Codda. Walk from there along the footpath through the moor heading northward. Pass over two streams. The hill in front of you is Leskernick. On its southern and western flanks are two settlements from the Middle Bronze Age, complete with roundhouses (hut circles) and field systems.

Note how some fields are covered with boulders and rocks, and could hardly have served an agricultural purpose. It is possible that some fields were reserved for the dead or spirits.

Neolithic–Late Iron Age

Warbstow Bury

GRID REFERENCE SX 201907

TO FIND Moderate   TO WALK Little

Take the A39 north of Camelford, and turn north-west up the A395, signposted for Launceston. At Hallworthy, take the northern road to Warbstow Cross and Canworthy Water. Just at the cusp of the hill going down to Warbstow Cross, the hillfort is on the left-hand side. The lay-by permits limited parking.

This impressive hillfort has multiple large banks and ditches, and a small long barrow in the centre. It is on the edge of the Culm Measures, the most northerly of Cornwall's moorlands, and overlooks the Ottery River.

Roman Period

Tintagel church – Roman milestone

GRID REFERENCE SX 050884

TO FIND Easy   TO WALK Little

From Camelford, head up the B3266 and, following the signs, change to the B3263 for Tintagel. In Tintagel, steer west through the main street. The church is signposted down a narrow road to the south-west. In the church is the Roman milestone.

The milestone bears the inscription 'IMP C G VAL LIC LICIN' – 'To the Emperor Caesar Gaius Valerius Licinius Licinianus'. Licinius was emperor from AD 308–24.

Late Medieval

Tintagel Castle

GRID REFERENCE SX 050892

TO FIND Easy   TO WALK Long

Danger Avoid in poor weather conditions

Take the route for Tintagel church as above, except continue down the main street for the car park near a gift shop. The signposts to the Castle indicate the route down the 'Vale of Avalon', which is forbidden to cars of the general public. Walk down to the bottom, where the ticket office and exhibition centre is located. English Heritage charges an entry fee.

The tall upstanding ruins are mainly Late Medieval (or 19th- and 20th-century restoration). However, on the northern and western flanks of the island, there are low drystone walls on terraces that represent at least 120 dwellings of the Early Medieval Period.

Late Medieval

Launceston Castle

GRID REFERENCE SX 330856

TO FIND Easy   TO WALK Moderate

Take the A388 off the A38 for Launceston. The road leads right up to the Castle gate. Entry is only by foot, however. Car parks are available elsewhere in the town. English Heritage charges an entry fee.

The Castle is of motte-and-bailey type. A stone keep and parts of the bailey wall survive. Some of the bailey buildings survive as foundations. In the adjacent town, there is a magnificent, highly decorated church and one of the town gates (Launceston was a walled town).

Post-Medieval

Stowe House and gardens

GRID REFERENCE SS 215112

TO FIND Moderate   TO WALK Moderate

From the A39 just before Kilkhampton, take the minor road to the west for Coombe. On the right-hand side before Stowe Barton Farm is a footpath leading to the east. The ruins of Stowe House and its associated gardens are to the south-east of the present-day buildings of Stowe Barton farm. Note the formal layout of this early phase of garden architecture of the late 17th century.

Industrial Period

Bude canal

GRID REFERENCE SS 204064 to SS 218037

TO FIND Easy   TO WALK Little–Moderate (if you follows the canal)

The surviving part of the canal begins at its opening at the harbour and goes southwards to Helebridge, where it passes under the A39. To the immediate east of the A39 road bridge is a basin and wharf area. The canal was designed to transport the lime-rich sands of the coast to the inland farms in order to 'sweeten' or reduce the acidity of the moorland soils.

Late Medieval and Consumer Age

Davidstow WWII American Airbase and Late Medieval longhouse settlement

GRID REFERENCE SX 150850 and SX 159844

TO FIND Easy   TO WALK Little–Moderate (to visit Late Medieval site)

Go north along the A39 from Camelford. After passing the B3314 turning to Slaughterbridge on the left side of the road, take the next turning on the right. The road passes right through the ruins of the WWII American airbase. Runways, a control tower and blast pens (square earthworks to prevent explosions from bombed aircraft affecting further aircraft) are just some of the upstanding features of the airbase.

Continue along the road and stop just before the farmhouse of Higher Penhale. Directly south on the edge of Crowdy Reservoir is the Late Medieval longhouse settlement. Low earthworks of turf mark out the houses. Be well prepared with waterproof footwear.

Museums and Heritage

The Historic Environment Service

The Historic Environment Service of Cornwall County Council is responsible for maintaining records of all the known archaeological sites and find spots in the County (including the Isles of Scilly). It also offers advice and information to the general public, academics and to the Council's planning department about Cornwall's archaeology. It is the first port of call for those planning research projects in Cornwall. The Service has its own archaeological unit that tenders along with other archaeological organisations for fieldwork projects resulting from development.
Historic Environment Section, (Cornwall Archaeological Unit), Cornwall County Council
Kennall Building, Old County Hall, Station Road, Truro TR1 3AY
Tel: +44 (0)1872 323603
Fax: +44 (0)1872 323811
Email: cau@planning.cornwall.gov.uk
www.cornwall.gov.uk/history/ab-hi30.htm

The Royal Cornwall Museum

This is the main museum of Cornwall. It houses a collection of local archaeology of all periods. There are also collections of natural history and geology, as well as art exhibits and foreign archaeology. The Museum stages some exhibitions specifically for children. Exhibits can now be viewed online via the CHAIN website (see entry for CHAIN below). Within the same building is the Royal Institution of Cornwall's Courtney Library. The library is well stocked with literature about many different aspects of Cornwall.
Opening hours: 10.00–17.00 Monday–Saturday (Last admission 16.30); free admission
Royal Cornwall Museum, River Street
Truro TR1 2SJ
Tel: +44 (0)1872 272205
Fax: +44 (0)1872 240514
Email: enquiries@royalcornwallmuseum.org.uk
www.royalcornwallmuseum.org.uk

CHAIN
(Cornwall Heritage Access Information Network)

CHAIN is a website for a number of museums and galleries in Cornwall. It provides online access to records and information of the collections held at the Royal Cornwall Museum, Penlee House Museum and Gallery, Falmouth Art Gallery, Wheal Martyn.
www.chain.org.uk/

Cornish Heritage Trust

The trust owns and curates a number of archaeological sites in Cornwall, as well as managing a number of English Heritage properties.
Hon Secretary Mrs Holden, Park View
Metherell, Callington

Email: cht@cornwallheritage.nildram.co.uk
www.cornwallheritage.nildram.co.uk/

English Heritage

English Heritage offers free entry to its sites for members (not just in Cornwall), free or reduced fees for events, reduced entry fees with some other organisations and a quarterly magazine.
UK:
English Heritage, Membership Department
Freepost WD214, PO Box 570, Swindon SN2 2UR
From overseas:
English Heritage, Membership Department
PO Box 570, Swindon SN2 2UR, UK
Tel: +44 (0)870 333 1182
Fax: +44 (0)1793 414 926
Email: members@english-heritage.org.uk

The National Trust

The trust owns and manages properties in Cornwall of historic and archaeological importance. Some properties are free and some charge fees for entry or parking.
The National Trust Cornwall Office, Lanhydrock
Bodmin PL30 4DE
Tel: 01208 265950, Fax: 01208 265959
www.nationaltrust.org.uk/regions/devoncornwall/

The Trevithick Trust

This is an organisation devoted to managing Cornwall's industrial heritage. It curates industrial sites and opens them to the general public. It is not the same as the Trevithick Society (see below). Membership entitles you to visit the sites under its care free, and you receive a newsletter too.
The Trevithick Trust, Trevithick Road
Pool, Redruth TR15 3NP
Tel / Fax 01209 210900
Email: info@trevithicktrust.com
Email for membership: members@trevithicktrust.com

SOCIETIES

Cornwall Archaeological Society (CAS)

The CAS provides archaeological walks, a lecture programme, an annual journal and a newsletter three times a year. The CAS can also help members seeking opportunities to participate in fieldwork, including excavation.
Cornwall Archaeological Society, Truro College
Tregye, Tregye Road, Carnon Downs, Truro TR3 6JH
www.cornisharchaeology.org.uk/

Trevithick Society

This is Cornwall's industrial archaeology and history society. It provides lectures, a quarterly newsletter and

an annual journal. It also carries out restoration and reconstruction projects. Free entry to a number of industrial archaeological sites is available to members. It is not the same as the Trevithick Trust (see above).
The Trevithick Society, Po Box No 62, Camborne TR14 7ZN
Email: membership@trevithick-society.org.uk
www.trevithick-society.org.uk/

The Young Archaeologists Club (YAC)
This is a club for children aged 8–16, though there is a scheme recently offered for the under-8s called 'YAC supporters' (with some restrictions on participation). The club offers a range of activities and information, including a quarterly magazine, free entry to monuments belonging to English Heritage, Cadw Welsh Historic Monuments, Historic Scotland and Environment and Heritage (Northern Ireland); details of National Archaeology days and residential holidays (9 years old upwards only).
Tony Blackman, YAC Cornwall Branch,
2 The Terrace, Cocks, Perranporth, Cornwall TR6 OAT
Tel: +44 (0)1872 572725
Email: tony@cocks.nildram.co.uk
www.britarch.ac.uk/yac/

OVERSEES ORGANISATIONS WITH AN INTEREST IN CORNISH HERITAGE

Australian Federation of Cornish Associations
The Cornish associations in Australia have a wide range of interests, which includes the archaeological heritage of Cornish communities in Australia.
Mr Chris Dunkerley
Tel: 61+2+9876.2893 or 9876.2618
Email: kevrenor@ozemail.com.au
http://members.ozemail.com.au/~kevrenor/afca.html

Cornish American Heritage Society (CAHS)
The society is involved in a range of activities to do with Cornwall and the Cornish settlements in North America and produces a quarterly newsletter, which includes Cornish heritage information.
Cornish American Heritage Society, 8494 Wesley Dr, Flushing, MI 48433-1165, USA
Cornish American Heritage Society
Box 286, Waterdown, ON L0R 2H0, Canada
www.cousinjack.org/

EDUCATION

Truro College
Truro College offers a two-year Foundation Degree in Archaeology in partnership with the University of Plymouth. Additionally, it offers an archaeology A-Level (both daytime and evening) and archaeological leisure courses.
Sylvia Dixon
Higher Education Admissions, Truro College
College Road, Truro TR1 3XX
Tel: +44 (0)1872 267061
Email: Sylviad@trurocollege.ac.uk
www.trurocollege.ac.uk/archaeology/

Bibliography

Guides to monuments
The most comprehensive, easy to use and understand guides (a little dated now):
Weatherhill, C. *Belerion: Ancient Sites of Land's End*. Alison Hodge, Penzance. 1981.
Weatherhill, C. *Cornovia: Ancient Sites of Cornwall and Scilly*. Alison Hodge, Penzance. 1985.
More up-to-date guides:
Johnson, N and Rose, P. *Cornwall's Archaeological Heritage*. Twelveheads Press, Truro. 1990.
Ratcliffe, J. and Johns, C. *Scilly's Archaeological Heritage*. Historic Environment Unit, Cornwall County Council & Twelveheads Press, Truro. 2003.
Current journals discussing Cornish archaeology:
Archaeology Alive, a popular journal produced at present for free by the Historic Environment Service explaining their current projects (also available online).
Cornish Archaeology, published by the Cornwall Archaeology Society.
The Journal of the Trevithick Society, concerned with industrial archaeology and history.

Regional studies
The Historic Environment Service's regional studies of archaeological landscapes are good local guides to the overall archaeological landscape:
Herring, P. and Rose, P. *Bodmin Moor's Archaeological Heritage*. Cornwall Archaeological Unit. Cornwall County Council, Truro. 2001.
Parkes, C. *Fowey Estuary Historic Audit*. Cornwall Archaeological Unit. Cornwall County Council, Truro. 2000.
Ratcliffe, J. *Fal Estuary Historic Audit*. Cornwall Archaeological Unit. Cornwall County Council, Truro. 1997.

Themed heritage guides
A good series of heritage books is published by Twelveheads Press, such as:
Tarrant, M. *Cornwall's Lighthouse Heritage*. Twelveheads Press, Truro. 2000.
Kittridge, A. *Cornwall's Maritime Heritage*. Twelveheads Press, Truro. 1991.
Lees, H. *Cornwall's Churchyard Heritage*. Twelveheads Press, Truro. 1996.

211

Notes and References

Introduction
1 D. Lowenthal *The Past is a Foreign Country*.
Cambridge University Press, Cambridge, 1984
2 The annual journal of the Cornwall Archaeological
Society
3 For more information on these ideas, see Chapter 7
(pp. 98–115) in M. Johnson *Archaeological Theory: An
Introduction*. Blackwell, Oxford 1999; and pp. 461 and
464 in C. Renfrew and P. Bahn (2nd ed.) *Archaeology:
Theories, Methods and Practice*. Thames and Hudson,
London 1996
4 Page 1 in P.V. Kirch and R.C. Green *Hawaiki,
Ancestral Polynesia : An Essay in Historical
Anthropology*. Cambridge University Press,
Cambridge, 2001
5 See Chapter 1, 'Creation', pp. 22 –39 in A. Voigt and
N. Drury *Wisdom from the Earth: The Living Legacy
of the Aboriginal Dreamtime*. Shambala, Boston, 1998
6 For more information on Cornish geology, see S.
Campbell, C.O. Hunt, J.D. Scourse, D.H. Keen, N.
Stephens (eds.) *Quaternary of South-west England*
(Geological Conservation Review S.). Kluwer
Academic Publishers, London, 1998; E.A. Edmonds,
M.C. McKeown and M. Williams *British Regional
Geology – South West England*. HMSO, London 1975;
E.D. Selwood, E.M. Durrance and C.M. Bristow (eds.)
The Geology of Cornwall and the Isles of Scilly.
University of Exeter Press, Exeter, 1998; and P. Stanier
Cornwall's Geological Heritage. Twelveheads Press,
Truro 1990
7 Page 34 in E.A. Edmonds, M.C. McKeown and M.
Williams *British Regional Geology – South West
England*. HMSO, London 1975
8 Page 13 in P. Berridge and A. Roberts 'The
Mesolithic period in Cornwall'. *Cornish Archaeology*.
25, 1986, pp. 7–34 and D. Naylor and P.M. Shannon
The Geology of Offshore Ireland and West Britain.
Graham & Trotman, London.
9 See M. Stoyle *West Britons: Cornish Identities and
the Early Modern British State*. University of Exeter
Press, Exeter, 2002.
10 D. Burnett *A Royal Duchy: Portrait of the Duchy of
Cornwall*. The Dovecote Press, Wimborne, Dorset,
1996.
11 Page 455 in T.C. Champion 'The appropriation of
the Phoenicians in British imperial ideology'. *Nations
and Nationalism* 7, 2001, pp. 451–65
12 W. Borlase, (2nd ed.) *Antiquities, Historical and
Monumental of the County of Cornwall*. Bowyer and J.
Nichols, London (re-pub. East Ardsley, Wakefield
Yorks.: EP Publishing Ltd and Cornwall County
Library) 1769
13 Ibid
14 Page 452 in Champion 2001
15 Ibid, pp.458–60
16 Ibid, p.461
17 Page 166 in H.O'Neill Hencken *The Archaeology of
Cornwall and Scilly*. Methuen, London, 1932.
18 N. Beagrie 'The St. Mawes Ingot'. *Cornish
Archaeology*. 22, 1983, pp. 107–11
19 Page 81 in S. Lancel (trans.. A. Nevill) *Carthage: A
History*. Blackwell, Oxford, 1997
20 Ibid, pp. 15–17 & 102–09
21 L. Thorpe (trans.) Geoffrey of Monmouth: *The
History of the Kings of Britain*. Penguin Books,
London, 1966.
22 J.C. Barnes (trans..) *Beroul's Romance of Tristran*;
translated [from the Italian]. Manchester University
Press, Manchester 1972; E. M. R. Ditmas *Tristan and
Iseult in Cornwall: The Twelfth-century Romance by
Beroul Re-told from the Norman French*. Forrester
Roberts, Gloucester, 1970.
23 Page 40 in Borlase 1769
24 e.g., see pp. 158–88 in L. Alcock, and G. Ashe
'Cadbury: is it Camelot?' In G. Ashe (ed.) *The Quest
for Arthur's Britain*. Pall Mall Press Ltd, London,
1968.
25 e.g., J.P. Mallory *In Search of the Indo-Europeans:
Language, Archaeology, and Myth*. Thames & Hudson,
London, 1991
26 J. Collis 'Celtic myths'. *Antiquity*. 71, 1997, pp.
195–201; S. James 'Celts, politics and motivation in
archaeology'. *Antiquity* 72, 1998, pp. 200–09
27 B. Anderson (rev. ed.) *Imagined Communities*.
Verso, London, 1991
28 J. Collis 'Celts and politics'. In P. Graves-Brown *et
al.* (eds) *Cultural Identity and Archaeology: the
construction of European Communities*, pp. 167–78.
Routledge, London, 1996; Collis 1997
29 James 1998
30 e.g., B.G. Trigger 'Alternative Archaeologies:
Nationalist, Colonialist, Imperialist'. *Man* 19, 1984, pp.
355–370
31 J.V.S. Megaw and M.R. Megaw 'Ancient Celts and
modern ethnicity'. *Antiquity* 70, 1996, pp. 175–81
32 H. Härke 'Archaeologists and migrations: A
problem of attitude?' *Current Anthropology* 39, 1998,
pp. 19–45
33 Collis 1997; James 1998; T.C. Champion 'Three
nations or one? Britain and the national use of the past'
In M. Diaz-Andreu and T.C. Champion (eds.)
Nationalism and Archaeology in Europe. UCL Press,
London, 1996, pp. 119–45; M. Chapman *The Celts: the
Construction of a Myth*. Macmillan, Basingstoke, 1992;
B. Cunliffe *The Ancient Celts*. Oxford University Press,
Oxford, 1997
34 R.G. Harvey, M.T. Smith, S. Sherren, L. Bailey and
S.J. Hyndam 'How Celtic are the Cornish?: A Study of
Biological Affinities'. *Man* 21, 1986, pp. 177–201
35 L. Laing, and J. Laing *Art of the Celts: From 700* BC
to the Celtic Revival. Thames and Hudson, London,
1992; A.C. Thomas *Celtic Britain*. Thames and
Hudson, London, 1997
36 A.C. Thomas *op cit*.
37 Pages 76–85 in A.C. Thomas *Christianity in Roman
Britain to* AD500. Batsford, London, 1993.

**Chapter One Natural and human worlds on the
edge of the Atlantic**
1 R.M. Jacobi. 'Early Flandrian hunters in the South
West'. *Proc. Devon Arch. Soc.* 37, 1979, pp. 48–93
2 C. Gamble *The Palaeolithic Societies of Europe*.
Cambridge University Press, Cambridge, 1999
3 There are many ethnographic examples of this:
aborigines in the Cape York Peninsula, Australia,
gather food plants over a wide area and then
concentrate them in particular clearings – D.R. Harris
'Land of plenty on Cape York Peninsula. Australian

Aborigines live without agriculture'. *The Geographical Magazine*, 48, 1976, pp. 657–61. Inuit people (and the archaeological cultures before them) in the Arctic regions of Canada and Greenland modified the routes of caribou deer to guide and concentrate the herds as part of their hunting strategy – pp.144 & 211 in R. McGhee *Ancient People of the Arctic*. University of British Columbia Press, Vancouver, 2001. They also used stone monuments (*Inuksuit*) as markers to show routes of migrating caribou – N. Hallendy *Inuksuit. Silent Messengers of the Arctic*. Douglas & McIntyre & University of Washington Press, Vancouver, 2000. As for fishing, Maori people in New Zealand kept shorelines like gardens – section 2.6.1 in the Waitangi Tribunal *Ngai Tahu Sea Fisheries Report 1992 (Wai 27)*. Waitangi Tribunal Report: 5 WTR. Brooker And Friend Ltd. Wellington, NZ, 1992 [WWW] www.knowledge-basket.co.nz/oldwaitangi/text/wai027s/verso_01.html (27/02/04). This meant concentrating various types of shellfish on different parts of the shore, creating an effect like horticultural allotments.

4 The harvester people are noted for their exploitation of large swathes of wild rice. This allowed them to harvest large surpluses, which were then stored in the same way that is usually associated with farming societies. See J.M. McClurken and C.E. Cleland (eds) *Fish in the Lakes, Wild Rice and Game in Abundance: Testimony on Behalf of Mille Lacs Ojibwe Hunting and Fishing Rights*. Michigan State University Press, East Lansing, MI, 2000; and T. Vennum *Wild Rice and the Ojibway People*, Minnesota Historical Press, St. Paul, Minnesota, 1988

5 Archaeologically, a similar culture has been identified in the Levant in the early part of the post-glacial. The 'Natufian' when first identified was thought to be one of the earliest farming cultures on the basis of plants and animals now used as domesticates, the storage facilities on sites and the permanent nature of settlement. More recently, it has become clear that they were sedentary hunter-gatherers and the immediate predecessors of the first farmers – see pp. 254–55 in B.M. Fagan *People of the Earth: An Introduction to World Prehistory*. Longman, Harlow, 1998

6 See p. 214 in M. Zvelebil 'Fat is a Feminist Issue: On Ideology, Diet and Health in Hunter-Gatherer Societies'. In M. Donald and L. Hurcombe (eds.) *Gender and Material Culture in Archaeological Perspective*, pp. 209–21, Palgrave Macmillan, Basingstoke, Hants., 2000.

7 See P.F. Whitehead 'Neolithic and Upper Palaeolithic working sites, Booby's Bay, Cornwall'. *Cornish Archaeol.* 12, 1973, pp. 5–18; and also, P.F. Whitehead. 'Booby's Point Working Site: A revised chronology'. *Cornish Archaeol.* 14, 1975, p. 118

8 Even as for north as Leeds! See L.G.A. *The Leeds Hippo. The LGA palaeontological icon*. Leeds Geological Association, 2001–04 [WWW] www.leedsgeolassoc.freeserve.co.uk/hippo.html (28/02/2004)

9 See B.R.G.M. *Carte géologique de la France et de la marge continentale à l'échelle de 1/1500 000*. Bureau de Récherche Géologiques et Minières, Orléans, 1980; and also, P. Gibbard *History of the northwest European rivers during the past three million years*.

Godwin Institute for Quaternary Research, University of Cambridge, 2004 [WWW] www-qpg.geog.cam.ac.uk/research/nweurorivers/ (25/02/2004)

10 Ibid

11 H.E. Balch 'Excavations at Wookey Hole and other Mendip Caves 1926–7'. *Antiquaries Journal* 8, 1928, pp. 193–210; C. Smith *Late Stone Age Hunters of the British Isles*. Routledge, London, 1992

12 R. Hosfield *Broom Excavations – September 2000 & September 2001*. Centre for the Archaeology of Human Origins, University of Southampton, 2002 [WWW] www.soton.ac.uk/~rth1/broom/broom.html (28/02/2004)

13 See p. 31 in J. Whetter *The History of Falmouth*. Dyllansow Truran, Redruth, Cornwall, 1981

14 C. Stringer 'Coasting out of Africa' *Nature* 405, 2000, pp. 24–27; Stringer, C. and C. Gamble *In Search of the Neanderthals*. Thames & Hudson, London, 1994

15 C. Stringer and C. Gamble 1994

16 See pp.76–82 in C. Smith 1992

17 Ibid

18 Page 13 in P. Berridge and A. Roberts 'The Mesolithic period in Cornwall'. *Cornish Archaeol.* 25, 1986, pp. 7–34 and D. Naylor and P.M. Shannon *The Geology of Offshore Ireland and West Britain*. Graham & Trotman, London

19 P.F. Whitehead 1973 & 1975

20 For the background to these changes, see M. Bell and M.J.C. Walker *Late Quaternary Environmental Change: Physical and Human Perspectives*. Longman, London 1992; and N. Roberts *The Holocene: an environmental history*. Blackwell, Oxford, 1998

21 For general information about Mesolithic stone tools including microliths, see C. Smith 1992 and J. Wymer *Mesolithic Britain*. Shire Publications, Princes Risborough 1991

22 Pages 114–115 in B. Cunliffe *Facing the Ocean: The Atlantic and Its Peoples, 8000 BC to AD 1500*. Oxford University Press, Oxford, 2001

23 For good overviews of the Neolithic in Europe, see J. Lichardus and M. Lichardus-Itten *Protohistoire de l'Europe. Le Néolithique et le Chalcolithique*. P.U.F., Paris 1985; H. Mueller-Karpe *Handbuch der Vorgeschichte. Band I. Altsteinzeit*. Beck, Munich, 1966; A. Whittle *Europe in the Neolithic: The creation of new worlds*. Cambridge University Press, Cambridge, 1996

24 See R. Bradley. *The Significance of Monuments: On the Shaping of Experience in Neolithic and Bronze Age Europe*. Routledge, London, 1998; and also, A. Whittle 1996

25 P. Rowley-Conwy 'Cemeteries, Seasonality and Complexity in the Ertebølle of Southern Scandinavia'. In M. Zvelebil, L. Dománska and R. Dennell (eds.) *Harvesting the Sea, Farming the Forest. The Emergence of the Neolithic Societies in the Baltic Region*. pp. 193–202, Sheffield Academic Press, 1998

26 S. Palmer (ed.) 'Culverwell Mesolithic Habitation Site, Isle of Portland, Dorset: Excavation report and research studies' *British Archaeological Reports* British Series 287 1999

27 See C. Smith 1992 and J. Wymer 1991

28 R.J. Schulting and M.P. Richards 'The use of stable isotopes in studies of subsistence and seasonality in the British Mesolithic' In R. Young (ed.), *Mesolithic*

Lifeways: Current Research from Britain and Ireland.
pp 55–65, University of Leicester Press, 2000
29 G.H. Smith 'The Lizard project: landscape survey
1978–1983'. *Cornish Archaeol.* 26, 1987, pp. 13–68
30 Berridge & Roberts 1986
31 N. Johnson and P. Rose *Bodmin Moor: An
archaeological survey. Vol. 1: The Human Landscape to
c.1800.* English Heritage & RCHME, London, 1994;
C. Tilley 'Rocks as resources: landscapes and power'.
Cornish Archaeol. 34, 1995, pp. 5–57
32 P. Herring and B. Lewis 'Ploughing up gatherer-
hunters: Mesolithic and later flints from Butterstor and
elsewhere on Bodmin Moor'. *Cornish Archaeol.* 31,
1992, pp. 5–14
33 P. Ashbee 'Ancient Scilly: retrospect, aspect and
prospect'. *Cornish Archaeol.* 25, 1986, pp. 186–219
34 R. Bradley 1998
35 P. Rowley-Conwy 1998
36 Page 24 in G.H. Smith 1987
37 Berridge and Roberts 1986, p. 20
38 See pp. 37–57 in C. Tilley *A Phenomenology of
Landscape.* Berg, Oxford, 1994
39 C. Tilley 1995
40 See also R. Bradley *An Archaeology of Natural
Places.* Routledge, London, 2000
41 Pages 78 and 115–16 in R. McGhee 2001
42 R.J. Schulting 'Aveline's Hole – An Early Mesolithic
Cemetery Site in the Mendips'. School of Archaeology
& Palaeoecology, Queen's University Belfast, n.d.
[WWW]
www.qub.ac.uk/arcpal/Rick%20Research/aveline's.html
(28/02/2004); R.J. Schulting, R.J. 'Welsh Mesolithic
Coastal Human Remains Project'. School of
Archaeology & Palaeoecology, Queen's University
Belfast, n.d. [WWW]
www.qub.ac.uk/arcpal/Rick%20Research/wales.html
(28/02/2004)
43 A. Chamberlain 'In this dark cavern thy burying
place'. *British Archaeology* 26, 1997 [WWW]
www.britarch.ac.uk/ba/ba26/ba26feat.html
(28/02/2004)
44 C.J. Caseldine 'Environmental change in Cornwall
during the last 13,000 years'. *Cornish Archaeol.* 19,
1980, pp. 3–16
45 I.G. Simmons, J.I. Rand and K. Crabtree 'A further
pollen analytical study of the Blacklane peat section on
Dartmoor, England'. *New Phytologist* 94, 1983, pp.
655–67
46 I.G. Simmons, J.I. Rand and K. Crabtree 'Dozmary
Pool, Bodmin Moor, Cornwall: A New Radiocarbon
dated Pollen Profile' In N.D. Balaam, B. Levitan and
Straker, V. (eds.) 'Studies in palaeoeconomy and
environment in South West England'. *British
Archaeological Reports* British Series 181, 1987, pp.
125–33
47 R.M. Jacobi, J.H. Tallis and P.A. Mellars 'The
southern Pennine Mesolithic and the ecological
record'. *Journal of Archaeological Science 3*, 1976, pp.
307–20
48 P.F. Burton and D.J. Charman 'Vegetation change in
lowland Cornwall: preliminary results from Crift
Down, near Lanlivery and Hoggs Moor, near
Lostwithiel'. *Cornish Archaeol.* 34, 1995, pp. 74–79;
Caseldine 1980; M.C.C. Walker and D. Austin 'Redhill
Marsh: A Site of possible Mesolithic activity on
Bodmin Moor'. *Cornish Archaeol.* 24, 1985, pp. 15–21

49 Schulting and Richards 2000
50 P. Ashbee 'Mesolithic Megaliths? The Scillonian
Entrance Graves: A New View'. *Cornish Archaeol.* 21,
1982, pp. 3–22
51 Such as in P.V. Kirch 'Transported landscapes'.
Natural History 91, 1982, pp. 32–35. Kirch is an
archaeologist working in Polynesia, who first described
this phenomenon
52 P. Trudgian 'Mesolithic flint scatters around Crowdy
Marsh'. *Cornish Archaeol.* 16, 1977, pp. 21–24
53 e.g., N. Johnson and A. David 'A Mesolithic Site on
Trevose Head and Contemporary Geography'. *Cornish
Archaeol.* 21, 1982, pp. 67–103; G.H. Smith and D.G.
Harris 'The Excavation of Mesolithic, Neolithic and
Bronze Age settlements at Poldowrian, St Keverne,
1980'. *Cornish Archaeol.* 21, 1982, pp. 23–66
54 J.M. Adovasio, O. Soffer and B. Klíma 'Upper
Palaeolithic fibre technology: interlaced woven finds
from Pavlov I, Czech Republic, c. 26,000 years ago'.
Antiquity 70, 1996, pp. 526–34
55 F.E.S. Roe 'Report on the cupped pebble'. In P.M.
Christie. 'Barrows on the North Cornish Coast:
wartime excavations by C.K. Croft Andrew,
1939–1944'. *Cornish Archaeol.* 24, 1985, pp. 23–121
56 Johnson & David 1982; Smith, G.H. 1987; Smith &
Harris 1982
57 Johnson and David 1982; G.H. Smith 'Excavation of
the Iron Age Cliff Promontory Fort and of Mesolithic
and Neolithic flint-working areas at Penhale, Holywell
Bay, near Newquay, 1983'. *Cornish Archaeol.* 27, 1988,
pp. 171–99; G.H. Smith 1987; Smith and Harris 1982
58 G.H. Smith 'Excavation at Windmill Farm,
Predannack Moor'. *Cornish Archaeol.* 23, 1984, p. 179;
C. Bonsall and P. Selby 'A collection of Mesolithic flints
from Crooklets, near Bude'. *Cornish Archaeol.* 14,
1975, p. 118
59 P. Berridge *Flint Report from Stithians Reservoir.*
Historic Environment Service, Cornwall County
Council: Unpublished manuscript, n.d.
60 G.H. Smith 'Excavations on Goonhilly Down, The
Lizard, 1981'. *Cornish Archaeol.* 23, 1984, pp. 3–48
61 See pp. 11–14 in H. Brody *The Other Side of Eden:
hunter-gatherers, farmers and the shaping of the
world.* Faber and Faber, London, 2001
62 J. Wymer 1991
63 R. Jacobi 1979
64 B. Cunliffe 2001
65 Pages 19 & 20 in Berridge & Roberts 1986
66 A. Fitter *An Atlas of the Wild Flowers of Britain
and Northern Europe.* Collins, London, 1978
67 D. Zohary and M. Hopf (2nd ed.). *Domestication of
plants in the Old World The origin and spread of
cultivated plants in West Asia, Europe, and the Nile
Valley.* Clarendon Press, Oxford, 1994

**Chapter two Neolithic culture in Cornwall: new
technologies and exchange**
1 J. Lichardus and M. Lichardus-Itten *Protohistoire de
l'Europe. Le Néolithique et le Chalcolithique.* P.U.F.,
Paris, 1985; H. Mueller-Karpe Handbuch der
Vorgeschichte. Band II. Jungsteinzeit. Beck, Munich,
1968; A. Whittle *Europe in the Neolithic: The creation
of new worlds.* Cambridge University Press, 1996
2 R. Bradley *The Significance of Monuments: On the
Shaping of Experience in Neolithic and Bronze Age
Europe.* Routledge, London, 1998

3 Ibid

4 Ibid

5 J. Thomas *Understanding the Neolithic*. Routledge, London, 1999

6 Bradley 1998; and S. Koerner and R. Gassón 'Historical Archaeology and New Directions in Environmental Archaeology.' In U. Albarella (ed.) *Environmental Archaeology: Meaning and Purpose.* Dordrecht: Kluwer, Dordrecht, 2001, pp. 177–210

7 Bradley 1998

8 R. Bradley *An Archaeology of Natural Places*. Routledge, London, 2000

9 Bradley 1998

10 Bradley 1998; J. Thomas *Time, Culture and Identity. An Interpretive Archaeology*. Routledge, London, 1996

11 c.f. C. Tilley *A Phenomenology of Landscape*. Berg, Oxford, 1994

12 c.f. C. Renfrew *Before Civilization – The Radiocarbon Revolution and Prehistoric Europe*. Penguin, Harmondsworth, 1973

13 J. Thomas 'Thoughts on the 'Repacked' Neolithic Revolution.' *Antiquity* 295, 2003, pp. 67–74

14 R.J. Mercer 'The Neolithic in Cornwall'. *Cornish Archaeol.* 25, 1986, pp. 35–80

15 P. Ashbee 'Mesolithic Megaliths? The Scillonian Entrance Graves: A New View'. *Cornish Archaeol.* 21, 1982, pp. 3–22; P. Ashbee 'Ancient Scilly: retrospect, aspect and prospect'. *Cornish Archaeol.* 25, 1986, pp. 186–219

16 e.g., G.H. Smith 'Excavation of the Iron Age Cliff Promontory Fort and of Mesolithic and Neolithic flint-working areas at Penhale, Holywell Bay, near Newquay, 1983'. *Cornish Archaeol.* 27, 1988, pp. 171–99

17 e.g., P. Berridge 'Flint Report from Stithians Reservoir'. Unpublished manuscript, n.d.

18 G.H. Smith 'The Lizard project: landscape survey 1978–1983'. *Cornish Archaeol.* 26, 1987, pp. 13–68

19 R.J. Schulting and M.P. Richards 'The use of stable isotopes in studies of subsistence and seasonality in the British Mesolithic' In R. Young (ed.), *Mesolithic Lifeways: Current Research from Britain and Ireland*. University of Leicester Press, 2000, pp. 55–65

20 Berridge n.d.

21 R.M. Jacobi 'Early Flandrian hunters in the South West'. *Proc. Devon Arch. Soc.* 37, 1979, pp. 48–93

22 T. Blackman 'Decorating the Landscape?' In C. Peters (ed.) 'Cornwall: A European Case Study in Identity'. *British Archaeological Reports* Int. Series, forthcoming

23 Schulting & Richards 2000; M.P. Richards and R.E.M. Hedges 'A Neolithic revolution? New evidence of diet in the British Neolithic'. *Antiquity* 73, 1999, pp. 891–897; M.P. Richards, R.J. Schulting and R.E.M. Hedges 'Sharp shift in diet at onset of Neolithic'. *Nature* 425, 2003, p. 366

24 See Mercer for his views, which I contradict here – R.J. Mercer 'Excavations at Carn Brea, Illogan, Cornwall'. *Cornish Archaeol.* 20, 1981, pp. 1–204; Mercer 1986

25 c.f. J.P. Mallory *In Search of the Indo-Europeans: Language, Archaeology, and Myth*. Thames & Hudson, London, 1991; A. Whittle 'Carn Brea: Evaluation and Implications'. *Cornish Archaeol.* 22, 1983, pp. 113–16

26 K.-Å. Aronsson Forest Reindeer Herding A.D.

1–1800. *An archaeological and palaeoecological study in Northern Sweden*. Umeå University Press, 1991; J. Forsyth *A History of the Peoples of Siberia. Russia's North Asian Colony 1581–1990*. Cambridge University Press, 1992

27 M.S. Copley *et al.* 'Dairying in Prehistoric Britain. Milking the organic residues.' *Conservation bulletin* (English Heritage) 45, 2004, pp. 24–25

28 c.f. A. Sherratt 'The secondary exploitation of animals in the Old World'. *World Archaeology* 15, 1983, pp. 90–104

29 Ashbee 1982; Ashbee 1986

30 Bradley 1998

31 e.g., Bradley 1998; Thomas 1999; C. Tilley 'Rocks as resources: landscapes and power'. *Cornish Archaeol.* 34, 1995, pp. 5–57

32 Mercer 1981

33 A. Whittle, J. Pollard and C. Grigson *The Harmony of Symbols: The Windmill Hill Causewayed Enclosure*. Oxbow Books, Oxford, 1999

34 M.C.C. Walker and D. Austin 'Redhill Marsh: A Site of possible Mesolithic activity on Bodmin Moor.' *Cornish Archaeol.* 24, 1985, pp. 15–21

35 P.F. Burton and D.J. Charman 'Vegetation change in lowland Cornwall: preliminary results from Crift Down, near Lanlivery and Hoggs Moor, near Lostwithiel'. *Cornish Archaeol.* 34, 1995, pp. 74–79

36 C.J. Caseldine 'Environmental change in Cornwall during the last 13,000 years'. *Cornish Archaeol.* 19, 1980, pp. 3–16

37 P. Berridge and A. Roberts 'The Mesolithic period in Cornwall'. *Cornish Archaeol.* 25, 1986, pp. 7–34

38 P. Herring and B. Lewis 'Ploughing up gatherer-hunters: Mesolithic and later flints from Butterstor and elsewhere on Bodmin Moor'. *Cornish Archaeol.* 31, 1992, pp. 5–14

39 Pages 32–37 in G.F. Smith 1987

40 Mercer 1981

41 R. Bradley and M. Edmonds *Interpreting the Axe Trade: Production and Exchange in Neolithic Britain*. Cambridge University Press, 1993; M. Russell *Neolithic Flint Mines in Britain*. Tempus, Stroud, Glos., 2001; Thomas 1999

42 Berridge & Roberts 1986; and see below for debate about jadeite

43 Berridge & Roberts 1986; Mercer 1986

44 Mercer 1986; R.J. Mercer 'The excavation of a Neolithic enclosure complex at Helman Tor, Lostwithiel, Cornwall'. *Cornish Archaeol.* 36, 1997, pp. 5–63

45 Mercer 1986

46 Ibid

47 A.R. Woolley, A.C. Bishop, R.J. Harrison and I.A. Kinnes 'European Neolithic jade implements: a preliminary mineralogical and typological study'. In T.H.McK. Clough and W.A. Cummins (eds) 'Stone Axe Studies' Vol 1, *CBA Research Report* No.23, 1979, pp. 90–96.

48 See R.V. Davis, H. Howard and I.F. Smith. 'The petrological identification of stone implements from south-west England. Sixth Report of the Sub-Committee of the South-Western Federation of Museums and Art Galleries.' In T.H.McK. Clough and W.A. Cummins (eds) 'Stone Axe Studies' Vol 2, *CBA Research Report* No 67, 1988, pp. 14–20. Davies *et al.* discuss 'jadeite' from south-west Britain. Vin Davis

(personal communication – October 2004) predicts that the some jadeite axes from Britain may be eclogite from Brittany or from the bottom of the English Channel (i.e. washed up on the beach!). He also informs me that this is still contentious and that recently, French archaeologist Pierre Petrequin has claimed evidence for an Alpine origin for jadeite axes in Brittany.

49 Mercer 1986

50 e.g., Ashbee 1982, 3–8

51 Page 50 in Mercer 1986

52 Page 68 in Mercer 1981

53 P. Dixon 'Crickley Hill', *Current Archaeol.* 76, 1981, pp. 145–6

54 Mercer 1986; Mercer 1997– though there is a question about the stratigraphy at Hembury

55 R.J. Mercer *Hambledon Hill – A Neolithic Landscape.* Edinburgh University Press, 1980

56 P. Herring *St Michael's Mount, Archaeological Works, 1995–8.* Cornwall Archaeological Unit, 2001

57 Mercer 1997

58 S. Gerrard *Dartmoor: Book of Dartmoor Landscapes through Time.* Batsford/English Heritage, London, 1997

59 N. Johnson and P. Rose *Bodmin Moor: An archaeological survey. Vol. 1: The Human Landscape to c. 1800.* English Heritage & RCHME, London, 1994

60 G.F. Walford 'Some thoughts on early enclosures in southeast Cornwall'. *Cornish Archaeol.* 37–8, 1998–9, pp. 130–1

61 Mercer 1997

62 e.g., C. Tilley, S. Hamilton, S. Harrison and E. Anderson *Nature, Culture, Clitter: distinguishing between cultural and geomorphological landscapes; the case of hilltop tors in south-west England.* Leskernick Homepage, University College London, n.d. [WWW] http://www.ucl.ac.uk/leskernick/articles/clitter/clitter.htm (28/02/2004)

63 Barbara Bender pers.com. 2002

64 B. Bender, S. Hamilton and C. Tilley *Stone Worlds, Alternative Narratives, Nested Landscapes.* Leskernick Homepage, University College London, n.d. [WWW] http://www.ucl.ac.uk/leskernick/articles/stone/stone.htm (28/02/2004)

65 Ibid; B. Bender, S. Hamilton and C. Tilley 'Leskernick: the biography of an excavation'. *Cornish Archaeol.* 34, 1995, pp. 58–73

66 Tilley 1995

67 Christopher Tilley has suggested that the tors were worshipped – p. 12 in Tilley 1995

68 e.g., Mercer 1986; C. Weatherhill *Cornovia: Ancient Sites of Cornwall and Scilly.* Alison Hodge, Penzance, 1985

69 Bradley 2000

70 Ashbee 1982; Mercer 1986

71 Russell 2001

72 Bradley 2000

73 Mercer 1981; Mercer 1986

74 Mercer 1981

75 e.g., recently J. Roberts and H. Quinnell 'The potential for a rapid, minimally-destructive method for the identification of archaeological ceramics – the results of a pilot study on Gabbroic Ware'. *Cornish Archaeol.* 37–8, 1998–9, pp. 126–7

76 D.P.S. Peacock 'The gabbroic pottery of Cornwall'. *Antiquity* 62, 1988, pp. 302–4; H. Quinnell 'The

Cornish gabbroic pottery: the development of a hypothesis'. *Cornish Archaeol.* 26, 1987, pp. 7–12

77 N. Federova 'Shamans, heroes and ancestors in the bronze castings of western Siberia.' In N. Price (ed.) *The Archaeology of Shamanism.* Routledge, London, 2001, pp. 56–64

78 For more information on Cornish geology, see S. Campbell, C.O. Hunt, J.D. Scourse, D.H. Keen and N. Stephens (eds.) *Quaternary of South-west England (Geological Conservation Review S.).* Kluwer Academic Publishers, London, 1998; E.A. Edmonds, M.C. McKeown and M. Williams *British Regional Geology – South West England.* HMSO, London 1975; E.B. Selwood, E.M. Durrance and C.M. Bristow (eds.) *The Geology of Cornwall and the Isles of Scilly.* University of Exeter Press, Exeter, 1998; and P. Stanier *Cornwall's Geological Heritage.* Twelveheads Press, Truro 1990

79 L. Harrod 'Gabbroic clay sources in Cornwall: a petrographic study of prehistoric pottery and clay samples'. *Oxford Journal of Archaeology* 23, 2004, pp. 271–86; and for her criticism of gabbro as a temper in pottery, see L. Harrad 'Experimental work' in *British Archaeology* 51, 2000 [WWW] http://www.britarch.ac.uk/ba/ba51/ba51lets.html (04/11/04)

80 E.A.K. Higginbotham 'Excavation at Woolley Barrow, Morwenstow". *Cornish Archaeol.* 10, 1077, pp. 3–16

81 P. Herring 'A Long Cairn on Catshole Tor, Altarnun'. *Cornish Archaeol.* 22, 1983, pp. 81–84

82 M. Parker Pearson *Bronze Age Britain.* Batsford/English Heritage, London, 1993

83 N.H. Andersen *The Sarup Enclosures. The Funnel Beaker Culture of the Sarup Site Including Two Causewayed Camps Compared to Contemporary Settlements in the Area and other European Enclosures.* Aarhus University Press, 1997

84 Page 216 in I. Heermann 'Ozeanien.' In F. Kussmaul (ed.) *Ferne Völker Frühe Zeiten. Kunstwerke aus dem Linden-Museum Stuttgart.* Band 1. Afrika, Ozeanien, Amerika. Verlag Aurel Bongers KG, Recklinghausen, 1982, pp. 131–221

85 Ashbee 1982

86 J. Barnatt *Prehistoric Cornwall: The Ceremonial Monuments.* Turnstone Press, Wellingborough, 1982

87 c.f. Andersen 1997

88 Ashbee 1986

89 I.F. Smith 'The Neolithic pottery.' In R.J. Mercer 'Excavations at Carn Brea, Illogan, Cornwall'. *Cornish Archaeol.* 20, 1981, pp. 161–85; and I.F. Smith 'The Neolithic pottery.' In R.J. Mercer 'The excavation of a Neolithic enclosure complex at Helman Tor, Lostwithiel, Cornwall'. *Cornish Archaeol.* 36, 1997, pp. 29–37

90 Pages 181–2 in Thomas 1996

Chapter three The age of the megaliths

1 For an outline of the divisions of the Bronze Age, see S. Needham 'Chronology and Periodisation in the British Bronze Age'. *Acta Supplementa Archaeologica* 1, 1996, pp. 121–40

2 J. Lichardus and M. Lichardus-Itten *Protohistoire de l'Europe. Le Néolithique et le Chalcolithique.* P.U.F., Paris, 1985; H. Mueller-Karpe *Handbuch der Vorgeschichte. Band II. Jungsteinzeit.* Beck, Munich,

1968; A. Whittle *Europe in the Neolithic: The creation of new worlds*. Cambridge University Press, Cambridge, 1996

3 c.f. J. Thomas 'Thoughts on the 'Repacked' Neolithic Revolution'. *Antiquity* 77, 2003, pp. 67–74

4 Lichardus & Lichardus-Itten 1985; M. Parker Pearson *Bronze Age Britain*. Batsford/English Heritage, London, 1993

5 T. Darvill *Prehistoric Britain*. Routledge, London, 1987 (repr. 1996)

6 Pages 90–91 in Darvill 1987

7 Ibid

8 Parker Pearson 1993

9 Ibid, p. 67

10 A. Burl *The Stone Circles of the British Isles*. Yale University Press, New Haven, 1976

11 A. Burl *Prehistoric Henges*. Shire Archaeology, Princes Risborough, 1991

12 R. Bradley *The Significance of Monuments: On the Shaping of Experience in Neolithic and Bronze Age Europe*. Routledge, London, 1998a

13 c.f. pp. 50–52 in Parker Pearson 1993

14 M. Green *A Landscape Revealed: 10,000 Years on a Chalkland Farm*. Tempus, Stroud, Glos., 2000

15 A. Gibson *Stonehenge & Timber Circles*. Tempus Stroud, Glos., 1998

16 C. Peters 'Cyberdreaming with Laris Pulenas: an afterlife beyond the Post-Modern'. In C.Finn & M. Henig (eds.) 'Outside Archaeology. Material culture and poetic imagination'. *British Archaeological Reports* Int. Series 999, 2001, pp. 41–52

17 For a good example of this, see J.G. Scott 'The Stone Circles at Templewood, Kilmartin, Argyll'. *Glasgow Archaeological Journal* 15, 1988–89, pp. 52–124

18 B.M. Fagan *People of the Earth: An Introduction to World Prehistory*. Longman, Harlow, 1998, p. 505

19 Parker Pearson 1993

20 From the site of Trundholm, see P. Gelling and H.E. Davidson *The Chariot of the Sun, and other symbols of the Northern Bronze Age*. J.M. Dent & Sons Ltd, London, 1969

21 Page 548 in A. Pollex 'Comments on the interpretation of the so-called cattle burials of Neolithic Central Europe'. *Antiquity* 73, 1999: 542–50

22 C. Lévi-Strauss *The Savage Mind*. Weidenfeld & Nicholson, London, 1966

23 N. Federova 'Shamans, heroes and ancestors in the bronze castings of western Siberia'. In N. Price (ed.) *The Archaeology of Shamanism*: 56–64. Routledge, London, 2001, pp. 56–64; J. Forsyth *A History of the Peoples of Siberia. Russia's North Asian Colony 1581–1990* Cambridge University Press, Cambridge, 1992

24 W. O'Brien *Bronze Age Copper Mining in Britain and Ireland*. Shire Archaeology, Princes Risborough, 1996; W. O'Brien 'Arsenical Copper in Early Irish Metallurgy'. In S.M.M. Young, A.M. Pollard, P. Budd and R.A. Ixer (eds.) 'Metals in Antiquity'. *British Archaeological Reports* Int. Series 792, 1999, pp. 33–42; and c.f. Russell, M. 2001. *Neolithic Flint Mines in Britain*. Stroud, Glos.: Tempus

25 Gerrard has attempted arguments for prehistoric tin streaming based on the difficulties of detection – see Chapter 1 of S. Gerrard *The Early British Tin Industry*. Tempus, Stroud, Glos., 2000

26 Page 26 in S. Timberlake 'Prehistoric copper mining in Britain'. *Cornish Archaeol.* 31, 1992, pp. 15–34

27 See Illustration 78 in Parker Pearson 1993

28 A. Sharpe 'Footprints of former miners in the far west'. *Cornish Archaeol.* 31, 1992, pp. 35–40

29 R.A. Ixer and R.A.D. Pattrick 'Copper-Arsenic Ores And Bronze Age Mining And Metallurgy With Special Reference To The British Isles'. In P.T. Craddock and J. Lang (eds.) *Mining and Metal Production Through the Ages*. The British Museum Press, London, 2003, pp. 9–20; J.P. Northover 'The earliest metalworking in southern Britain'. *Der Anschnitt* 9, 1999, pp. 211–25

30 A. Sheridan and A. Shortland '"...beads which have given rise to so much dogmatism, controversy and rash speculation": faience in Early Bronze Britain Age and Ireland'. Chapter 21 in I.N.G. Shepherd and G.J. Barclay (eds.) *Scotland in Ancient Europe*. University of Edinburgh Press, Edinburgh, 2004

31 Ibid

32 P.M. Christie 'Cornwall in the Bronze Age'. *Cornish Archaeol.* 25, 1986, pp. 81–110

33 P. Ashbee 'Bant's Carn, St Mary's, Isles of Scilly'. *Cornish Archaeol.* 15, 1976, pp. 11–26

34 P. Bonnington 'Cemetery Mounds in Cornwall and Anglesey'. In C. Peters (ed.) 'Cornwall: A European Case Study in Identity'. *British Archaeological Reports* Int. Series, forthcoming

35 S.J. Staines *Soils in Cornwall II: Sheet SW53 (Hayle)*. Soil Surv. Rec. No. 57, 1979

36 D. Dudley 'Woolley Barrow, Morwenstow'. In 'Excavation News, 1967–8'. *Cornish Archaeol.* 7, 1968a, p. 80

37 V. Russell and P.A.S. Pool 'Excavation of a Menhir at Try, Gulval'. *Cornish Archaeol.* 3, 1964, pp. 15–26

38 G. Eogan *The Accomplished Art: Gold and Gold-working in Britain and Ireland During the Bronze Age*. Oxbow Books, Oxford, 1995; J.J. Taylor 'Lunulae reconsidered'. *Proc. Prehist. Soc.* 36, 1970, pp. 38–81

39 Eogan 1995

40 J. Thomas *Time, Culture and Identity. An Interpretive Archaeology*. Routledge, London, 1996; J. Thomas *Understanding the Neolithic*. Routledge, London, 1999

41 Peters 2001

42 C. Tilley *A Phenomenology of Landscape*. Berg, Oxford, 1994

43 A. Ellison 'The Pygmy Vessel' in F.M. Griffith 'Archaeological Investigations at Colliford Reservoir, Bodmin Moor, 1977–78'. *Cornish Archaeol.* 23, 1984, pp. 79–81; Parker Pearson 1993

44 Parker Pearson 1993, 94–95; Sheridan and Shortland 2004. British faïence is recognisable by its turquoise colour – see A. Sheridan 'Supernatural power dressing'. *British Archaeology* 70, 2003 [WWW] www.britarch.ac.uk/ba/ba70/feat3.shtml (06/03/04)

45 Sheridan *op cit*.

46 A. Shortland 'Making a talisman' *British Archaeology* 70, 2003 [WWW] www.britarch.ac.uk/ba/ba70/feat3.shtml (06/03/2004)

47 Sheridan, 2003

48 Ibid

49 Page 98 in P.M. Christie 1986; M. Parker Pearson 'The production and distribution of Bronze Age pottery in south-west Britain'. *Cornish Archaeol.* 29, 1990, pp. 5–32; c.f. D.F. Williams 'A Note on the Petrology of the Beaker'. In N. Thomas and S.

Hartgroves 'A Beaker Cist Grave at Harrowbarrow'. *Cornish Archaeol.* 29, 1990, p. 59

50 Christie 1986

51 Parker Pearson 1990

52 Sheridan 2003; Sheridan and Shortland 2004

53 Gibson 1998

54 A. Burl *Prehistoric Astronomy and Ritual*. Shire Archaeology, Princes Risborough, 1983; C. Ruggles *Astronomy in Prehistoric Britain and Ireland*. Yale University Press, New Haven, 1999; C. Tilley 'Rocks as resources: landscapes and power'. *Cornish Archaeol.* 34, 1995, pp. 5–57

55 F. Peters 'The possible use of West Penwith menhirs as boundary markers'. *Cornish Archaeol.* 29, 1990, pp. 33–42

56 J. Barnatt 'Lesser Known Stone Circles in Cornwall'. *Cornish Archaeol.* 19, 1980, pp. 17–29

57 Page 24 in P. Herring and P. Rose *Bodmin Moor's Archaeological Heritage*. Cornwall County Council, Truro, 2001

58 Page 124 in A. Burl *The Stone Circles of the British Isles*. Yale University Press, New Haven, 1976; p. 69 in R.J. Mercer 'The Neolithic in Cornwall'. *Cornish Archaeol.* 25, 1986, pp. 35–80

59 Page 65 in Mercer 1986

60 Page 71 in Mercer 1986

61 Page 63 in Mercer 1986

62 Green 2000

63 A. Watson *Megalithic Sound and Landscape: an introduction to recent research at Neolithic sites*. Reading University, 2001 [WWW] www.neolithic.reading.ac.uk/index.htm (06/03/2004); A. Watson and D. Keating 'Architecture and sound: an acoustic analysis of megalithic monuments in prehistoric Britain'. *Antiquity* 73, 1999, pp. 325–36

64 C. Weatherhill *Cornovia: Ancient Sites of Cornwall and Scilly*. Alison Hodge, Penzance, 1985

65 A. Preston-Jones 'The Men-an-Tol reconsidered'. *Cornish Archaeol.* 32, 1993, pp. 5–16

66 Page 48 in I. Cooke *Mermaid to Merry Maid: a Journey to the Stones*. Men-an-Tol Studio, Penzance, 1987

67 Ian Cooke in Preston-Jones 1993, p. 13

68 Barnatt 1980

69 c.f. R. Bradley 'Ruined buildings, ruined stones: enclosures, tombs and natural places in the Neolithic of south-west England'. *World Archaeology* 30, 1998b: 13–22; Bradley 1998a; R. Bradley *An Archaeology of Natural Places*. Routledge, London, 2000; Thomas 1996; Thomas 1999

70 Preston-Jones 1993

71 Barnatt 1980

72 Ibid

73 J. Barnatt *Prehistoric Cornwall: The Ceremonial Monuments*. Turnstone Press, Wellingborough, 1982; Bradley 1998a – older literature used to date menhirs to later the Early and Middle Bronze Ages because of these later cists

74 Russell & Pool 1964

75 H. Miles and T.J. Miles 'Excavations on Longstone Down, St Stephen in Brannel and St Mawan'. *Cornish Archaeol.* 10, 1971, pp. 5–31

76 G. Orwell *Animal Farm*. Harcourt, Brace and Co., New York, 1946

77 Bradley 1998b

78 J. Ratcliffe and C. Parkes 'Lost and Found on Chapel Down'. *Cornish Archaeol.* 28, 1989, pp. 259–60

79 Pages 85–86 in Barnatt 1982

80 Page 25 in Herring & Rose 2001; N. Johnson and P. Rose *Bodmin Moor: An archaeological survey*. Vol. 1: *The Human Landscape to c. 1800*. English Heritage & RCHME, London, 1994; Tilley 1995

81 A.C. Thomas and B. Wailes 'Sperris Quoit, the excavation of a new Penwith chambered tomb'. *Cornish Archaeol.* 6, 1967, pp. 9–23

82 Page 24 in H. Miles 'Barrows on St Austell granite'. *Cornish Archaeol.* 14, 1975, pp.5–82

83 Page 29 in C. Weatherhill *Belerion: Ancient Sites of Land's End*. Alison Hodge, Penzance, 1981

84 S. Hartgroves 'The cup-marked stones of Stithians reservoir'. *Cornish Archaeol.* 26, 1987, pp. 68–69

85 Cooke 1987

86 P. Trudgian 'Cupmarked stones from a barrow at Starapark, near Camelford'. *Cornish Archaeol.* 15, 1976, pp. 48–49

87 D. Dudley 'Tregiffian, St Buryan'. In 'Excavation News, 1967–8'. *Cornish Archaeol.* 7, 1968b, p. 80

88 C. Waddington 'Cup and Ring Marks in Context'. *Cambridge Archaeological Journal* 8, 1998, pp. 29–54

89 See L. Grinsell 'Round barrows and burials of the 'Wessex' earlier Bronze Age in Cornwall'. *Cornish Archaeol.* 33, 1994, pp. 36–39; and J.E.R. Trahair 'A Survey of Cairns on Bodmin Moor'. *Cornish Archaeol.* 17, 1978, pp. 3–24 for detailed explanations.

90 Pages 5–12 in Miles & Miles 1971

91 C. Tilley, S. Hamilton, S. Harrison and E. Anderson *Nature, Culture, Clitter: distinguishing between cultural and geomorphological landscapes; the case of hilltop tors in south-west England*. Leskernick Homepage, University College London, n.d. [WWW] www.ucl.ac.uk/leskernick/articles/clitter/clitter.htm (28/02/2004)

92 Page 101 in Christie 1986

93 Christie *op cit*.; p.130 in P.M. Christie 'A Barrow Cemetery on Davidstow Moor, Cornwall: wartime excavations by C.K. Croft Andrew'. *Cornish Archaeol.* 27, 1988, pp. 27–169

94 Page 34 in Christie 1988

95 Page 14 in G.H. Smith 'Excavations on Goonhilly Down, The Lizard, 1981'. *Cornish Archaeol.* 23, 1984, pp. 3–48

96 Pages 147–148 in D. Harris and P. Trudgian 'The Excavation of Three Cairns at Stannon, Bodmin Moor'. *Cornish Archaeol.* 23, 1984, pp. 141–55

97 Page 36 in P.M. Christie 'Barrows on the North Cornish Coast: Wartime excavations by C.K. Croft Andrew 1939–1944'. *Cornish Archaeol.* 24, 1985, pp. 23–121

98 G.H. Smith 1984

99 P.M. Christie 'Crig-a-mennis: a Bronze Age barrow at Liskey, Perranzabuloe, Cornwall'. *Proc. Prehist. Soc.* 26, 1960, pp. 76–97

100 P. Ashbee 'The excavation of Tregulland Barrow, Treneglos Parish, Cornwall'. *Antiq. Journ.* 38, 1958, pp. 174–196; G.H. Smith 1984

101 G.H. Smith *op cit*.

102 Site CRIVA, p. 70 in F.M. Griffith 'Archaeological Investigations at Colliford Reservoir, Bodmin Moor, 1977–78'. *Cornish Archaeol.* 23, 1984, pp. 49–139

103 The Cornwall Historic Environment Service's audits have produced a detailed picture of past landscapes.

Chapter four Settled farming communities in the ancestral landscape

1 For a discussion of the Bronze Age chronology see S. Needham 'Chronology and Periodisation in the British Bronze Age.' *Acta Supplementa Archaeologica* 1, 1996, pp. 121–140; and for an overview of the Cornish Bronze Age, see P.M. Christie 'Cornwall in the Bronze Age.' *Cornish Archaeol.* 25, 1986, pp. 81–110

2 J.P. Northover 'The earliest metalworking in southern Britain.' *Der Anschnitt* 9, 1999, pp. 211–25

3 For more detailed explanations of early metallurgy, see H. Hodges *Artifacts: An Introduction to Early Materials and Technology.* Duckworth, London, 1989; and S.U. Wisseman and W.S. Williams *Ancient technologies and archaeological materials.* Gordon and Breach Science Publishers, Langhorne, Pa., 1994

4 Page 313 in A. Harding 'Reformation in Barbarian Europe, 1300–1600'. In B. Cunliffe (ed.) *The Oxford Illustrated Prehistory of Europe.* Oxford University Press, Oxford, 1994, pp.304–335

5 p. 106 in G. Eogan *The Accomplished Art: Gold and Gold-working in Britain and Ireland During the Bronze Age.* Oxbow Books, Oxford, 1995

6 Ibid

7 c.f. R. Osgood 'Britain in the age of warrior heroes.' *British Archaeology* 46, 1999 [WWW] http://www.britarch.ac.uk/ba/ba16/ba16feat.html (21/03/04)

8 e.g., S. Gerrard *Dartmoor.* English Heritage/Batsford, London, 1999

9 See R. Bradley, R. Entwistle and F. Raymond *Prehistoric Land Divisions on Salisbury Plain. The work of the Wessex Linear Ditches Project.* English Heritage, London 1994; and B. Cunliffe *Iron Age Communities in Britain.* Routledge, London, 1991

10 J. Collis *The European Iron Age.* Routledge, London, 1984

11 Collis 1984; and S. Laval *History of Carthage.* Blackwell, Oxford 1997

12 G. Barker & T. Rasmussen *The Etruscans.* Blackwell, Oxford, 1998

13 c.f. Collis 1984

14 Page 13 in J. Girard *Principles of Environmental Chemistry.* Jones & Bartlett, Sudbury, MA, USA, 2004

15 Pages 186–192 in E.R. Wolf *Europe and the People Without History.* University of California Press, Berkeley, 1992

16 Fig. 38 in N. Johnson and P. Rose *Bodmin Moor: An archaeological survey. Vol. 1: The Human Landscape to c. 1800.* English Heritage & RCHME, London, 1994

17 Page 31 in P. Herring and P. Rose *Bodmin Moor's Archaeological Heritage.* Cornwall County Council, Truro, 2001

18 Page 29 Ibid

19 Fig. 42 in Johnson and Rose 1994

20 J.A. Nowakowski 'Trethellan Farm, Newquay: the excavation of a lowland Bronze Age settlement and Iron Age cemetery.' *Cornish Archaeol.* 30, 1991, pp. 5–242

21 Pages 316–7 in Harding 1994; V. Straker 'Charred Plant Macrofossils' pp.166–179 in J.A. Nowakowski 1991; and P. Gilbert and V. Straker 'Assessment of Charred Plant Macrofossils' p.38 in A.M. Jones *et al.* 'The excavation of a Later Bronze Age Structure at Callestick', *Cornish Archaeol.* 37 & 38, 1998–9,
pp.5–55

22 Ibid

23 Gerrard 1999 & S. Gerrard *The Early British Tin Industry.* Tempus, Stroud, Glos., 2000

24 For a discussion of pottery distributions see M. Parker Pearson 'The production and distribution of Bronze Age pottery in south-west Britain.' *Cornish Archaeol.* 29, 1990, pp. 5–32; M. Parker Pearson *Bronze Age Britain.* Batsford/English Heritage, London, 1993

25 There are numerous environmental studies that show this using a wide range of techniques and methods. See M. Bell and M.J.C. Walker *Late Quaternary Environmental Change: Physical and Human Perspectives.* Longman, London 1992; and N. Roberts *The Holocene: an environmental history.* Blackwell, Oxford, 1998

26 E. Maltby and C.J. Caseldine 'Environmental Reconstruction at Colliford.' In F.M. Griffith 'Archaeological Investigations at Colliford Reservoir, Bodmin Moor, 1977–78.' *Cornish Archaeol.* 23, 1984, pp. 92–117

27 Herring & Rose 2001, 35

28 Herring & Rose 2001; Johnson & Rose 1994; H. Quinnell 'Cornwall during the Iron Age and Roman Period' *Cornish Archaeol.* 25, 1986, pp. 111–134; C. Weatherhill *Cornovia: Ancient Sites of Cornwall and Scilly.* Alison Hodge, Penzance, 1985

29 Caseldine 1980; H. Miles 'Excavations at Killibury hillfort, Egloshayle 1975–6.' *Cornish Archaeol.* 16, 1977, pp. 89–121

30 Page 44 in P. Herring 'The cliff castles and hillforts of West Penwith in the light of recent work at Maen Castle and Treryn Dinas.' *Cornish Archaeol.* 33, 1994, pp. 40–56

31 Pages 43–48 in Johnson and Rose 1994

32 Pages 48 and 50 in Johnson and Rose 1994

33 R. Bradley *The Significance of Monuments: On the Shaping of Experience in Neolithic and Bronze Age Europe.* Routledge, London, 1998

34 c.f. Herring 1994

35 Cunliffe 1991

36 H. Quinnell *Excavations at Trethurgy Round, St Austell: Community and Status in Roman and Post-Roman Cornwall*, Cornwall County Council, Truro, 2004

37 Bradley *et al.* 1994

38 Weatherhill 1985

39 Page 139 in A. Preston-Jones and P. Rose 'Medieval Cornwall.' *Cornish Archaeol.* 25, 1986, pp. 135–185

40 Pete Herring pers.com. 04/2003

41 Page 139 in Preston-Jones and Rose 1986

42 G.H. Smith and D.G. Harris 'The Excavation of Mesolithic, Neolithic and Bronze Age settlements at Poldowrian, St Keverne, 1980'. *Cornish Archaeol.* 21, 1982, pp. 23–66

43 Nowakowski 1991

44 M.S. Copley *et al.* 'Dairying in Prehistoric Britain. Milking the organic residues.' *Conservation bulletin* (English Heritage) 45, 2004, pp. 24–25

45 Johnson & Rose 1994

46 Page 111 in T. Darvill *Prehistoric Britain.* Routledge, London, 1987 (repr. 1996).

47 A.M. Jones *et al.* 1998–9

48 D. Dudley 'An excavation at Bodrifty, Mulfra, near Penzance.' *Archaeological Journal* 113, 1956, pp. 1–32;

and C. Weatherhill *Belerion: Ancient Sites of Land's End*. Alison Hodge, Penzance, 1981

49 I. Thomas 'The excavations at Kynance Cove, 1953–60.' *The Lizard*: 1.4, 1960, pp. 5–16

50 Herring & Rose 2001, 29 & 36

51 A. Sharpe 'Treryn Dinas: cliff castles reconsidered.' *Cornish Archaeol.* 31, 1992, pp. 65–68

52 For further discussion of similar sites elsewhere, see R. Bradley *An Archaeology of Natural Places*. Routledge, London, 2000

53 G. Cooney 'Introduction: seeing land from the sea.' *World Archaeology* 35, 2003–2004, pp.323–328

54 For further comments on the spiritual qualities of water bodies, see G. Cooney *Landscape of Neolithic Ireland*. Routledge, London, 2000; p. 230 in G. Cooney and E. Grogan *Irish Prehistory: A Social Perspective*. Wordwell, Dublin, 1999

55 Nowakowksi 1991, 45 & 203

56 Nowakowski 1991, 205

57 Nowakowski 1991, 204–5

58 Sites GM IX and X

59 A.C. Thomas in Nowakowksi 1991, 203

60 H. Quinnell 1986

61 R. Maclean 'The Fogou: in investigation of function' *Cornish Archaeol.* 31, 1992, pp. 41–64

62 P.M. Christie 'The excavation of an Iron Age souterrain and settlement at Carn Euny, Sancreed, Cornwall.' *Proceedings of the Prehistoric Society* 44, 1978, pp. 309–434

63 See Weatherhill 1981

64 Pages 118–119 in H. Quinnell 1986, pp. 111–134

65 Barbara Bender pers. comm. 2001

66 c.f. C. Peters 'Cyberdreaming with Laris Pulenas: an afterlife beyond the Post-Modern.' In C.Finn & M. Henig (eds.) 'Outside Archaeology. Material culture and poetic imagination'. *British Archaeological Reports* Int. Series 999, 2001, pp. 41–52; C. Tilley, S. Hamilton, S. Harrison and E. Anderson *Nature, Culture, Clitter: distinguishing between cultural and geomorphological landscapes; the case of hilltop tors in south-west England*. Leskernick Homepage, University College London, n.d. [WWW] http://www.ucl.ac.uk/leskernick/articles/clitter/clitter.htm (28/02/2004); and C. Tilley 'Rocks as resources: landscapes and power'. *Cornish Archaeol.* 34, 1995, pp. 5-57

Chapter five Citizens of the Empire: *Romanitas* in Cornwall

1 Even within the British province there was diversity, see A. Sargent 'The North-South divide revisited: thoughts on the character of Roman Britain' *Britannia* XXXIII, 2002, pp. 219–26

2 Authors like Virgil, Cicero, Livy, Catullus, Caesar, Horace, Tacitus, Pliny the Elder, Pliny the Younger and Ovid – translations are available in the Penguin Classics series, for example.

3 Page 53 in E. Swift *The End of the Western Roman Empire. An Archaeological Investigation*. Tempus, Stroud, Glos., 2000

4 See H. Chadwick *The Early Church: Story of Emergent Christianity from the Apostolic Age to the Dividing of the Ways Between the Greek East and the Latin West*. Penguin, Harmondsworth, 2005; J. Knight *The End of Antiquity. Archaeology, Society and Religion AD 235–700*. Tempus. Stroud, Glos., 1999; and

A.C. Thomas *Christianity in Roman Britain to AD 500*. Batsford, London, 1981

5 See the poems in H. Isbell (trans..) *The Last Poets of Imperial Rome*. Penguin, Harmondsworth, 1971 – such as Nemesianus' *Cyngetica* (The Hunt) or Ausonius' *Mosella* (The Moselle river)

6 A tribal unit created by the Romans, though not necessarily existing previously.

7 P. Salway *A History of Roman Britain*. Oxford University Press, Oxford, 1997

8 These words, 'I came, I saw, I conquered', came from the triumph Caesar celebrated in Rome following a successful campaign in what is now Turkey – see section 37 of Chapter 1 'Julius Caesar', pp. 13–53 in G. Suetonius *The Twelve Caesars* (trans.. R.Graves). Penguin, Harmondsworth, 1989

9 Pages 97–114 in J. Caesar *The Conquest of Gaul* (trans.. S.A. Handford). Penguin, Harmondsworth, 1982

10 B. Cunliffe *Hengistbury Head, Dorset. Volume 1: The Prehistoric and Roman Settlement 3500 BC–AD 500*. Oxbow, Oxford, 1987; and Illustration 9.27, p. 404 in B. Cunliffe *Facing the Ocean. The Atlantic and its Peoples*. Oxford University Press, Oxford, 2001

11 Marcus Tullius Cicero, the lawyer, politician and philosopher. The reference is in a letter to his friend Atticus where he discusses the news from his brother who was serving on Caesar's campaign in Britain – pp. 175–76 in Cicero *Cicero's Letters to Atticus* (trans.. D.R. Shackleton Bailey), Penguin, Harmondsworth, 1978

12 P.R. Davis 'Some navigational considerations of pre-medieval trade between Cornwall and North-West Europe' *Cornish Archaeol.* 36, 1997, pp. 129–37; and pp. 32–47 in P. Marsden *Ships and Shipwrecks* English Heritage/Batsford, London, 1997

13 Pages 32–28 in P. Marsden *Ships and Shipwrecks*. Batsford/English Heritage, London, 1997

14 B. Cunliffe *Danebury*. Batsford/English Heritage, London, 1993; Cunliffe, B. 1991. *Iron Age Communities in Britain*. London: Routledge

15 Cunliffe 1991

16 For the political background to the Roman conquest, see pp. 3–52 in P. Salway 1997

17 R.T. Brooks 'The Excavation of the Rumps Cliff Castle, St Minver, Cornwall'. *Cornish Archaeol.* 13, 1974, pp. 5–50

18 A. Sharpe 'Treryn Dinas; cliff castles reconsidered' *Cornish Archaeol.* 31, 1992, pp. 65–68; and P. Herring 'The cliff castles and hillforts of West Penwith in the light of recent work at Maen Castle and Treryn Dinas' *Cornish Archaeol.* 33, 1994, pp. 40–56

19 A.S.R. Gordon 'The excavation of Gurnard's Head, an Iron Age cliff castle in Western Cornwall', *Archaeological Journal* 97, 1940, pp. 96–111; and J. Nowakowski *National Trust Archaeological Survey of Gurnard's Head*. Cornwall Archaeological Unit, Truro, 1986

20 Gordon 1940; and Nowakowski 1986

21 Brooks 1974

22 Sharpe 1992 and Herring 1994

23 H. Quinnell 'A sense of identity: distinctive Cornish stone artefacts in the Roman and post-Roman periods'. *Cornish Archaeol.* 32, 1993, pp. 29–46 – as far as Richborough, Kent (p.40) and Pudding Lane, London (p. 41)

24 J. Ratcliffe 'Duckpool, Morwenstow: A Romano-British and early medieval industrial site and harbour' *Cornish Archaeol.* 34, 1995, pp. 81–171

25 Cunliffe 1991

26 H. Quinnell 'Cornwall during the Iron Age and Roman Period'. *Cornish Archaeol.* 25, 1986, pp. 111–34; P.M. Carlyon 'Finds from the earthwork at Carvossa, Probus' *Cornish Archaeol.* 26, 1987, pp. 103–44

27 Charles Thomas and Henrietta Quinnell have suggested that Cornwall may have formed a sub-canton or semi-autonomous region of the *civitas*. The problem, however, is that there is no example anywhere else in the Roman Empire of such an arrangement, nor any surviving Latin word for a subdivision of a *civitas*. The theory relies on reading backwards from Early Medieval times when Cornwall was indeed a political unit, but rests on no evidence from the Roman period itself. See A.C. Thomas 'The Character and Origins of Roman Dumnonia' In A.C. Thomas (ed.) 'Rural Settlement in Roman Britain', *CBA Research Report* 7, 1966, pp. 74–98; p. 1 of H. Quinnell; and H. Quinnell 1986

28 O.J. Padel *Cornish Place-Name Elements*. English Place-Name Society, Nottingham

29 S.A. Butcher 'Roman Nornour, Isles of Scilly: a reconsideration' *Cornish Archaeol.* 39–40, 2000–1, pp.5–11; and S.A. Butcher 'Excavations at Nornour, Isles of Scilly, 1969–73: the pre-Roman settlement' *Cornish Archaeol.* 17, 1978, pp. 29–112

30 C.H. Roseman *Pytheas On the Ocean*. Chicago, 1994; and pp. 306–08 in Cunliffe 2001

31 J. Collis *The European Iron Age*. Routledge, London, 1997; Cunliffe 1987

32 Even in the Late Roman period, there appears to have been relatively few coins in circulation – see S.M. Pearce 'Late Roman coinage in South-West Britain' *Transactions of the Devonshire Association* 102, 1970, pp. 19–34

33 A. Fox and W.L.D. Ravenhill 'The Roman fort at Nanstallon, Cornwall' *Britannia* 3, 1972, pp. 56–111; A. Fox and W.L.D. Ravenhill 'Excavation of the Roman Fort at Tregear, Nanstallon, 1965: Interim Report'. *Cornish Archaeol.* 5, 1966, pp.; A. Fox and W.L.D. Ravenhill 'Excavation of The Roman Fort At Tregear: Second Interim Report'. *Cornish Archaeol.* 6,1967, pp.; A. Fox and W.L.D. Ravenhill 'Excavation of The Roman Fort at Tregear: Third Interim Report'. *Cornish Archaeol.* 7,1968, pp.; A. Fox and W.L.D. Ravenhill 'Excavation of The Roman Fort At Tregear: Fourth Interim Report'. *Cornish Archaeol.* 9,1970, pp.;

34 B.H.St.J. O'Neil 'The Roman Villa at Magor Farm, near Camborne, Cornwall' *Journal of the Royal Institution of Cornwall* 24, 1933–1934, Appendix 1–59

35 Quinnell 1986

36 L.H. Threipland 'An excavation at St Mawgan-in-Pydar, North Cornwall' *Archaeological Journal* 113, 1956, pp. 33–81

37 D. Harris 'Excavation of a Romano-British round at Shortlanesend, Kenwyn, Truro' *Cornish Archaeol.* 19, 1980, pp. 63–75

38 A. Saunders and D. Harris 'Excavation at Castle Gotha, St Austell' *Cornish Archaeol.* 21, 1982, pp. 109–53

39 A. David 'Merthen, Constantine'. *Ancient Monuments Laboratory Report* Geophysics G7/80, AML, London, 1980; D. Harvey 'The Double Fort at Merthen, Constantine' *Cornish Archaeol.* 9, 1970, pp.103–106; and p. 28 in A. Reynolds *Helford Estuary Historic Audit*, Cornwall Archaeological Unit, Cornwall County Council, Truro, 2000

40 See also the site of Trevinnick, A. Fox and W.L.D. Ravenhill 'Excavation of a rectilinear earthwork at Trevinnick, St Kew, 1968' *Cornish Archaeol.* 8, 1969, pp. 89–97

41 Henrietta Quinnell has suggested that the rectilinear enclosures may date to the Late Iron Age (LIA – 200 BC until AD 43) because sherds of South West Decorated Ware were found at the enclosure at Carvossa, near Probus. That these sherds were found in a later context, however, suggests that they were either heirlooms, or had been lying in ploughsoil near the site. No features at Carvossa could date to the LIA. See p. 122 in Quinnell 1986; see also H.L. Douch and S.W. Beard 'Excavations at Carvossa, Probus, 1968–1970: preliminary report'. *Cornish Archaeol.* 9, pp. 93–97; and Carlyon 1987

42 H. Quinnell *Excavations at Trethurgy Round, St Austell: Community and Status in Roman and Post-Roman Cornwall*, Cornwall County Council, Truro, 2004; H. and T. Miles 'Excavations at Trethurgy, St Austell: interim report' *Cornish Archaeol.* 12, 1973, pp. 25–30

43 D.P.S. Peacock 'A Romano-British salt working site at Trebarveth, St Keverne' *Cornish Archaeol.* 8, 1969, pp. 47–65

44 Because older material appears in later contexts, they lay the same dating traps as the rectilinear enclosures. For example, South West Decorated Ware pottery sherds at Chysauster are likely to have come from an earlier LIA roundhouse settlement on the same site

45 H. O'Neill Hencken 'Excavations at Chysauster 1931' *Archaeologia*, 83, 1933, pp. 237–84; H. O'Neill Hencken *The Archaeology of Cornwall and Scilly*. Methuen, London, 1932

46 P.M. Christie 'The excavation of an Iron Age souterrain and settlement at Carn Euny, Sancreed, Cornwall' *Proceedings of the Prehistoric Society* 44, 1978, pp. 309–434

47 A. Guthrie 'Excavation of a settlement at Goldherring, Sancreed, 1958–61' *Cornish Archaeol.* 8, 1969, pp. 5–39

48 J. Wood 'A new perspective on West Cornwall courtyard houses' *Cornish Archaeol.* 36, 1997, pp. 95–106

49 Pages 186–88 in D. Perring *The Roman House in Britain*. Routledge, London, 2002; and E.W. Black 'Villa Owners: Romano-British Gentlemen and Officers' *Britannia* XXV, 1994, pp. 99–110

50 Page 192 in Perring 2002

51 P. Ashbee 'Halangy Down, St. Mary's, Isles of Scilly, Excavations 1964–1977' *Cornish Archaeol.* 35, 1996, pp. 2–201; P. Ashbee 'Halangy Porth, St. Mary's, Isles of Scilly, Excavations 1975–76' *Cornish Archaeol.* 22, 1983, pp. 3–46; P. Ashbee 'Excavations at Halangy Down, St. Mary's, Isles of Scilly, 1969–1970' *Cornish Archaeol.* 9, 1970, pp. 69–76; P. Ashbee 'Excavations at Halangy Down, St. Mary's, Isles of Scilly, 1967 and 1968' *Cornish Archaeol.* 7, 1968, pp. 24–32; P. Ashbee 'Excavations at Halangy Down, St. Mary's, Isles of Scilly, 1965 and 1966' *Cornish Archaeol.* 5, 1966, pp.

20–27; P. Ashbee 'Excavations at Halangy Down, St. Mary's, Isles of Scilly, 1964. Interim Report' *Cornish Archaeol.* 4, 1965, pp. 36–40

52 J. Wood 1997

53 M. Lyons *The Totem and the Tricolour. A Short History of New Caledonia since 1774.* New South Wales University Press. Kensington, Sydney, 1986

54 Pages 320–321 in R.P. Whimster 'Iron Age burial in Southern Britain' *Proceedings of the Prehistoric Society* 43, 1977, pp. 317–327

55 c.f. Weatherhill, C. 1985. *Cornovia: Ancient Sites of Cornwall and Scilly.* Penzance: Alison Hodge

56 J. Wood 1997

57 Butcher 1978 & 2000–01

58 Pages 15–16 in Butcher 2000–01

59 Pages 152–153 in A.C. Thomas *Exploration of a Drowned Landscape. Archaeology and History of the Isles of Scilly.* Batsford, London, 1985

60 Ratcliffe 1995; H. Quinnell 'The Pottery' in Ratcliffe 1995, pp. 120–23; and H. Quinnell 'Copper alloy objects' in Ratcliffe 1995, pp. 132–34

61 P.M. Carlyon 'Kilhallon – an update' *Cornish Archaeol.* 37–38, 1998–9, pp. 132–36; P.M. Carlyon 'A Romano-British site at Kilhallon, Tywardreath: excavation in 1975' *Cornish Archaeol.* 21, 1982, pp. 155–70

62 Quinnell 1986

63 R.B. Warner 'The Carnanton tin ingot' *Cornish Archaeol.* 6, 1967, pp. 29–31

64 P. Ashbee 1996

65 Pages 60–61 in R.G. Collingwood *The Archaeology of Roman Britain.* Bracken Books, London 1996 (originally published 1930 by Methuen, London)

66 Page 87 in N. Johnson 'The Bolster Bank, St Agnes – A Survey' *Cornish Archaeol.* 19, 1980, pp. 77–88

67 D. Perring 'Gnosticism in fourth-century Britain: the Frampton mosaics reconsidered' *Britannia* XXXIV, 2003, pp. 97–127

68 N.M. Sharples *Maiden Castle.* English Heritage/Batsford, London, 1992; R.E.M. Wheeler *Maiden Castle, Dorset.* Society of Antiquaries, London, 1943

69 There are parallels for this pagan resistance elsewhere in Britain, see M. Fulford 'Links with the Past: Pervasive 'Ritual' Behaviour in Roman Britain' *Britannia* XXXII, 2001, pp.199–218

70 Johnson 1980

71 Herring 1994

Chapter six The age of saints in a frontier land

1 See H. Chadwick *The Early Church: Story of Emergent Christianity from the Apostolic Age to the Dividing of the Ways Between the Greek East and the Latin West.* Penguin, Harmondsworth, 2005; J. Knight *The End of Antiquity. Archaeology, Society and Religion AD 235–700.* Tempus. Stroud, Glos., 1999

2 D.H. Farmer *The Oxford Dictionary of Saints.* 2nd ed. Oxford University Press, Oxford, 1987

3 L. Olson *Early Monasteries in Cornwall.* Woodbridge, 1989; L.M. Bitel *Isle of the Saints: monastic settlement and Christian community in early Ireland.* Cork University Press, 1990

4 T. Charles-Edwards 'Early Medieval Kingships in the British Isles' in S. Basset (ed.) *The Origins of Anglo-Saxon Kingdoms.* Leicester University Press, Leicester, 1989, pp.28–39

5 T. Burkitt and A. Burkitt 'The Frontier Zone and the Siege of Mount Badon: A review of the Evidence for their Location'. *Proceedings of the Somerset Archaeological and Natural History Society* 134, 1991, pp. 81–93; L. Alcock and G. Ashe, G. 'Cadbury: is it Camelot?' In G.Ashe (ed.) *The Quest for Arthur's Britain.* Pall Mall Press Ltd, London, 1968, pp. 155–88; Pearce, S.M. 1978. *The Kingdom of Dumnonia. Studies in History and Tradition in South Western Britain. AD 350–1150.* Padstow, Cornwall: Lodenek Press

6 D. Hill and A.R. Rumble (eds) *The Defence of Wessex: The Burghal Hidage and Anglo-Saxon Fortifications.* Manchester University Press, 1996; and D. Hill 'The Burghal Hidage: The Establishment of a Text'. *Medieval Archaeology* XIII, 1969, pp. 84–92

7 A.D. Saunders 'Lydford Castle, Devon'. *Medieval Archaeol.* 24, 1980, pp. 123–64

8 Charles Thomas has put up an alternative idea that Tintagel may have been Purocoravis (or more correctly Durocornovium) – named on a Roman road list known as the Ravenna Cosmography – and that two milestones found on the nearby mainland suggest that it could have been a local tax collection point. However, apart from Exeter, none of the stations on the road in question are known with any certainty, so this is all highly speculative. See a copy of the Ravenna Cosmography on www.roman-britain.org/ravenna.htm

9 Page 186 in S.M. Pearce *The Archaeology of South West Britain.* Collins, London, 1981

10 E. Campbell 'The archaeological evidence for external contacts: imports, trade and economy in Celtic Britain AD 400–800'. In K.R. Dark (ed.) *External Contacts and the Economy of Late Roman and Post-Roman Britain.* The Boydell Press, Woodbridge, 1996, pp. 83–96

11 J.M. Wooding 'Cargoes in trade along the Western Seaboard'. In K.R. Dark (ed.) *External Contacts and the Economy of Late Roman and Post-Roman Britain.* The Boydell Press, Woodbridge, 1996, pp. 67–82

12 Soft wood resins were used as a sealant for wine vessels – see p. 61 in C. Heron and A.M. Pollard 'The analysis of natural resinous materials from Roman amphoras'. In E.A. Slater and J.O. Tate (eds) 'Science in Archaeology Glasgow 1987. Proceedings of a conference on the application of science to archaeology'. *British Archaeological Reports* British Series 196, 1988

13 A.C. Thomas '"Gallici Nautae de Galliarum Provinciis" – A Sixth/Seventh Century Trade with Gaul, Reconsidered'. *Medieval Archaeology* XXXIV, 1990, pp. 1–26

14 Page 92 in A. Bowman 'Post Roman imports in Britain and Ireland: A maritime perspective'. In K.R. Dark (ed.) *External Contacts and the Economy of Late Roman and Post-Roman Britain.* The Boydell Press, Woodbridge, 1996, pp. 97–108

15 C.D. Morris 'Tintagel Island 1991: interim report' *Cornish Archaeol.* 31, 1992, pp. 131–34; C.D. Morris 'Tintagel Island 1994: an interim report' *Cornish Archaeol.* 36, 1997, pp. 208–14

16 Page 142 in E. Okasha 'A supplement to Corpus of Early Christian Inscribed Stones of South-west Britain' *Cornish Archaeol.* 37–38, 1998–99, pp. 137–52

17 The Catholic Community Forum (ed.) (n.d.) *A Supplement to the Life of John the Almsgiver, our*

saintly father and Archbishop of Alexandria, written by Leontius, Bishop of Neapolis in the island of Cyprus. [WWW] www.catholic-forum.com/saints/stj68002.htm (15/04/04)

18 Pages 183–96 and 209–21 in A.C. Thomas *And Shall These Mute Stones Speak? Post-Roman Inscriptions in Western Britain.* University of Wales Press, Cardiff, 1994

19 A.C. Thomas *Celtic Britain.* Thames & Hudson, London, 1997

20 Pages 197–200 in A.C. Thomas 1994

21 Pages 27–39 in A.C. Thomas 1994

22 Pages 41–49 in A.C. Thomas 1994

23 A.C. Thomas *Christianity in Roman Britain to AD 500.* Batsford, London, 1981

24 C. Bourke Patrick: *The Archaeology of a Saint.* HMSO, London, 1993

25 O.J. Padel Cornish *Place-Name Elements.* English Place-Name Society, Nottingham

26 Preston-Jones and Rose 1986

27 Härke, H. 1995. 'Finding Britons in Anglo-Saxon graves'. *British Archaeology* 10 [WWW] www.britarch.ac.uk/ba/ba10/ba10feat.html (03/04/2004)

28 E-ware is also absent from Tintagel – see p. 103 in A. Bowman 1996

29 C.f. W. Davies *Patterns of Power in Early Wales.* Clarendon Press, Oxford, 1990; and p. 105 in M. Swanton (ed.) *The Anglo-Saxon Chronicle.* J.M. Dent, London, 1996

30 Hill and Rumble 1996; and Hill 1969

31 Preston-Jones and Rose 1986

32 A.C. Thomas' Settlement-History in early Cornwall I: The Antiquity of the Hundreds'. *Cornish Archaeol.* 3, 1964, pp. 70–79

33 A. Preston-Jones 'Decoding churchyards'. *Cornish Archaeol.* 33, 1994, pp. 71–95

34 A. Preston-Jones and A. Langdon 'St Buryan crosses' *Cornish Archaeol.* 36, 1997, pp. 107–25

35 S. Gerrard *The Early British Tin Industry.* Tempus, Stroud, Glos., 2000

36 A.C. Thomas Christian Celts, *Messages and Images.* Tempus, Stroud, Glos., 1998

37 Against that Elizabeth Okasha (1998–99) has pointed out that little of the text is clearly legible, so any such reading must be treated with caution.

38 R. Bruce-Mitford Mawgan Porth: *A Settlement of the Late Saxon Period on the North Cornish Coast – Excavations 1949–52, 1954 and 1974.* English Heritage/Batsford, London, 1997

39 D. Dudley and E.M. Minter 'The Excavation of a Medieval Settlement at Treworld, Lesnewth, 1963'. *Cornish Archaeol.* 5, 1966, pp. 34–58

40 P. Ashbee 'Ancient Scilly: retrospect, aspect and prospect'. *Cornish Archaeol.* 1986, 25, pp. 186– ; A.C. Thomas *Exploration of a Drowned Landscape. Archaeology and History of the Isles of Scilly.* Batsford, London, 1985

41 See Chapter 6, pp.128–47 in Galliou, P. and Jones, M. 1996. *The Bretons.* Oxford: Blackwell

42 Galliou and Jones 1996

43 P.-R. Giot, P. Guigon and B. Merdrignac *The British Settlement of Brittany.* Tempus, Stroud, Glos., 2004; and P.-R. Giot, L. Fleuriot and G. Bernier *Les Premiers Bretons: la Bretagne du Ve siècle à l'an mil.* Editions Jos, Châteaulin, Brittany, 1985

44 Martin Henig's review of Giot *et al.* 2004 is scathing and finds little new or really convincing archaeological evidence to substantiate their ideas – see M. Henig 'British Bretons'. *British Archaeology* 72, 2003 [WWW] www.britarch.ac.uk/ba/ba72/book.shtml#book3 (20/10/2004)

45 See B. Cunliffe *Facing the Ocean: The Atlantic and Its Peoples, 8000 BC to AD 1500.* Oxford University Press, 2001

46 P.-R. Giot *et al.* 2004; and P.-R. Giot *et al.* 1985

47 G. Hutchinson 'The Bar-lug Pottery of Cornwall'. *Cornish Archaeol.* 18, 1979, pp. 81–104; Thomas 1997

48 Hutchinson 1979

49 P.-R. Giot *et al.* 2004; and P.-R. Giot *et al.* 1985

50 Grimmer, M. 2001. 'Saxon Bishop and Celtic King: Interactions between Aldhelm of Wessex and Geraint of Dumnonia'. *The Heroic Age* 4 [WWW] www.mun.ca/mst/heroicage/issues/4/Grimmer.html (16/04/2004)

Chapter seven Late Medieval floruit: the Earldom, the Church and the State

1 The idea that this frontier idea continued into the Late Medieval is briefly discussed in R. Higham 'Public and Private Defence in the medieval South West: Town, Castle and Fort'. In R. Higham (ed.) *Security & Defence in South-West England Before 1800* University of Exeter Press, 1987, pp. 27–49

2 J. Carley 'The Origins of the Earldom of Cornwall'. *Journal of the Royal Institution of Cornwall* New Series II, Vol IV, 2003, pp. 29–38

3 Beroul's *Romance of Tristran*; translated [from the Italian] by John C. Barnes. Manchester, Manchester University Press; New York, Barnes & Noble, 1972; Ditmas, E. M. R. *Tristan and Iseult in Cornwall: The Twelfth-century Romance by Beroul Re-told from the Norman French.* Forrester Roberts, Gloucester, 1970

4 A.C. Thomas 'The Context of Tintagel: a new model for the diffusion of post-Roman Mediterranean imports' *Cornish Archaeol.* 27, 1998, pp. 7–25; A.C. Thomas *Tintagel, Arthur and Archaeology.* Batsford/English Heritage, London, 1993

5 See C. Peters 'When King Arthur met the Pisky and the Knocker: Cornish Dreamtime or Nightmare'. In C. Peters (ed.) 'Cornwall: A European Case Study in Identity'. *British Archaeological Reports* Int. Series *forthcoming*; and for the association of these moorlands with Arthur, see pp. 28–29 in O.J. Padel 'The Nature of Arthur'. *Cambrian Medieval Celtic Studies* 27, 1994, pp. 1–31

6 Page 12 in *English Heritage Restormel Castle.* English Heritage, London, 1996.

7 See the discussion of such arguments in R. Higham 'Castles in Devon'. In S.C.Timms (ed.) *Archaeology of the Devon Landscape.* Devon County Council, 1980, pp. 70–80; R. Higham 'Early castles in Devon, 1068–1201' *Château Gaillard*, IX–X, 1982, pp. 101–16; Higham 1987

8 G. Beresford 'The medieval manor of Penhallam, Cornwall'. *Medieval Archaeol.* 18, 1974, pp. 90–145

9 A. Preston-Jones and P. Rose 'Week St Mary: town and castle'. *Cornish Archaeol.* 31, 1992, pp. 143–53

10 A. Preston-Jones 'Kilkhampton Castle: Archaeology, History, Management' *CAU Report No. 1988R003.* Cornwall County Council, Truro, 1988

11 A. Reynolds 'Kilkhampton Castle Farm. An archaeological and historical assessment'. CAU Report No. 1999R046. Cornwall County Council & The National Trust, 1999

12 N.V. Quinnell 'Upton Castle'. *RCHM Field Survey Section Recording and Report Form – Antiquity* No. SX 27 NW 35. (Copy with Cornwall County Council Historic Environment Service, Truro), 1982

13 B. Weiler 'Image and Reality in Richard of Cornwall's German Career'. *English Historical Review.* 113, 1998, p. 1111

14 P. Herring 'Cornish Medieval Deer Parks' In R. Wilson-North (ed.) *The lie of the land: aspects of the archaeology and history of the designed landscape in the south west. Exeter* The Mint Press and the Devon Gardens Trust, 2003

15 A. Saunders 'Excavations at Launceston Castle 1970–76: interim report' *Cornish Archaeol.* 16, 1977, pp. 129–37; A. Saunders 'Launceston Castle Excavations in 1981 – an interim report. *Cornish Archaeol.* 21, 1982, pp. 187–8; A. Saunders *Launceston Castle.* HBMCE, London, 1984

16 P. Rose 'The medieval garden at Tintagel Castle'. *Cornish Archaeol.* 33, 1994, pp. 170–82

17 See A. Richardson 'Gender and Space in English Royal Palaces c. 1160 – c. 1547. A Study in Access Analysis and Imagery'. *Medieval Archaeology XLVII*, 2003, pp. 131–65; and R. Gilchrist *Gender and Archaeology: Contesting the Past.* Routledge, London, 1999

18 in P. Payton *Cornwall. A History.* Cornwall Editions, Fowey, 2004

19 P. Beresford Ellis *Cornish language and its literature: a history.* Routledge & Kegan Paul, London, 1974

20 Page 46 in P. Payton *The Making of Modern Cornwall: Historical Experience and the Persistence of Difference.* Dyllansow Truran, Redruth, 1992

21 Section 4.2 of the Domesday Book – C. & F. Thorn (eds) *Domesday Book. Cornwall.* Phillimore, Chichester, 1977

22 J.A. Buckley *Medieval Cornish Stannary Charters. 1201–1507.* Penhellick Publications, Pool, Camborne, 2001

23 N.J.G. Pounds 'The Duchy Palace at Lostwithiel, Cornwall'. *Archaeol J.* 136, 1979, pp. 203–17

24 A. Preston-Jones and P. Rose 'Medieval Cornwall'. *Cornish Archaeol.* 25, 1986, pp. 135–85

25 Preston-Jones and Rose 1986

26 M. Tangye *Carn Brea. Brief history and guide.* Dyllansow Truran, Redruth, 1981

27 J. Whitaker 'Lanyhorn Castle and its Lords'. *Journal of the Royal Institution of Cornwall* 9.3, 1888, pp.425–48

28 J.J. Rogers 'Carminow of Carminow'. *Journal of the Royal Institution of Cornwall* 5, 1875, pp.231–35

29 C. Henderson *St Columb Major, Church and Parish.* King's Stone Press, Shipston-on-Stour, 1930

30 Whitaker 1888; and J. Redley *Ruan Lanihorne Parish Recalled from Records, Writings and Hearsay.* J. Redley, Ruan Lanihorne, 1995

31 J.P. Greene *Medieval monasteries.* Leicester University Press, 1992

32 J. Gossip *St Thomas' Priory, Launceston, Cornwall. Archaeological Survey.* Cornwall Archaeological Unit, Cornwall County Council, Truro, 2001

33 L. Olson and A. Preston-Jones 'An ancient cathedral of Cornwall? Excavated remains east of St Germans Church' *Cornish Archaeol.* 37–38, 1998–99, pp. 153–69

34 P. O'Hara 'Bodmin Priory'. *Cornish Archaeol.* 24, 1985, p. 212

35 Preston-Jones and Rose 1986

36 Page 7 and 15 in C. Parnell *The Book of Truro.* Halsgrove, Tiverton, 2004

37 Preston-Jones and Rose 1986

38 Page 26 in D. Austin, G.A.M. Gerrard and T.A.P. Greeves 'Tin and Agriculture in the middle ages and beyond: landscape archaeology in St Neot Parish, Cornwall'. *Cornish Archaeol.* 28, 1989, pp. 5–251

39 Pages 19–26 in J. Ratcliffe *Fieldwork in Scilly 1991 and 1992.* Cornwall Archaeological Unit, Cornwall County Council, Truro, 1993

40 For more on Perranzabuloe, see A. Preston-Jones *The Old Church of St Piran, Perranzabuloe.* Cornwall Archaeological Unit, Cornwall County Council, Truro, 1994

41 Olson and Preston-Jones 1998–99

42 D.B. Hague 'Early lighthouses in Cornwall'. *Cornish Archaeol.* 6, 1967, pp. 64–67

43 C. Johns and N. Thomas *An Archaeological Evaluation of the Proposed New Library Site, Bodmin, Cornwall.* Cornwall Archaeological Unit, Cornwall County Council, Truro, 1995; C. Thorpe *Mount Folly Square, Bodmin, Cornwall.* Cornwall Archaeological Unit, Cornwall County Council, Truro, 2001

44 Preston-Jones and Rose 1986

45 Austin, Gerrard and Greeves 1989

46 p. 187–188 in L.E. Elliott-Binns *Mediaeval Cornwall.* Methuen, London, 1955; R. Carew *Survey of Cornwall.* Tamar Books, Redruth, 2000 (original ed. 1602)

47 Page 23 in M. Kowaleski *Local Markets and Regional Trade in Medieval Exeter.* Cambridge University Press 2003

48 p. 187–88 in Elliott-Binns 1955

49 Page 99 in Payton 2004; and p. 19 in P. Payton *Cornwall's History. An introduction.* Tor Mark, Redruth, 2002

50 e.g., A. Preston-Jones 'The Excavation of a Long-Cist Cemetery at Carnanton, St Mawgan, 1943'. *Cornish Archaeol.* 23, 1984, pp. 157–77

51 P. Sheppard *The Historic Towns of Cornwall, an archaeological survey.* CCRA, Truro, 1980

52 Preston-Jones and Rose 1986; and Elliott-Binns 1955

53 M. Spriggs 'The Cornish Language, Archaeology, and the Origins of the English Theatre'. In M. Jones (ed.) *Traces of ancestry: studies in honour of Colin Renfrew.* McDonald Institute Monographs, Cambridge, 2004, pp. 143–61

54 e.g., p. 212 in B. Murdoch 'The Cornish medieval drama'. In R. Beadle (ed.) *The Cambridge Companion to Medieval English Theatre.* Cambridge University Press, 1994, pp. 211–39

55 Page 154 in Spriggs 2004

56 P. Stead 'Investigations at Nos 4–6 Pydar Street, Truro' *Cornish Archaeol.* 37–38, 1998–99, pp. 178–85

57 Cornwall Historic Environment Service *Cornwall & Scilly Urban Survey.* Cornwall County Council, Truro, 2004 [WWW] www.historic-cornwall.org.uk/ (10/12/2004)

58 Preston-Jones and Rose 1986

59 See also the excavation report of the leper hospital at St Leonard's, near Launceston – P. Harding, S. Ainsworth, J. Gater, and C. Johns 'The evaluation of a medieval leper hospital at St Leonards, Cornwall'. *Cornish Archaeol.* 36, 1997, pp. 138–50

60 J. Mattingly 'Stories in the Glass – Reconstructing the St Neot Pre-Reformation Glazing Scheme'. *Journal of the Royal Institution of Cornwall* New Series II, Vol. III, 2000, pp. 9–55

61 C. Parkes *Fowey Estuary Historic Audit*. Cornwall Archaeological Unit, Cornwall County Council, Truro, 2000

62 M. Bell and M.J.C. Walker *Late Quaternary Environmental Change: Physical and Human Perspectives*. Longman, London 1992; and N. Roberts *The Holocene: an environmental history*. Blackwell, Oxford, 1998

63 S. Gerrard *Dartmoor: Book of Dartmoor Landscapes through Time*. English Heritage/Batsford, London, 1997

64 G. Beresford 'Old Lanyon, Madron: a deserted medieval settlement. The late E. Marie Minter's excavations of 1964'. *Cornish Archaeol.* 33, 1994, pp. 130–69; E.M. Minter 'Lanyon in Madron: Interim Report of the Society's 1964 Excavation'. *Cornish Archaeol.* 3, 1964, pp. 44–45

65 D. Dudley and E. M. Minter 'Medieval village at Garrow Tor, Bodmin Moor, Cornwall'. *Medieval Archaeology*, VI, 1963, pp. 272–94

66 Preston-Jones and Rose 1986

67 J.A. Nowakowski and P. Herring 'The Beehive Huts of Bodmin Moor'. *Cornish Archaeol.* 24, 1985, pp. 185–95

68 Pounds 1979

69 P. Mayer 'Calstock and Bere Alston silver-lead mines in the first quarter of the 14th century'. *Cornish Archaeol.* 29, 1990, pp. 79–95

70 Preston-Jones and Rose 1986; M. Tangye 'A huer's hut, Cribbin Head, Penberth, St Levan'. *Cornish Archaeol.* 33, 1994, pp. 183–86

71 J. Ratcliffe and C. Johns *Scilly's Archaeological Heritage*. Historic Environment Unit, Cornwall County Council, Truro, 2003

72 R.T Taylor and J. Allan 'Addendum: A note on the petrology of Cornish potteries' *Cornish Archaeol.* 37–38, 1998–99, pp. 186–89; H.L. Douch 'Cornish earthenware potters' *Journal of the Royal Institution of Cornwall* new ser. 6, 1969, 33–64

73 Preston-Jones and Rose 1986

74 P. Marsden *Ships and Shipwrecks* English Heritage/Batsford, London, 1997

Chapter eight Capitalism and class conflict

1 See B. Anderson *Imagined Communities. Reflections on the Origin and Spread of Nationalism*. (rev. ed.) Verso, London, 1991

2 Ibid

3 Even farming was becoming geared to surpluses – see U. Albarella and S.J.M. Davis 'Mammals and birds from Launceston Castle, Cornwall: decline in status and the rise of agriculture'. *Circaea* 12, 1996, pp. 1–156

4 John Rashleigh of Menabilly, for example, financed and promoted the extension of Cornish fisheries to take in the seas off Newfoundland, Canada – J.

Scantlebury 'John Rashleigh and the Newfoundland Cod Fishery, 1608–20' *Journal of the Royal Institute of Cornwall* New Series II, Vol. VIII, 1978, pp. 61–71

5 Pages 59–60 in R. Morton Nance *A Glossary of Cornish Sea-Words*. The Federation of Old Cornwall Societies, 1963

6 Page 47 in Morton Nance 1963

7 R. Hunt *Popular Romances of the West of England*. John Camden Hotten, London, 1865; W. Bottrell *Traditions and Hearthside Stories of West Cornwall*. Llanerch Enterprises, Dyfed, 1989; M.A. Courtney *Cornish feasts and folk-lore: revised and reprinted from the folk-lore society journals, 1886–87*. Beare & Son, Penzance, 1890

8 Pages 522–23 & 527–33 in B. Cunliffe *Facing the Ocean: The Atlantic and Its Peoples, 8000 BC to AD 1500*. Oxford University Press, Oxford, 2001

9 M. Boyle *Lighthouses. Four Countries – One Aim*. B & T Publications, Southampton, 1996

10 J. Mattingly 'A Note on Cornish –Breton Links'. *Institute of Cornish Studies Associates' Newsletter*, 2nd series, No. 4, May 1995

11 Page 101 in P. Payton *Cornwall. A History*. Cornwall Editions, Fowey, Cornwall, 2004

12 D. Smart *The Cornish Fishing Industry – a brief history*. Tor Mark Press, Penryn, 1992

13 Page 121 in M. Kurlansky *Salt: A World History*. Penguin, London, 2002; Chapter XXIX in L. Brochet *La Vendée à travers les ages*. Res Universis, Paris, 1991 (original 1902)

14 R.Platt *Smugglers' Britain. The Ordnance Survey Guide*. Cassell, London, 1991

15 M. Tangye 'A seventeenth century fish cellar at Porth Godrevy, Gwithian'. *Cornish Archaeol.* 30, 1991, pp. 243–52

16 Page 51 in G. Pawley White *A Handbook of Cornish Surnames*. Dyllansow Truran, 1972

17 Tangye 1991

18 Ibid

19 R. Linzey *Fortress Falmouth*. English Heritage, London, 2000; and D. Harris and J. Andrew 'An Ancient Wall at Pendennis Point, Falmouth'. *Cornish Archaeol.* 24, 1985, pp. 183–84

20 V. Fenwick & A. Gale *Historic Shipwrecks: Discovered, Protected & Investigated*. Tempus, Stroud, Glos., 1999

21 T. Pawlyn *The Falmouth Packets 1689–1851*. Truran Books, Truro, 2003

22 Pages 126–27 in Fenwick and Gale 1999; P. McBride and R. Larn *Admiral Shovell's Treasure and Shipwreck in the Isles of Scilly*. P. McBride and R. Larn, 1999

23 P.W.J. McBride, R. Larn and R. Davis 'A Mid-17th Century Merchant Ship-wreck near Mullion; interim report'. *Cornish Archaeol.* 10, 1971, pp.75–78

24 Pages 50–51 in Fenwick and Gale 1999

25 Anderson 1991

26 It was called *De animantis subterranibus*

27 G.Agricola *De Re Metallica*. (Trans.. H.C. and H.L. Hoover). Dover Publications, New York, 1912 (original 1556)

28 The Roche example is from the records of the Cornwall Historic Environment Service (PRN 19836) and the Boscarne example in a medieval display case of the Royal Cornwall Museum

29 The figurine is in a medieval display case in the

Royal Cornwall Museum
30 R. Carew *Survey of Cornwall*. Tamar Books, Redruth, 2000 (original ed. 1602); R. Hunt 1865; W. Bottrell 1989; M.A. Courtney 1890
31 Pages 33 and 35 in A. Sharpe *St Just. An Archaeological Survey of the Mining District*. Volume I. Cornwall Archaeological Unit, Cornwall County Council, Truro, 1992
32 A. Sharpe *The Minions Survey*. Cornwall Archaeological Unit, Cornwall County Council, Truro, 1989; P. Herring and P. Rose *Bodmin Moor's Archaeological Heritage*. Cornwall County Council, Truro, 2001
33 S. Gerrard 'Retallack: a Late Medieval Tin Milling Complex in the Parish of Constantine and its Cornish Context'. *Cornish Archaeol.* 24, 1985, pp. 175–82
34 Herring and Rose 2001
35 C.E. Lazareth and J.-C.C. Mercier 'Geochemistry of ballast granites from Brouage and La Rochelle, France: evidence for medieval to post-medieval trade with Falmouth, Cornwall, and Donegal, Ireland'. In A.M. Pollard (ed.) *Geoarchaeology: exploration, environments, resources*. Geological Society, London, Special Publications 165, 1999, pp. 123–37.
36 A. Sharpe *Pendinas Castle*. Cornwall Archaeological Unit, Cornwall County Council, Truro, 1989; and pp. 82–83 in Volume 1 of Linzey 2000
37 Pages 31–35 in D.E. Pett *The Parks and Gardens of Cornwall*. Alison Hodge, Penzance, 1998
38 See D. Crossley *Post-medieval archaeology in Britain*. Leicester University Press, 1990
39 Page 33 in R. Carew 2000 (original ed. 1602)
40 P. Herring and E. Berry 'Stonaford'. *Cornish Archaeol.* 36, 1997, pp. 151–75
41 Page 51 in P. Herring and P. Rose *Bodmin Moor's Archaeological Heritage*. Cornwall County Council, Truro, 2001
42 G. Beresford 'Old Lanyon, Madron: a deserted medieval settlement. The late E. Marie Minter's excavations of 1964'. *Cornish Archaeol.* 33, 1994, pp. 130–69
43 N. Johnson and P. Rose *Bodmin Moor: An archaeological survey. Vol. 1: The Human Landscape to c. 1800*. English Heritage & RCHME, London, 1994
44 Figure 63 in Johnson and Rose 1994
45 J.A. Nowakowski and P. Herring 'The Beehive Huts of Bodmin Moor'. *Cornish Archaeol.* 24, 1985, pp. 185–95
46 M. Bell and M.J.C. Walker *Late Quaternary Environmental Change: Physical and Human Perspectives*. Longman, London 1992; and N. Roberts *The Holocene: an environmental history*. Blackwell, Oxford, 1998
47 G. Smith 'Excavations on Goonhilly Downs, the Lizard, 1981'. *Cornish Archaeol.* 23, 1984, pp. 3–48
48 Page 152 in A. Preston-Jones and P. Rose 'Medieval Cornwall'. *Cornish Archaeol.* 25, 1986, pp. 135–85
49 Pages 107–10 in Crossley 1990
50 Sharpe 1989; and pp. 82–83 in Volume 1 of Linzey 2000.
51 A.D. Saunders and T. Miles 'King Charles' Castle, Tresco'. *Post Medieval Archaeology* 4, 1970: N. Quinnell 'A 16th Century Outwork to King Charles' Castle, Tresco'. *Cornish Archaeol.* 17, 1978, pp. 142–43
52 Pages 202–203 in Pett 1998

53 R.W. Wilson-North 'Stowe: the country house and garden of the Grenville family'. *Cornish Archaeol.* 32, 1993, pp. 112–27; and pp. 225–226 in Pett 1998
54 Page 94 in W. Lake *A Complete Parochial History of the County of Cornwall*. Vol. IV. John Camden Hotten, London, 1872. However, Gilbert claims they were found in two separate niches – p. 364 in D. Gilbert *The Parochial History of Cornwall*. Vol. III. J.B. Nicholas and Son, London, 1838
55 Page 28 in S.V. Daniell *The Story of Cornwall's Churches*. Tor Mark Press, Penryn, 1988; pp. 66 and 83 in H. Miles Brown *What to look for in Cornish Churches*. David & Charles, Newton Abbot, 1973
56 A. Langdon *Stone Crosses in North Cornwall*. (2nd ed.) Federation of Old Cornwall Societies, 1996; A. Langdon *Stone Crosses in Mid Cornwall*. Federation of Old Cornwall Societies, 1994; A. Langdon *Stone Crosses in East Cornwall*. Federation of Old Cornwall Societies, 1996; A. Langdon *Stone Crosses in West Penwith*. Federation of Old Cornwall Societies, 1997; A. Langdon *Stone Crosses in West Cornwall (including the Lizard)*. Federation of Old Cornwall Societies, 1999
57 See C. Straffon *Fentyntow Kernow. In Search of Cornwall's Holy Wells*. Meyn Mamvro, St Just, 1998; A. Lane-Davies *Holy Wells of Cornwall*. Federation of Old Cornwall Societies, 1970
58 Pages 6 and 8 in D. Shearlock *Truro Cathedral*. Pitkin Pictorials, Andover, Hants., 1986
59 Page 74 in W. Lake *A Complete Parochial History of the County of Cornwall*. Vol. III. John Camden Hotten, London, 1870

Chapter nine Cornwall and the diaspora: a world industrial culture
1 P. Payton *Cornish Overseas*. Alexander Associates, Fowey, 1999
2 J. Collis *Celts: Origins, Myths and Inventions*. Tempus, Stroud, Glos., 2003
3 D. Gregory *Brute New World : The Rediscovery of Latin America in the Early 19th Century*. I.B.Tauris, London, 1993
4 S.P. Schwartz *Creating the cult of "Cousin Jack": Cornish miners in Latin America 1812–1848 and the development of an international mining labour market*. University of Exeter. n.d. [WWW] www.ex.ac.uk/projects/cornishlatin/workingpapersandb ibliography.htm (11/11/04)
5 P. Taylor *The Toll-houses of Cornwall*. Federation of Old Cornwall Societies, Penryn, 2001
6 Pages 18–19 in C. Parkes *Fowey Estuary Historic Audit*. Cornwall Archaeological Unit, Cornwall County Council, Truro, 2000.
7 Pages 114–15 in V. Fenwick and A. Gale *Historic Shipwrecks. Discovered, Protected and Investigated*. Tempus, Stroud, Glos., 1999
8 Pages 32–33 in M. Tarrant *Cornwall's Lighthouse Heritage*. Twelveheads Press, Truro, 2000
9 Pages 58–61 in C. Noall *The Book of St Ives*. Baron Books, Buckingham, 2000
10 Page 62 in R. Cole *Roseland Heritage Coast Historic Audit*. Cornwall Archaeological Unit, Cornwall County Council, Truro, 2000
11 Pages 34–35 in J. Ratcliffe and C. Johns *Scilly's Archaeological Heritage*. Historic Environment Unit, Cornwall County Council, Truro, 2003

12 Pages 13–19 in C. Rowe *Marconi at The Lizard*.
Trevithick Society, 2000
13 Page 17 in R.P. Laity *St Ives in the 1800's*. Wordens
of Cornwall, Penzance, 1973; p. 59 in E. Murt.
Downlong Days. A St Ives Miscellany. St Ives Printing
and Publishing Company, St Ives, 1994
14 A. Pye and F. Woodward *The Historic Defences of
Plymouth*. Cornwall County Council, 1996
15 Named after the then prime minister, Palmerston.
16 C. Buck *Tregantle Fort*. Cornwall Archaeological
Unit, Cornwall County Council, Truro, 1999; and
pages 80–84 in Pye and Woodward 1996
17 Taylor 2001; p. 28 in A. Sharpe *St Just. An
Archaeological Survey of the Mining District*. Volume
I. Cornwall Archaeological Unit, Cornwall County
Council, Truro, 1992; and p. 105 in A. Guthrie
Cornwall in the Age of Steam. Tabb House, Padstow,
1994
18 B. James *Tales of the Tinner's Way*. Dyllansow
Truran, Truro, 1988; and pp. 78–81 in C. Weatherhill
Belerion. Ancient Sites of Land's End. Alison Hodge,
Penzance, 1981
19 Guthrie 1994
20 B. Young and B.D. Stamp *Bude Canal. Past and
Present*. Bill Young, Bude, 1997
21 J.R. Smith *The Luxulyan Valley: walking the
tramway track*. Cornwall County Council, Truro, 1992;
J.R. Smith *et al. The Luxulyan Valley: An
Archaeological and Historical Survey*. Cornwall
Archaeological Unit, Cornwall County Truro, 1988; J.
Lewis *A Richly Yielding Piece of Ground. The history
of Fowey Consols Mine*. Cornish Hillside Publications,
St Austell, 1997; J. Keast *The King of Mid-Cornwall:
The Life of Joseph Thomas Treffry 1782–1850*.
Dyllansow Truran, Redruth, 1982
22 Pages 62–74 in A. Burton *Richard Trevithick. Giant
of Steam*. Aurum Press, London, 2000; pp. 115–116 in
J. Rowe *Cornwall in the Age of the Industrial
Revolution*. 2nd ed. Cornish Hillside Publications, St
Austell, 1993; and p. 63 in E. Vale *The Harveys of
Hayle*. D. Bradford Barton, Truro, 1966
23 Pages 40–41 in P. Payton *Cornwall's History. An
introduction*. Tor Mark, Redruth, 2002
24 E.T. MacDermot *History of the Great Western
Railway. Vol. I '1833–1863'*. Great Western Railway,
London, 1927
25 Pages 38–39 in R.K. Morriss *The Archaeology of
Railways*. Tempus, Stroud, Glos., 1999
26 Copper still had to be sent to South Wales for
smelting though, because of the lack of coal in
Cornwall – see S. Hughes. *Copperopolis. Landscapes
of the Early Industrial Period in Swansea*. RCAHM
Wales, Aberystwyth, 2000
27 Page 112 in D.B. Barton *History of Tin Mining and
Smelting in Cornwall*. D. Bradford Barton, Truro,
1967; C. Thorpe *Dolcoath, Chapel Road, Cornwall.
Geotechnical site investigation, archaeological
recording*. Cornwall Archaeological Unit, Cornwall
County Council, Truro, 2000
28 P. Joseph 'Tin dressing sites in the Western Cot
Valley, St Just'. *Journal of the Trevithick Society* 30,
2003, pp. 54–73
29 Pages 18–20 in R.M. Barton *A History of the
Cornish China-Clay Industry*. D. Bradford Barton,
Truro, 1966; pp. 91–92 in Guthrie 1994; and pp. 44–45
in N. Johnson and P. Rose *Cornwall's Archaeological

Heritage*. Twelveheads Press, Truro, 1997
30 J. Smith *Cornwall's China Clay Heritage*.
Twelveheads Press, Truro, 1992; P. Herring and J.R.
Smith *The Archaeology of the St Austell China Clay
Area. An Archaeological and Historical Assessment*.
Cornwall Archaeological Unit, Cornwall County
Council, Truro, 1991
31 L. Mayers *Balmaidens*. The Hypnatia Trust,
Penzance, 2004.
32 Cornwall County Council *Cornwall Landscape
Assessment*. Truro, 1996
33 Tangye, M. 1994. 'A huer's hut, Cribbin Head,
Penberth, St Levan'. *Cornish Archaeol*. 33: 183–86
34 Page 276 in S. Baring-Gould *A book of the west—
Cornwall*. Methuen, London,1899 (republished by
Wildwood, London: 1981); and pp. 9–10 in A. Kittridge
Cornwall's Maritime Heritage. Twelveheads Press,
Truro, 1991
35 Pages 178 & 200 respectively in C. Parkes 2000. For
Ethy, see also p. 65 in C. Parkes and P. Herring
'Archaeological Survey'. In P. Herring (ed.) *Ethy Park,
St Winnow. Historic Landscape Survey*. Cornwall
Archaeological Unit, Cornwall County Council, Truro,
1998
36 M. Tangye "Hulls' in Cornwall: a survey and
discussion'. *Cornish Archaeol*. 12, 1973, pp. 31–52
37 Page 72 in B. Dunstan *The Book of Falmouth and
Penryn*. Barracuda Books, Chesham, Bucks., 1975; and
p. 130 in J. Ratcliffe *Fal Estuary Historic Audit*.
Cornwall Archaeological Unit, Cornwall County
Council, Truro, 1997
38 T. Miles 'The Pottery'. In P.M. Christie 'A Post-
Medieval Cottage at Carn Euny, Sancreed'. *Cornish
Archaeol*. 18, 1979, pp. 117–19
39 S.P. Schwartz 'Cornish Migration to Latin America:
A Global and Transnational Perspective'. Unpublished
doctoral thesis, University of Exeter, 2003
40 D.B. Barton *The Cornish Beam Engine*. D.Bradford
Barton, Truro, 1969
41 D. Bick 'Evolution of the Pre-Cornish Beam Engine
House'. *Industrial Archaeology Review* XXI, 1999, pp.
121–35
42 P.M. Christie 'A Post-Medieval Cottage at Carn
Euny, Sancreed'. *Cornish Archaeol*. 18, 1979, pp.
105–23
43 Frank Chester in Christie 1979
44 L. Biek 'Report from the soot from F.3', p.122 in
Christie 1979; pp.110–12 in Christie 1979
45 J. Allen 'The Cornish round chimney in Australia'.
Cornish Archaeol. 6, 1967, pp. 68–73; J. Allen 'The
archaeology of nineteenth century British imperialism:
an Australian case study'. *World Archaeology* 5, 1973,
pp. 44–60
46 I. Auhl *The Story of the 'Monster Mine'. The Burra
Burra Mine and its townships 1845–1877*. District
Council of Burra Burra, Burra Burra, Australia, 1986;
Heritage SA. *Burra: State Heritage Area*. Heritage
South Australia, Department for Environment and
Heritage, n.d.
47 Pages 75–98 in G.J. Drew and J.E. Connell *Cornish
Beam Engines in South Australian mines*. Dept. of
Mines and Energy, South Australia, Adelaide, 1993
48 A. Simmons 'Red Light Ladies: settlement patterns
and material culture on the mining frontier'.
Anthropology Northwest No. 4. Department of
Anthropology, Oregon State University, 1989;

D.L.Hardesty 'The Archaeology of Mining and Miners: A View From the Silver State'. *Society for Historical Archaeology*, Special Publication Series No. 6, 1988; C. Judge 'Reconstructing The Social Dimension: Miners Bay, Industrial Settlement 1844–1854'. Unpublished M.A. Thesis, University Of Auckland, 2003

49 C. Judge 2003. See also R. Clough 'Documents And Digs: Investigation Of The Copper And Clay Industries In New Zealand'. *Australian Historical Archaeology* 7, 1989, pp. 3–9; R. Clough 'The Archaeology Of The Historic Copper Industry On Kawau Island'. *Australian Historical Archaeology* 9, 1991, pp. 45–48; R. Clough 'The Last Roast: Archaeology Of The Historic Copper Industry Of Kawau Island 1843–1855'. *Archaeology In New Zealand* 35(3), 1992, pp. 141–54

50 Page 156 in S. Schwartz and R. Parker *Lanner: A Cornish Mining Parish*. Halsgrove, Tiverton, 1998

51 Ibid

52 Pages 278–79 in W. Lake *A Complete Parochial History of the County of Cornwall*. Vol IV, John Camden Hotten, London, 1872

53 Page 113 in H. Mc Cabe *Houses and Gardens of Cornwall*. Tabb House, Padstow, 1988

54 H. Lees *Cornwall's Churchyard Heritage*. Twelvehead Press, Truro, 1996

55 Ibid

56 Ibid

57 J. Lake, J. Cox and E. Berry *Diversity & Vitality. The Non-Conformist Chapels of Cornwall*. Cornwall Archaeological Unit, Cornwall County Council, Truro, 2001

58 The best example of a Quaker Meeting House is that at Come-to-Good, built in 1710 of cob with a thatched roof

59 Quoted from p. 252 in A.K. Hamilton Jenkin *Cornwall and its People*. David and Charles, Newton Abbott, 1945 (rev. ed. 1970)

60 Page 27 in J. Lake, J. Cox and E. Berry 2001

61 Lake, Cox and Berry 2001

62 Ibid

63 Page 73 in J. Lake, J. Cox and E. Berry 2001

64 D.Pirrie, S.H. Hughes and G.S. Camm 'Late Holocene sedimentation due to mine waste discharge, Fal Estuary'. In J.D. Scourse and M.F.A. Furze (eds.) *The Quaternary of West Cornwall*. Quaternary Research Association, London, 1999

65 Page 59 in P. Stanier *Stone Quarry Landscapes. The Archaeology of Quarrying in England*. Tempus, Stroud, Glos., 2000; pp. 34, and 120–21 in M. Messenger *Caradon & Looe. The Railways and Mines*. Twelveheads Press, Truro, 2001

66 R. Hunt *Popular Romances of the West of England*. John Camden Hotten, London, 1865; W. Bottrell *Traditions and Hearthside Stories of West Cornwall*. Llanerch Enterprises, Dyfed, 1989; M.A. Courtney *Cornish feasts and folk-lore: revised and reprinted from the folk-lore society journals, 1886–87*. Beare & Son, Penzance, 1890

67 Page 180 in W. Borlase *Antiquities, Historical and Monumental of the County of Cornwall*. 2nd ed., Bowyer and J. Nichols, London, 1769 (re-pub. EP Publishing Ltd, East Ardsley, Wakefield Yorks. and Cornwall County Library)

68 J. Nicholas 'Verses on the Logging Rock (1815)'. *Cornish Archaeol.* 12, 1973, pp. 55–56

69 Lake, Cox and Berry 2001; and J.K. Lander 'The Early Days of Teetotalism in Cornwall'. *Journal of the Royal Institution of Cornwall* New Series II, Vol. IV, pp. 85–100

70 C. Judge 2003

71 P. Herring 'A folly on Kit Hill'. *Cornish Archaeol.* 28, 1989, pp. 252–258; P. Herring and N. Thomas *The Kit Hill Survey*. Cornwall Archaeological Unit, Cornwall County Council, Truro, 1990

72 B. Acton *History of Truro. Volume 3: Exploring the City – and Around*. Landfall Publications, Devoran, Truro, 2003

73 A good example with the concern with such etiquette is – *A Lady of Distinction Regency Etiquette; The Mirror of Graces (1811)*. (Facsimile of the 1811 publication). R. L. Shep, Fort Bragg, CA., 1997

74 V. and B. Acton *History of Truro. Volume 1: From Coinage Town to Cathedral City*. Truro: Landfall Publications, Devoran, Truro, 1997

75 For views and discussion of the stuccoed interiors, see pp. 96–99 in A.E. Richardson and C. Lovett Gill *Regional Architecture of the West of England*. Halsgrove, Tiverton, 2001 (original ed. 1924)

76 M. Tangye 'Rock-cut baths in Cornwall'. *Cornish Archaeol.* 36, 1997, pp. 186–200

77 Ibid

78 At this period, it would have been measured out in feet and inches

79 D.E. Pett *The Parks and Gardens of Cornwall*. Alison Hodge, Penzance, 1998

80 Pages 219–21 in Pett 1998; and pp. 31–35 in Mc Cabe 1988

81 Pages 135–37 in Pett 1998

82 Pages 60–62 in Pett 1998

83 Pages 29–32 in Pett 1998; and pp. 37–49 in R. King *Tresco. England's Island of Flowers*. Constable, London, 1985

Chapter ten Discovering 'vanishing' and 'enchanted' Cornwall in the recent past

1 J. Benson *The Rise of Consumer Society in Britain, 1880–1980*. Longman, London, 1994

2 J.E. Packer *The Porthcurno story. Porthcurno Museum of Submarine* Telegraphy, Porthcurno, 1996

3 C. Johns 'Marconi Bungalow' *Cornish Archaeol.* 37–38, 1998–99, pp. 216–17; N. Thomas 'Marconi Wireless Station' *Cornish Archaeol.* 39–40, 2000–01, pp. 203

4 G. Bussey *Marconi's Atlantic Leap*. Marconi Communications, Coventry, 2001

5 C. Johns *Goonhilly Satellite Earth Station*. Cornwall Archaeological Unit, Cornwall County Council, Truro, 1998

6 Pages 128 and 130 in P. Hancock *Cornwall at War 1939–1945*. Halsgrove, Tiverton, 2002

7 A. Tennyson 'Idylls of the King'. In *Poetical Works of Alfred Lord Tennyson*. Macmillan & Co. Ltd, London, 1899, pp. 308–475

8 D. Du Maurier *Vanishing Cornwall*. Gollancz, London, 1967; and D. Du Maurier *Enchanted Cornwall: Her Pictorial Memoir*. Michael Joseph, London, 1989

9 W.S. Gilbert and A. Sullivan *The Pirates of Penzance in Full Score*. Dover Publications, New York, 2001

10 C. Fox *Stanhope Forbes And The Newlyn School*. David & Charles, Newton Abbot, 1993

11 P. Curtis *Barbara Hepworth*. Tate Gallery
Publishing, London, 1998

12 Page 85 in P. Payton *The Making of Modern
Cornwall*. Dyllansow Truran, Redruth, 1992

13 M. Stratton and B. Trinder *Twentieth Century
Industrial Archaeology*. E & FN Spon, London, 2000

14 E.W.A. Edmonds 'The Camborne and Redruth
Tramway'. *Journal of the Trevithick Society* 29, 2002,
pp. 3–47

15 Ibid

16 J. Betjeman *Cornwall (Shell Guide)*. Architectural
Press, London, 1934

17 S. Baring-Gould *A Book of the West – Cornwall*.
Methuen, London, 1899 (re-pub. 1981, London:
Wildwood)

18 p. 183 in M. Tangye 'A huer's hut, Cribbin Head,
Penberth, St Levan'. *Cornish Archaeol.* 33, 1994, pp.
183–86; p. 122 in H.L. Douch *Old Cornish Inns and
their place in the social history of Cornwall*. D.
Bradford Barton, Truro, 1966

19 M. Tangye 'A seventeenth century fish cellar at
Porth Godrevy, Gwithian'. *Cornish Archaeol.* 30, 1991,
pp. 243–52

20 p. 78–79 in B. Gray *Oh my dear life!* Headland
Hotel, Newquay, 2002

21 B. Earl *The Cornish Arsenic Industry*. Pool,
Redruth, 1996

22 A. Sharpe *An archaeological survey of Levant
Calciners*. Cornwall Archaeological Unit, Cornwall
County Council, Truro, 1994

23 B. Earl *Cornish Explosives*. Trevithick Society,
Cornwall, 1978

24 B. Earl and J.R. Smith *National Explosives, Upton
Towans, Hayle. An Archaeological and Historical
Assessment*. Cornwall Archaeological Unit, Cornwall
County Council, Truro, 1991

25 T. Brooks *Castle-an-Dinas 1916–1957: Cornwall's
Premier Wolfram Mine*. Cornish Hillside Publications,
St Austell, 2001

26 A. Fairhurst 'Mining the Sea: The Extraction of
Bromine from Sea Water at Hayle'. *Journal of the
Trevithick Society* 26, 1999, pp. 3–29

27 e.g., p. 29 in D.E. Pett *The Parks and Gardens of
Cornwall*. Alison Hodge, Penzance, 1998

28 D. Smart *The Cornish Fishing Industry, a brief
history*. Tor Mark Press, Penryn, 1992

29 pp. 45–46 in M. Tangye 'Hulls' in Cornwall: a
survey and discussion. *Cornish Archaeol.* 12, 1973, pp.
31–52

30 B. Cole and R. Durak *Railway Posters 1923–1947*.
Science Museum, London, 1992

31 A.M. Broadley *The Cornish Riviera, Great Western
Railway*. GWR, London, 1904

32 e.g., pp. 214–15 in J.T. Salmon *A Field Guide to the
Native Trees of New Zealand*. Reed Methuen,
Auckland, New Zealand, 1986

33 40% of Cornish plant species are alien, in fact – see
p. 9 in C.N. French, R.J. Murphy and M.G.C. *Atkinson
Flora of Cornwall*. Wheal Seton Press, Camborne

34 Page 38 in J. Ratcliffe *Fal Estuary Historic Audit*.
Cornwall Archaeological Unit, Cornwall County
Council, Truro, 1997; Gray 2002

35 Gray 2002

36 N. Tangye *The Story of Glendorgal. A Personal
View*. Dyllansow Truran, Redruth, 1984; and Sarah
McNaughton pers.comm. 2004

37 Pages 33–34 in S. McNaughton 'What does the
archaeological evidence reveal about the human usage
through time, of the coastal zone between Trevelgue
Head and Griffin Point?' Truro College & The
University of Plymouth: Unpublished HND
Dissertation, 2004

38 Gray 2002

39 D. Hannigan *Francis Frith's Around Penzance*.
Frith Book Company, Salisbury, Wilts., 1999

40 Heritage SA. *Burra: State Heritage Area*. Heritage
South Australia, Department for Environment and
Heritage, n.d.

41 Todd, A.C. 1977. Search for Silver: Cornish Miners
in Mexico, 1824–1947. Padstow: Lodenek Press; p. 7 in
S.B. Smith 'The Rolt Memorial Lecture 2001. The
Development of Industrial Museums within
Landscapes'. *Industrial Archaeology Review* XXIV,
2002, pp. 5–10

42 Pages 10–11 in Todd 1977

43 Pages 44–56 in Todd 1977

44 Page 46 in P. Payton *Cornwall's History. An
introduction*. Tor Mark, Redruth, 2002; H. Harradance
The life and works of Silvanus Trevail. The Silvanus
Trevail Society, Luxulyan, 1998; pp. 30–31 in H.
Hambly *North Cornwall Reflections*. Bossiney Books,
St Teath, Bodmin, 1992; for a description of the
interior, Alex. Matthews *King Arthur's Castle Hotel,
Tintagel, Cornwall*. Alex. Matthews, London, 1920

45 The plan appears in a report written in July 1940 by
the SS General Werner Best – see T. Crago 'SS
Kernow?' *Newsletter of the Cornish History Network*
15, 2002, pp. 1 & 5.

46 p. 11 in G. Williamson *The SS: Hitler's Instrument
of Terror*. Motorbooks International, Osceola, WI,
USA, 1994

47 For a recent edition, see R.L. Stevenson *Treasure
Island*. Penguin, Harmondsworth, 1994

48 For example, see p. 495 in W. Page (ed.) *The
Victoria History of the County of Cornwall*. Vol. I
(reprint) William Dawson & Sons, Folkestone, Kent,
1975 (original 1906)

49 Page 252 in P. Payton *Cornwall. A History*.
Cornwall Editions, Fowey, Cornwall, 2004

50 B. Deacon, A. George and R. Perry *Cornwall at the
Crossroads*. Cornish Social and Economic Research
Group, Redruth, 1988

51 N.J.G. Pounds 'The Duchy Palace at Lostwithiel,
Cornwall'. *Archaeol J.* 136, 1979, pp. 203–17

52 Page 264 in Payton 2004

53 B. Deacon, D. Cole, and G. Tregidga *Mebyon
Kernow and Cornish Nationalism*. Welsh Academic
Press, Cardiff, 2003

54 Pages 150–51 in B. Biscoe 'The Hungry Beast. A
personal view of Keskerdh Kernow and the media'. In
S. Parker (ed.) *Cornwall Marches On! Keskerdh
Kernow 500*. Keskerdh Kernow Ltd, Cornwall, 1998,
pp. 149–61

55 See the webpages available – Natural Environment
Service Cornwall Hedge Group. Cornwall County
Council, Truro, 2004 [WWW]
www.cornwall.gov.uk/meetings/hedge/default.htm
(01/10/2004)

56 P. Herring and E. Bull 'Cornish hedges' *Cornish
Archaeol.* 37–38, 1998–99, pp. 207–08

57 S. Hall *The Cornish Pasty*. Agre Books, Bridport,
Dorset, 2001

List of Subscribers

Adams, Anne
  Dauntsey Lock, Wiltshire
Adlam, Tania
  Taupo, Central Plateau, New
  Zealand
Ahrens, Jim
  Falmouth, Cornwall
Allen, Madeleine
  Houghton, West Sussex
Allinson, Sir Leonard
  Wendron, Cornwall
Alvarez-Buylla, Mrs Mary
  Guildford, Surrey
Amphlett, Mr and Mrs P. N.
  Great Hallingbury, Hertfordshire
Andrewartha, W.
  Caulfield, VIC, Australia
Annear, John Marshall
  Dulwich, London
Annear, Mark O'Donovan Poon
  Dulwich, London
Annear, Nicholas Marshall Poon
  Dulwich, London
Arumugasamy, Mrs E.
  Leytonstone, London
Ashbee, Paul, MA, D.Litt, FSA,
  FRSAI
  Chedgrave, Norwich
Ashby, Brian Sterry
  Mousehole, Cornwall
Ashman, Marjorie W.
  West Leederville, WA, Australia
Ashworth, R.
  Epping, VIC, Australia
ASKi (UK) Ltd
  Marazion, Cornwall
Atkins, Thelma and Alan
  Newbury, Berkshire
Attree, Colin and Audrey
  Wrotham, Kent
Avery, Stuart
  Christchurch, New Zealand
Axton, Bryan Edward
  West Molesey, Surrey

Baker, Owen A.
  Rosevidney, Cornwall
Ball, Edwin J.
  Niagara Falls, ON, Canada
Ball, Jonathan MBE
  Bude, Cornwall
Bardell, Jon and Chel
  Deloraine, TAS, Australia
Barker, Ashley
  Penzance, Cornwall
Baskott, Mike
  Kingsand, Cornwall
Bawden, Michael
  Rickmansworth, Hertfordshire

Baxter, John
  Trebetherick, Cornwall
Baylis, A.R.L.
  Newton Ferrers, Cornwall
Beardsell, Andrew B.
  Brighouse, West Yorkshire
Beautyman, Paul
  An Agaidh Mhòr, Scotland
Beeman, R.J.
  Polwheveral, Cornwall
Beer, Keith E.
  Doddiscombsleigh, Devon
Bell, Michael and Ann
  Wadebridge, Cornwall
Bellis, John
  Sale, Cheshire
Benallack, William G.
  Lansing, MI, USA
Bennett, Stephen
  Stanton, Suffolk
Bennett, William Gordon
  Torrance, CA, USA
Benney, Barry
  Budock Water, Cornwall
Berryman, William
  Stafford, Staffordshire
Bessant, Loraine and Roger
  Knutsford, Cheshire
Bishop, Andrew L.
  Wimbledon, London
Blackman, Tony
  Perranporth, Cornwall
Blake, Michael
  Gweek, Cornwall
Bolitho, Dr Elaine E.
  Ngaio, Wellington, New Zealand
Botterill, Anne and Deryck
  Torquay, Devon
Bourdeaux, Canon Michael
  Iffley, Oxfordshire
Bournemouth University, Talbot
  Campus Library
  Poole, Dorset
Bowden, Clive Eric
  Witney, Oxfordshire
Bowden, Harold H.
  Callington, Cornwall
Bowlin, Lerona
  Stockton, CA, USA
Bowman, Ron
  Escondido, CA, USA
Bray, John
  Victoria, BC, Canada
Bray, Robert
  Bradley Stoke, Bristol
Brewer, Collin William
  Sladesbridge, Cornwall
Broom-Smith, Mary
  Castle Douglas, Scotland

Brown, J.A.
  Limpley Stoke, Bath
Brown, Kelvin
  Saltash, Cornwall
Brown, Mrs Rosemary
  St Austell, Cornwall
Brown, Mrs Shelby
  North Hill, Cornwall
Brown, Wella
  Saltash, Cornwall
Burley, Christine
  Canterbury, Kent
Burnside, Commodore Ian, OBE
  RAN (Rtd)
  Reid, ACT, Australia
Burrow, K.J.
  Bideford, Devon
Burt, Andrew and Toni
  St Just in Penwith, Cornwall
Burt, E. Laura
  St Columb, Cornwall
Busby, Graham D.
  St Mellion, Cornwall
Byrns, Marilyn J.
  Port MacDonnell, SA, Australia

C C C Celt
  Bucks County, PA, USA
Campbell, Dulcie J.
  Beckenham, WA, Australia
Carbis, In-Pensioner John C.
  Chelsea, London
Cardiff University
  Cardiff, Wales
Carrithers, Kathryn Toy
  Bellevue, WA, USA
Carwithen, F.A.
  Addleston, Surrey
Catling, Canon R.M.
  Exmouth, Devon
Chantry, P.A.
  St Austell, Cornwall
Chapman, Frank W.
  Clowance, Cornwall
Chenoweth, Doris J.
  Mobile, AL, USA
Clarke (née Annear), Rosemary
  Doreen
  Dulwich, London
Clynick, P.R.R.
  Crewkerne, Somerset
Coates, Simon
  Perranporth, Cornwall
Cock, Owen W.N.
  Pinner, Middlesex
Cole, Mrs Maureen
  Ladock, Cornwall
Coleman, Ada
  Forest Hill, VIC, Australia

Colenso-Dunne, C.G.
  Portchester, Hampshire
Conner, Marlene
  Chandler, AZ, USA
Cook, Robert Knight
  Longford, TAS, Australia
Cooke, Anita
  Mylor Churchtown, Cornwall
Cooke, Ian McNeil
  Mel-an-Tol Studio, Cornwall
Coombe, Canon Michael Thomas
  Exmouth, Devon
Coombes, Brian and Janet
  Bodmin, Cornwall
Coon, George Vernon
  Ashburton, Devon
Corbet, Sally
  St Buryan, Cornwall
Cornwall Inscriptions Project
  Redruth, Cornwall
Cornwall Library Service
Corotto, June Goyne
  Lancaster, PA, USA
Cothey, Dr V.J.
  St Ives, Cornwall
Couch, Sallyann
  Harrowbarrow, Cornwall
Coulson-Thomas, Professor Colin J.
  Mullion, Cornwall
Coutts, John M.
  Orpington, Kent
Cowling, Mark Graham
  New Plymouth, Taranaki, New
  Zealand
Cowling, Russell Maurice
  New Plymouth, Taranaki, New
  Zealand
Cox, Raymond and Patricia
  Halesowen, West Midlands
Croggon, Richard
  Buninyong, VIC, Australia
Crosfill, Martin
  Heamoor, Cornwall
Cullis, Paul J.
  Folkestone, Kent
Curnow, Ann L.
  Las Vegas, NV, USA
Curnow, E.L. and G.E. and
  Manning, Mrs R.,
  Estates of Clarks Beach,
  Auckland, New Zealand
Curnow, Howard
  St Hilary, Cornwall
Curnow, Professor William C.
  Pullenvale, QLD, Australia

Dadda, Miss J.A.
  Poole, Dorset
Dainty (née Chirgwin), Beryl
  Rothwell, Northants

Davies, Peter
  Bodmin, Cornwall
Davies, Peter Wilton
  Trehane Mill, Cornwall
Davis, Jan
  Lemon Grove, CA, USA
Davis, Vin
  York, Yorkshire
Day, Andrew
  Bodmin, Cornwall
Day, Dianne
  Victoria, BC, Canada
Dellow, Adrienne
  Saffron Walden, Essex
Dennis, Stephen
  Bridgetown, WA, Australia
Dingle, Mrs Mary
  Bundaberg, QLD, Australia
Donohew, Alistair Timothy
  Grampound, Cornwall
Double, Mrs H.R.
  St Austell, Cornwall
Downing, Des
  Falmouth, Cornwall
Driver, Roger
  Ding Dong, Cornwall
Duinker, Pauline S. Carveth
  Mississauga, ON, Canada
Dungey, P.
  Threemilestone, Cornwall
Dunkerley (Kevrenor), Chris
  Epping, NSW, Australia
Dunn, Geoff
  Tywardreath, Cornwall
Dymond, A.J.
  Launceston, Cornwall

Eade, Patricia M.
  Glen Waverley, VIC, Australia
Ealey, SallyAnn
  St Keverne, Cornwall
Eastlake, Les
  St Tudy, Cornwall
Eddy, John W., FRCS, FRCOG
  Colchester, Essex
Ede, Roger M.
  Kingskerswell, Devon
Edwards, James Eustice
  Malmesbury, Wiltshire
Eich, Clive
  Luxulyan, Cornwall
Ellis (Johnson), Jocelyn
  The Lizard, Cornwall
Ellis, Robin
  Camborne, Cornwall
Evans, David J.
  Sevenoaks, Kent

Fairhurst, Arthur
  Maidenhead, Berkshire

Fawdry, John Berryman
  Devoran, Cornwall
Ferrett, Malcolm John
  St Neots, Cambridgeshire
Field, David and Elaine
  Indian Queens, Cornwall
Field, Robert and Ceza
  Brightwell cum Sotwell, Oxon
Finnemore, Michael J.
  Ashby de la Zouch, Leicestershire
Fogwill, Marilynn A.
  Edmonton, AB, Canada
Foster, Joyce
  Truro, Cornwall
Freeman (née Hichens), Mary
  Enfield, Middlesex
Frost, Peter R.
  Jurbise, Belgium
Fryer, Mr and Mrs David
  Polgooth, Cornwall

Garwood, Paul
  Hinckley, Leicestershire
Gentle, Raymond
  Tideford, Cornwall
George, Richard L.
  North Huntingdon, PA, USA
Gillingham, John Ellery
  Troon, Cornwall
Gillis, Ann
  Pencorse, Cornwall
Glanfield, P.
  Falmouth, Cornwall
Glasswell, Patricia and John
  Trebetherick, Cornwall
Goodall, Anne
  Stockton-on-Tees
Govan, Thelma Maude
  Ballarat, VIC, Australia
Gray, James
  Norton Sub Hamdon, Somerset
Greaves, Nigel M.
  Tavistock, Devon
Griffin, Tristan V.
  Alvaston, Derby
Griffiths, G.E.
  Creech-St-Michael, Somerset
Grimshaw, Kareen
  Te Aroha, North Island, New
  Zealand
Grist, Michael W.
  Llantwith Major, Vale of
  Glamorgan
Gummow, Joseph
  Stratford, ON, Canada

Hall, Nigel
  East Harptree, Bristol
Hambly-Staite, Keith and Aldyth
  Feock, Cornwall

ARCHAEOLOGY
OF CORNWALL

Hancock, Helen
   Barry, Vale of Glamorgan
Hancock, John A.
   Perranporth, Cornwall
Hancock, M.T.G.
   Barry, South Glamorgan
Hanson, Jeremy
   Bromley, Kent
Harbour, Derek
   Minions, Cornwall
Harding, Paul and Rachel England
   Foxhole, Cornwall
Harper, S. Hebdige, S.
   Newquay, Cornwall
Harris, Jennifer M.
   Pompton Plains, NJ, USA
Harry, M.A.D.J.
   Praa Sands, Cornwall
Harvey, Kevin William
   Pontardawe, Swansea
Hatton, Jane
   Mawnan Smith, Cornwall
Hawke, Ann and Andrew
   Llanilar, Aberystwyth
Hawkey, Robert C.
   Calgary, AB, Canada
Hayter, Zoë
   Falmouth, Cornwall
Hendy, Lynne
   St Austell, Cornwall
Hichens, R.E.
   Flushing, Cornwall
Hichens, R.T.S.
   Calenick, Cornwall
Hicks, Roger David
   Callington, Cornwall
Hitchens, T. Neil
   Trescowe, Penzance
Hockley, Michael
   Falmouth, Cornwall
Holland, Sir Geoffrey
   St Ives, Cornwall
Holmes, Jonathan J.
   Pendeen, Cornwall
Hoskins, John H.
   Sioux Falls, SD, USA
Houghton, D.J.
   St Keverne, Cornwall
Howlett, Jonathan
   Worthing, West Sussex
Hughes, John Vivian
   Port Talbot, West Glamorgan
Hugh-Jones, Bridget
   St Buryan, Cornwall
Hulett, Abigail
   Wadebridge, Cornwall
Hulett, Carol F.
   Wadebridge, Cornwall
Hunt, Gordon
   East Kilbride, Scotland

James, Dr Bryony
   Auckland, New Zealand
James, John F.
   London
Janes, Daniel
   Bangor, Wales
Jarvis, Ann
   Oakley, Bedfordshire
Jee, E.
   Devoran, Cornwall
Jenkin, Albert E.
   Pottstown, PA, USA
Jenkin, Ann Trevenen
   Hayle, Cornwall
Jennings, William R.
   Pasadena, CA, USA
Jewell, C.R.
   Bude, Cornwall
Johnson, Dr and Mrs W.H.
   Bodmin, Cornwall
Juleff, Kitto
   Appledore, Kent
Juleff, Lyn
   Kedron, QLD, Australia

Keast, John
   Warleggan, Cornwall
Kent, Dr Alan M.
   Probus, Cornwall
Kessell, Bettina Grace
   Killara, NSW, Australia
Kinsmen, Revd Barry
   Padstow, Cornwall
Kitto, Robert J.
   West Lakes, SA, Australia
Knight, Lillian
   Sydney, NSW, Australia
Konik, Daniel
   Constantine, Cornwall
Kopp, Rita Bone
   Ashland, OH, USA

Leach, Peter E., FSA
   St Mawes, Cornwall
Leggat, Dr and Mrs Peter
   West Looe, Cornwall
Littleton, Paul A.
   Weybridge, Surrey
Long, Anne C.M.
   St Just, Cornwall
Lorigan, Catherine
   Reading, Berkshire
Luxton, Mrs R. June
   Lower Tremar, Cornwall
Lyall, J.C.
   Perranwell Station, Cornwall

Mackie, Rachel Keigwin
   London
Maddern, Allan J.
   Andover, Hampshire

Manclus, Jo
   Truro, Cornwall
Marley, Jane
   Falmouth, Cornwall
Marrone, Jackie Lee
   Denver, CO, USA
Marshall, Barbara
   Wollongong, NSW, Australia
Marshall, Brian Roberts
   Farnham, Surrey
Martin, Kevin and Judy
   Fowey, Cornwall
Martin, Mrs R.E.
   Trevone, Cornwall
Mason, A.J.
   Leegomery, Shropshire
Matthews, Marilyn J.
   Golden, CO, USA
Matthews, Duncan Paul
   Liskeard, Cornwall
Mayman, I.
   Talland Bay, Cornwall
McClelland, William E.
   Fallbrook, CA, USA
McGivern, Adrian
   Oakley, Bedfordshire
McNaughton, Sarah
   Boscombe, Dorset
Meeson, John and Ann
   Bodrigan, Cornwall
Meeson, Mark
   Chipping Norton, Oxon
Meeson, Peter
   Tregoodwell, Cornwall
Megaw, Emeritus Professor J.V.S.
   and Dr M. Ruth
   Adelaide, SA, Australia
Meyer, Revd Canon C.J.
   Newquay, Cornwall
Michell, Len
   St Mary's, Isles of Scilly
Miles, David
   London
Monk, Denzil
   Penzance, Cornwall
Moon, Robin
   High Wycombe, WA, Australia
Moore, Andrew M.T.
   Pittsford, NY, USA
Morgan, Miss M.Y.
   Truro, Cornwall
Morrab Library
   Penzance, Cornwall
Morris, William A.
   London
Moyle, Terry
   South Darenth, Kent
Moyse, R.M.
   London
Mullett, Jan
   Falmouth, Cornwall

Murley, Windsor B.
Hopewell Jct, NY, USA
Murton, Darren
Illogan, Cornwall
Mynott, Robert F.
Trumpington, Cambridge

Nankivell, Edmund
Hassocks, West Sussex
Nethercott, Elizabeth
Torpoint, Cornwall
Nethersole, Nigel E.
Redruth, Cornwall
Newlyn, Evelyn S.
Scarborough, ME, USA
Nicholas, Katrina-Rhiannon
Watford, Hertfordshire
Nobbs, Richard
Kingston upon Thames, Surrey
Northey, Eve
Ilminster, Somerset

O'Brien, Vern T.
Palmerston, NT, Australia
O'Carroll, John
Padstow, Cornwall
O'Connor, M.J. and C.B.
St Ervan, Cornwall
O'Rell, Michael
Manhattan Beach, CA, USA
Olds, Ken
Penzance, Cornwall

Paër-Gotch, B.E. de St
St Pinnock, Cornwall
Palamountain, Brian Anthony
Atawhai, Nelson, New Zealand
Parish, Graham P.
Penrose Burden, Cornwall
Parnell, David and June
Worcester Park, Surrey
Pascoe, J.D.
Etobicoke, ON, Canada
Paul, Peter T.
Red Cliffs, VIC, Australia
Payn, D.S.
Mevagissey, Cornwall
Pentreath, Dr R.J.
Bath, Somerset
Perry, Cynthia L.
San Diego, CA, USA
Perry, Margaret
Crow's Nest, Cornwall
Perry, Mrs P.A.
Bere Alston, Devon
Perry, Richard J.
San Diego, CA, USA
Perry, William
San Diego, CA, USA
Peters, Brian and Barbara
Helston, Cornwall

Peters, David and Gill
Falmouth, Cornwall
Pethybridge, Mrs John
Rock, Cornwall
Phillips, John A.
Kendal, Cumbria
Pike, Jean
Nuthampstead, Hertfordshire
Pill, Colin
Southville, Bristol
Pilsbury, Graham
Camborne, Cornwall
Playle, John
Hammersmith, London
Porte, Stuart
Stockwell, London
Post, Margaret Mary James
Stafford, TX, USA
Pringle, David and Sarah
Hong Kong
Proffitt, David
Looe, Cornwall
Pryor, Robin J.
St Andrews Beach, VIC, Australia

Queensland, Cornish Association of
Wishart, QLD, Australia
Quick, Malcolm J.
Plymouth, Devon
Quinnell, Henrietta
Exeter, Devon

Raddy, Darren James
West Looe, Cornwall
Raddy, Laura-Jane
West Looe, Cornwall
Raddy, Luke Adam
West Looe, Cornwall
Rashleigh, Carole
Breage, Cornwall
Read family
Clevedon, North Somerset
Reed, Henry
Barrow-upon-Soar, Leicestershire
Rhodes, Mrs S.L.
Castallack, Cornwall
Richards, F. Stephen J.
St Tudy, Cornwall
Richards, Geoff and Angela
Egloshayle, Cornwall
Richards, Keith and Marilyn
Weston-super-Mare, North
Somerset
Riding, C.R.
Gorran Haven, Cornwall
Riley, M.J.
Forrest Hill, Auckland, New
Zealand
Rilstone, Jules
Penally, Pembrokeshire

Roberts, Colin
Trentham, Staffordshire
Roberts, Mr and Mrs G.G.
Mickleton, Gloucestershire
Rodda, Adrian F.
Camborne, Cornwall
Rogers, Angela
Peel, Isle of Man
Rogers, Jeremy
Sandhurst, Berkshire
Rogers, Mary H.
Devizes, Wiltshire
Roseland Care Limited
Tregony, Cornwall
Roskilly, Rachel
St Keverne, Cornwall
Rovellotti, Fabrizio
Quarona, VC, Italy
Royal Cornwall Polytechnic
Society, The
Falmouth, Cornwall
Rule, Laurence
Camborne, Cornwall
Rundle, Mrs Gillian
Liskeard, Cornwall
Rutter, W.
Falmouth, Cornwall

St Aubyn, James
St Michael's Mount, Cornwall
Sanders, Judith Gail Rickard
Santa Rosa, CA, USA
Sandoe, Jill
Stockton on Forest, Yorkshire
Sandrey, Eric F.
Ennis, County Clare
Schoolar, Ian R.
Coventry, Warwickshire
Scott, Mrs Jane
Treluggan, Cornwall
Scullion, Edward G.
Peterborough, Cambridgeshire
Searle, Peter C.
Oakwood, Leeds
Seccombe, Sir Vernon
Saltash, Cornwall
Shaw, Hilary
Port Navas, Cornwall
Shepperd, M.J.
Port Navas, Cornwall
Shimmield, Linda
Mt Osmond, SA, Australia
Sinclair, Sir George
South Minack, St Levan
Skewes, William F.
Evergreen, CO, USA
Sleeman, Dr Andrew
County Wicklow, Ireland
Smale, David Christopher
Chelmsford, Essex

Smelt, Maurice
  Penzance, Cornwall
Smith, Diana
  Shortlanesend, Cornwall
Smith, Sir John, CH, CBE
  Shottesbrooke Park, Berkshire
Smitheram, Mary Lou
  Santa Barbara, CA, USA
Smitheram, William H.
  Santa Barbara, CA, USA
Snedden, Professor Richard J.
  Malvern, VIC, Australia
Snell, Dr Lawrence S., FSA
  South Zeal, Devon
Spencer, Lloyd
  Cubert, Cornwall
Spriggs, Professor Matthew
  Canberra, ACT, Australia
Standing, Judith
  Bateman, WA, Australia
Stanley, Jane
  Little Polgooth, Cornwall
Stephens, Anne Honeychurch
  Lake Hopatcong, NJ, USA
Stephens, Dr F. Graham
  Portreath, Cornwall
Stephens, W.J.
  Prestwood, Buckinghamshire
Stevens, Jean Barrieu
  San Clemente, CA, USA
Stewart, Betty Hosking
  Bakersfield, CA, USA
Stirk, Carole
  Crawley, West Sussex
Swiggs, John Noel
  Par, Cornwall
Symons, John C.
  Malvern Wells, Worcestershire
Szweda, Dr Stephen Anthony
  Corsham, Wiltshire

Taperell, Ken
  South Benfleet, Essex
Thomas, Bruce MacA
  Forestville, NSW, Australia
Thomas, Joe
  Illogan, Cornwall
Thomas, Professor K.D.
  London
Thomas, Mrs M.J.
  St Neot, Cornwall
Thomas, Nicholas
  Newlyn, Cornwall
Thomas. William Davy
  St Albert, AB, Canada
Thompson, Fiona
  Lostwithiel, Cornwall
Thorne, Graham
  Maldon, Essex
Toms, Don
  Lead, SD, USA

Tonkin, Lindsay Evelyn
  Eldene, Wiltshire
Tonkin, W. John
  St Austell, Cornwall
Towey, Anne Elizabeth
  Charlton Kings, Gloucestershire
Trefusis, Nicholas
  Flushing, Cornwall
Tregonning, Graham L.
  Standish, Lancashire
Treleven, K.R.
  Colchester, Essex
Tremain, Harold
  Yuma, AZ, USA
Tremain, Rob
  Launceston, Cornwall
Tremain Wiekhorst, Verona
  Yuma, AZ, USA
Tremaine, Dudley
  Glastonbury, Somerset
Tremewen, J.
  Doncaster, VIC, Australia
Trethewey, Gerald Roy
  Port Huron, MI, USA
Trevarthen, Alec and Emma
  Falmouth, Cornwall
Trevelyan, Raleigh
  St Veep, Cornwall
Trevenna, T.J. and M.
  St Mawgan, Cornwall
Trevenna, Tim and Val
  St Dennis, Cornwall
Treverrow, Barry
  Devizes, Wiltshire
Trevivian, Jacqueline
  Veryan, Cornwall
Treweek, Miss S.
  Sutton, Surrey
Trewhella, John
  Marazion, Cornwall
Trezona, Barbara
  Lake Ridge, VA, USA
Truro College
  Truro, Cornwall
Tschirschky, M., MA
  Frankfurt, Germany
Turner, F. Joy
  Lostwithiel, Cornwall
Turney, Simon J.
  Penzance, Cornwall

Unger, Elizabeth
  Manhattan, KS, USA
University of Exeter
  Exeter, Devon
Upfold, Mr and Mrs J.
  Treloquithack, Cornwall
Venning, John
  Callington, Cornwall
Voaden, Dr Denys J.
  College Park, MD, USA

Voaden, Jeremy
  Blockley, Gloucestershire

Wade, Dr Mary
  Cheadle Hulme, Chesire
Wagstaff, Robert and Helen
  Bayers, France
Wakeford, Robert John
  Burcott, Buckinghamshire
Ward, Patrick John
  Tolgullow, Cornwall
Watkins, Brian E.
  North York, ON, Canada
Wheeler, Anna
  Redruth, Cornwall
Wheeler, Miss Norma
  Truro, Cornwall
Whiffin, June
  Blackburn South, VIC, Australia
White, A.J.
  Brittany, France
White, Penny McGuire
  Mentone, VIC, Australia
Whitford, Percy, JP, MRAeS
  Datchet, Berkshire
Whitman, Mrs J.
  Jamison, PA, USA
Wiblin, C.N.
  St Leven, Cornwall
Williams, Professor H.P.
  Winchester, Hampshire
Williams, John L.
  Hamlyn Heights, VIC, Australia
Williams, Mr and Mrs Michael C.
  Probus, Cornwall
Williams, Roger
  Marazion, Cornwall
Wills, Margaret and Trevor
  Gulval, Cornwall
Wilshaw, Mrs Jean
  Roche, Cornwall
Wilson, Anne
  Deniliquin, NSW, Australia
Winslade, R.G.
  Carnon Downs, Cornwall
Winter, Carl
  St Keyne, Cornwall
Wood, A.D., MA
  Liskeard, Cornwall
Woods, Mary Kinder
  Grantham, Lincolnshire
Woodward, Joe
  Gwarnick, Cornwall
Woon, C.D.
  London
Wright, Trevor
  Perranporth, Cornwall
Yates, J.V.
  Trelights, North Cornwall
Zuber, Hans
  Fowey, Cornwall

Index

References in *italic* are to illustrations or their captions, and maps.

AUTHOR'S ACKNOWLEDGEMENTS

I would like to thank in particular the team from Cornwall Editions Ltd, especially Yvonne McFarlane, Roger Bristow and Maurice Smelt, for all their help in this venture.

The staff of the Historic Environment Service, especially Steve Hartgroves, have been most cooperative and encouraging in providing valuable resources and time. I am also grateful for the many stimulating discussions I have had with Pete Herring, Andy Jones and Jacqui Nowakowski. Likewise, the staff of the Royal Cornwall Museum have provided resources and ideas, especially Anna Tyacke, Robert Cook and Margaret Morgan.

Thanks are also due to my employer, Truro College, for the opportunity to work in my homeland and to study and teach its archaeology.

For useful discussions on Cornish archaeology I am grateful to Garry Tregidga and Treve Crago of the Institute of Cornish Studies; Tony Blackman of the YAC; Rod Clough of Clough Associates Ltd (Heritage Consultants), Auckland, New Zealand; Patrick Laviolette of University College London; and Matthew Spriggs, Professor of Archaeology at the Australian National University, Canberra (and a Cousin Jack to boot!). My students, too, past and present, have often provided me with interesting insights, recently especially Sarah McNaughton, Lynne Hendy and Doug Smith.

Finally, I thank my wife, son, parents, friends and family for their continual understanding and encouragement.

The publishers would like to thank the following people for their assistance in the preparation of this book:

Allan Rees and ARKA Graphics, who created the maps; David Ashby and Eric Thomas who created the illustrations; Steve Hartgroves at Historic Environment Service, Cornwall County Council for much help and loan of images from the HES archives; Jonathan Holmes at Penlee House; Mike Tippett, Cornwall County Council; Polly Buston at Sonia Halliday Photographs; Janet Bord of the Fortean Picture Library; Ian McNeil Cooke; Karen Forster at Atmosphere Picture Library; Daphne Razazan; Sharron Schwartz; Rob Cook; Jane Marley and Emma Lloyd at the Royal Cornwall Museum; photographers Simon Cook, Geoff Hitchens, Mike Newman and John Watton.